★ **AUTHENTIC TEXAS** ★

NUMBER NINETEEN

Clifton and Shirley Caldwell Texas Heritage Series

MARCIA HATFIELD
DAUDISTEL
&
BILL WRIGHT

Authentic

TEXAS

★ PEOPLE OF THE BIG BEND ★

Photographs by
BILL WRIGHT

Foreword by
J. P. BRYAN

UNIVERSITY OF TEXAS, AUSTIN

Publication of this work was made possible
in part by support from Clifton and Shirley
Caldwell and a challenge grant from the
National Endowment for the Humanities.

Requests for permission to reproduce material from this work
should be sent to:
    Permissions
    University of Texas Press
    P.O. Box 7819
    Austin, TX 78713-7819
    http://utpress.utexas.edu/index.php/rp-form

♾ The paper used in this book meets the minimum requirements
of ANSI/NISO Z39.48-1992 (R1997) (Permanence of Paper).

PCN: 2013945249

ISBN: 978-0-292-74915-3 (cl.: alk. paper)
ISBN: 978-0-292-75304-4 (pbk.: alk. paper)

Cataloging data is available from the Library of Congress.

doi:10.7560/749153

For the people of the Big Bend

Contents

~~~

Foreword

Marcia Hatfield Daudistel and Bill Wright have followed a different trail in attempting to define the lure of the landscape of the Big Bend region of Texas. This is not a book of pictures of the land where the hot breath of the Chihuahuan Desert is a constant companion as it rolls over the shoulders of the omnipresent inspiration of the Rocky Mountains. It is a book about people, some might say, about the characters that live there. In their lives, they inhabit in what many call the last bastion of a frontier. Is it possible to find there what the authors call "Texas exceptionalism"? This is roughly defined in the true grit of the West and Texas as independence, self-sufficiency, an appreciation of the land, and the careful stewardship of both land and community. The answer to these questions, as their creative research reveals, is not a whimpered "maybe" but a chorus of "yesses"!

To plumb this question, the authors sought guidance in the faces and lives of a select group of its inhabitants who are wonderfully captured by the eye and lens of Bill and Marcia's astute compilation of more than forty individual interviews. The counties of Jeff Davis, Presidio, Brewster, and a small part of Reeves County embrace their subjects. The towns, which you will find by beginning at Balmorhea and meandering in a gradual circle going south to Valentine, to Marfa, to Presidio, to Redford, to Terlingua, through the Big Bend Park, up to Marathon, then Alpine, and, lastly, to Fort Davis and nearby Limpia Crossing are home to the subjects. The small communities thoughtfully described in their essence by the authors are held in place by more than six million acres of high desert landscape. It is a land of unremitting space with an audience of less than twelve thousand occupants to behold nature's orchestrated wonders in the sky above and on the earth below. This is not only the least-populated part of Texas but also one of the least-populated regions in the lower forty-eight states. Most of those who live there would like to keep it that way. They have come to appreciate, through an adherence to a less-modern lifestyle, that all change is not progress. Importantly, the people who live here and the land they live on share something in common. They are both unique. That is quite an accomplishment because it is achieved in a state that itself is mythically different from those with which it is joined in a Union and among people in Texas for whom extraordinary conduct is not the exception but the norm.

John Steinbeck, Nobel Prize winner (1962), had this to say: "Texas is a nation in every sense of the word. It has been described as a state of mind, a mystique, an obsession." There is no doubt Texas has been the breeding ground for generations of individuals who, when asked, "Where are you from?" are pleased to respond, "I am from Texas." Why does there exist this quality of exceptionalism and pride in Texans and in the lives of Bill and Marcia's subjects? First, it finds itself in the chemistry of five hundred years of history shaped by thousands of visible and invisible heroes, a history so colorful that if written as fiction would be discarded as unbelievable. Texas simply has the finest history of any state in the United States.

Creditability for this statement is supported by the fact that more books have been written about Texas than any state in the Union. Second is the impact of the land where this history was forged. When pioneers crossed the ninety-eighth meridian, which runs through the Cotton Bowl, historians like Walter Prescott Webb said it changed peoples' view not just of the land they beheld but themselves.

For the first time in five hundred years of Western migration, pioneers were no longer confined by a forested country but were instead witnesses to thousands of miles of tallgrass and shortgrass prairies, punctuated by some of the most beautiful mountains in the world. People began to see their opportunities not as limited by geography or circumstances but as unlimited. You see the remnants of that inspiration reflected in the personalities of those captured in *Authentic Texas: People of the Big Bend*. Marcia and Bill's insightful work is one more compelling piece of evidence of how our historical heritage and the land continue to influence future generations of Texans. They follow the footprints of millions of Texans who preceded them to this country. The invisible heroes of the past become

visible in the conduct of Bill and Marcia's chosen generation as they live out lives marked by purpose and reverence to neighbor, community, and country. But maybe there is an even more special incentive for individual excellence for those who share time in this remote and remarkable place, which gets to the heart of Bill and Marcia's search for Texas exceptionalism. Famed philosophers have noted that nothing affects people more profoundly than the desert, not even the sea, and nothing seems to incline them so powerfully toward great thoughts unless it is the mountains.

I read long ago that deserts and mountains play important roles in the lives of prophets, saints, and artists. Their epiphanies take place on the tops of mountains or in the middle of deserts. They bring their messages to the world after descending from one or emerging from the other. It seems invariable that their creative thoughts and inspiration come from a high-altitude, dry, or barren place.

In the Big Bend, one can be simultaneously on the top of the mountain and in the heart of a desert. You need not be prophet, artist, or saint to submit to the influence of the land. It can positively touch all of us, regardless how humble our calling in life.

Those who come under the spell of this place are by modern standards willing to live with less but paradoxically receive more. Less rain, less water, less urban entertainment, less shopping convenience, and less superficiality. Then more comes in quiet, in solitude, in visual inspiration, in studied reflection, in the absence of meaningless social endeavor, in the freedom to be one's self and independent. Life is free to develop a rhythm with nature, with time, and with season. All of these simple but profound pleasures are shared in part with our rural counterparts of a bygone era.

The individuals sought out by Bill and Marcia and captured on picture and page are christened with names like Mike, Jean, Chuy, Clyde, Lonn, Eduardo, Verena, Denise, Johnny, Jim, and Bonnie; they participate, as many have before them, in a common communion with the land and the history made upon it. Though time and social pressure may reduce their numbers, this land of mountains and desert and the long view will continue to influence future generations of Texans. They may not be able to articulate with poetic precision the words that say this place inspired them, but it will have, nonetheless. How will we know? By the lives they live, in a country that promises so little but gives so much.

Each individual in this book can attest to one thing: this place changed them; they did not change it.

My wife Mary Jon and I were drawn to this remote area of desert landscape by the simple ambition to own a ranch. Something larger than a postage stamp, which was all we could afford in our place of first choice, South Texas. We went west in our quest and found a lot less—a lot less rain, a lot less green, a lot less civilization, and, importantly, a lot less costly land. Our first purchase was Chalk Draw Ranch, placed stoically and picturesquely in the desert on the northern tip of the tongue of the Big Bend National Park—and in our price range. About six months later, recognizing that our primitive ranch circumstances might be measurably improved by a home in Marathon with amenities unavailable at the ranch—like electricity, phone, television, sufficient water for washing clothes and a nearby grocery store—we bought the Gage Hotel, believing this would be a wonderful compromise for our city dwelling.

Certainly in none of these early experiences did we demonstrate even a remote sign of the exceptionalism found in such forceful evidence among Bill and Marcia's featured subjects. We were just being pushed along by the energy of our circumstances. But over the years, this place, like the soft hands of the potter, changed the posture of our purpose. We committed a large measure of our available resources to improving the land, but with the concerns of a conservationist, not the legalism of an environmentalist. We sought a balance between a pristine landscape and land that bears the footprint of ranching endeavor. We came to appreciate that, at the core, we raise grass, not cattle, a timeless method of harvesting the energy of the sun. We are foremost stewards of the land and all that occupies it.

We have come to understand that we have a privileged time to say grace over the environment and a desire to leave it better than we found it.

In our embrace of the Trans-Pecos, the Gage became once again a Hotel and not our home. It is, however, a home briefly to thousands of visitors who share our infatuation with a land that awaits in dramatic repose for those who look close enough to share in its wonders.

The land we tend to is now better than we found it. The grass waves at us in thanksgiving. We restored the Hotel. In doing so, something more important was done than saving a building. The soul of a small community was restored. So in our personal experience, I can say we have taken from our time in the Marathon community and we have given back, but when the scales are balanced we will have received more from the experience than we can ever offer in return.

J. P. BRYAN

★ AUTHENTIC TEXAS ★

Introduction

Like many ideas for a book, this one was born at a party, from a lively discussion between old friends, and took shape over plates of red chile enchiladas. Twenty-six writers from the anthology *Literary El Paso* had gathered to sign books in El Paso and celebrate at a dinner at Marcia's home. Bill is one of the contributors, so he traveled from his home in Abilene for the event. We worked together on his two Native American books, *The Tiguas: Pueblo Indians of Texas* and *The Texas Kickapoo: Keepers of Tradition*, during Marcia's time at Texas Western Press. After those books were published, we discussed doing a project together again, this time as co-authors.

Marcia had passed through Valentine, Texas, three times on the way to and from the Way Out West Book Festival in Alpine and never saw a human being. Although the spectacular scenery of the Big Bend was very impressive, the persistent questions in her mind were "Where are the people?" and "Why do they come here and why do they stay?" So she asked Bill.

He had often mulled over the same questions. His first trip to the desert was in 1951 when, as a high school student, he traveled with his friends to the new Big Bend National Park. After a long weekend of exploration, hiking the Chisos

Mountains, discovering secret springs, and finding giant pines on the mountaintops, he was hooked. But even then, he couldn't imagine why anyone would (or comfortably could) live there. He felt the harsh desert regions of West Texas had not been receptive to human occupation and that the scarcity of water, and the extremes of temperature, made it unattractive in terms of comfort and sustainability.

The Big Bend doesn't have the trout streams of Colorado or the sunny, sandy beaches of Florida or California. Instead, this vast expanse of the great Chihuahuan Desert is naturally populated only by plants and animals that have adapted to extreme conditions, protecting themselves with spines or fangs. Why would anyone want to live here unless they had to? Between Marcia's literary curiosity about people and her love of good stories and Bill's photographic curiosity about people and his love of good stories, the idea for this book ignited.

It is only the progress of technology that has enabled human beings to sustainably occupy this harshly beautiful land. The earliest inhabitants were clustered around areas of natural water or transited the area in search of migratory game. Their scattered remains indicate a hardscrabble, tenuous existence. As you travel away from the Rio Grande and its now-capricious supply of water, human occupation is now dependent on wells or surface tanks and other mechanisms to provide water for man and animals. It would seem that the only realistic areas suitable for human occupation, economically speaking, would be those offering mining or ranching opportunities. Yet most of the small towns of the Big Bend continue to maintain their population numbers and even grow at a slow but steady rate. We knew the answers to our original questions—why people come to stay and, when and if they do leave, what is responsible for their departure—would be only speculation unless we went to find out.

There are already many books on the natural wonders of the Big Bend, but there are very few in-depth books on the experiences of the people who choose this area as their home. We decided to interview some of the inhabitants of the desert communities of the Big Bend: Fort Davis, Alpine, Presidio, Redford, Marfa, Balmorhea, Valentine, Terlingua and Study Butte, Marathon, and the Big Bend National Park. Through these discussions we hoped to find out what motivated people to come and, more importantly, to stay. We wondered if possibly these inhabitants, who accepted the inconveniences of living in these remote areas, facing difficulties that required their own skills to overcome, represent the greatest concentration of the fundamental character that has helped to make Texas an exceptional place.

What is Texas "exceptionalism"? Texans have traditionally regarded themselves as a different breed of people, manifesting traits of self-reliance, friendliness, and neighborliness not usually found in the general population. We wondered if these traits, and the need for them, had diminished over time in the sprawling urban centers of Texas. Does a search for a simpler, less-stressful existence prompt a move to smaller communities? We wondered if age was a factor in a longing for a Mayberry-like community.

Closely related to Texas exceptionalism is a belief in the existence of an "authentic" Texas, which in our definition refers to the values (or imagined values) of independence and self-reliance that inspired the early settlers of the state and fostered the expansion and development from early days until now. Certainly those values are present in all parts of the state and nation in areas with more services available, but perhaps it is concentrated in the Big Bend area, where living is indeed simpler in some ways but more complicated in others. Are there common traits among the people of the Big Bend that make them truly exceptional with the same traits that have characterized Texans for decades? Do our modern interconnected lives make it unnecessary to live the same self-reliant lives of the early settlers of Texas? Does the Texas spirit still exist, and are modern-day Texans just facing different obstacles?

Texas has always been a mythic place of vast open spaces, cowboys, cattle, and tough, independent men and women. Since urban sprawl has taken over previously luxuriously open space and growing corporations have brought people to Texas from elsewhere, that original image has been lost in much of the state, but in West Texas, we found, it is still alive and well. Do the people of the Big Bend, in fact, possess the character traits of what is believed to be authentic Texas?

In contemplating the lives of the people we would interview, we became acutely aware of our own assumptions about what makes a good life. We tried to imagine life without modern chain stores, coffee shops, big box stores, and instant availability to services a phone call away. Even though it is easier to live in a more populated area when emergencies occur, these people have chosen the inconvenience of limited services. What is life like when the nearest Walmart is 150 miles away? Do they miss it? What do they do when the plumbing doesn't work? We wondered if people who chose to live in these remote areas were by nature more independent or self-sufficient or whether they became that way by living there. A person living in a more urban environment would answer these questions differently: a twenty-four-hour plumber is available by only picking up the phone. Not an option in the Big Bend.

Armed with questions, we began to identify our subjects. We wanted year-round residents of the Big Bend who made a commitment to live there permanently, although we found some who began with second homes quickly made a permanent move. We were also intrigued with the people who were born and raised there, moved away for military service or jobs, but came home to stay, sometimes after many years away. We wanted a mix of age groups; we expected a large number of newly retired baby boomers, and they were there, but we were wrong to assume they would be the largest group.

What was the attraction for people who were not raised there, who had never previously called the Big Bend home? As our project unfolded, we discovered how deeply the spectacular scenery had affected the newcomers to the area and how much it influenced their decision to move there. Phrases such as "it is good for the soul" and "I just knew this is where I was supposed to be" were typical of their comments about their physical surroundings.

Beautiful mountains, a sky full of stars, spectacular sunsets and sunrises made it easy to believe in the power of scenery on the human spirit. In the midst of all the physical beauty of the Big Bend, strong community ties were formed. Again and again we heard that newcomers and long-time residents alike participated in the life of their towns, whether for civic or church activities, or simply were support to one another in times of need. Some found it fittingly ironic that those who live in big cities frequently create communities in cyberspace, finding those with common interests through the Internet that they communicate with regularly, yet have never met their next-door neighbors. So, in a crowded city full of people, you can easily be unknown and isolated, yet in the geographical isolation of the Big Bend, with far fewer people, you are known in the community. We were told several times that the downside of that was that everyone really did know everything about everyone else. Bad behavior would not go unnoticed.

Although most of the towns of the Big Bend have cable television, Internet, and cell-phone coverage, some do not. We found that the ones that do aren't always reliable, and somehow that isn't the problem we would perceive it to be elsewhere. Some people are very comfortable living entirely "off the grid."

Over the next two years we scheduled trips to the Big Bend for photographs and interviews, using Fort Davis as our base. Bill is a familiar face in these communities and has a second home in Limpia Crossing, a rural development north of Fort Davis. Marcia loves the historic Hotel Limpia, so Fort Davis was a practical and centrally located place to set out from each day.

We decided the interview trips should be

three to four days in length in order to cover the distances between communities. We were given the names of possible subjects by people such as Ramon Renteria of the *El Paso Times*, who grew up in Valentine. Bill asked the people he knew in Fort Davis, and since he had been coming to the Big Bend for decades, he had contacts in most of the towns we wanted to cover. As we began the interview process, the people we interviewed told us stories of people who should be included. We were aware that many people in the Big Bend needed to look us over before consenting to an interview. Contact by e-mail or telephone explaining our project would not result in permission to interview; a first trip to meet our potential subjects in order to interview them on a second trip was necessary.

We quickly realized that the communities were very different from one another. Everyone we spoke with had an opinion of how they differed. Terlingua is characterized as attracting ex-hippies and fiercely independent people. Donald Judd's Chinati Foundation in Marfa ensures a steady stream of artists in residence and interns and has attracted artists, writers, and gallery owners. Considered avant-garde and sophisticated, Marfa has lured people from New York City and other urban areas. Many have second homes and arrive by private jet. Alpine, with the hospital, supermarket, an Ace hardware store, Sul Ross State University, and a population of 6,000, is acknowledged as the big city of the Big Bend. Fort Davis is developing a reputation as a baby-boomer retiree town, with people fleeing Houston, Austin, Dallas, and other crowded areas for more peaceful surroundings.

Presidio, across the Rio Grande from Ojinaga, Mexico, is experiencing a surge in its population with the increase of border-patrol and law-enforcement personnel. Valentine is a very small town with a mix of long-time residents and younger families with children. Frequently, the parents work more than one job. Redford, an agricultural area across the international border from the Mexican village of El Mulato, has experienced the closing of businesses and schools in their tiny community. Marathon, considered the gateway to the Big Bend, has the Gage Hotel, one of the town's biggest employers, and is characterized as especially tightly knit.

The best stories of any area of Texas are the ones written about or told by the people who live there. The Big Bend itself has been the subject of many books of photography and guidebooks, but very few have been about the people who love this favored place. We were privileged to be welcomed by the people we interviewed, who shared their stories of returning to their original homes, with their family ties, or the people who made the leap of faith to make a life in an unknown place. Their reasons for making this part of West Texas their home are as varied as the people themselves.

We found that life in the Big Bend is not an acquired taste, either you love it or you don't. Sometimes visitors to the area decide to move there, under the spell of the scenery and the quiet, but find that a permanent way of life that does not include sophisticated medical care and the amenities of urban life is an insurmountable obstacle.

We were frequently told that the decision to live there was nearly instantaneous, much like love at first sight, overwhelming, inconvenient, and sometimes irrational. More than a few of our subjects first visited the Big Bend as children and vowed they would live there as adults. They returned to live there, sometimes several decades later.

Bill's love of the Big Bend has lasted six decades, but Marcia was a newcomer to the area. The first evening she sat on the porch of the Limpia Hotel in a rocking chair, looking at a sky full of stars, hearing the chimes from the Jeff Davis County Courthouse clock, she felt an inexplicable familiarity and connection with this place. She felt as if she had come home. This has been the experience of many who came from other cities and decided to stay.

The conversations we had lacked idle chatter and were very thoughtful and carefully considered. At first, we thought this was because most of the people interviewed were highly educated, formally or informally, but we were told several times when we remarked on this that isolation from traffic jams, noise, and the busyness of city life gave them the ultimate gift of time to think, look around, and appreciate the here and now of their lives.

Without access (except by Internet) to luxury goods, things to clutter up your life are much less important here. There is no need to impress others. If, in fact, the spirit of Texas is independence, self-sufficiency, appreciation of the land, and the careful stewardship of it, then that spirit is alive and well in the communities of the Big Bend. The popular notion of what real Texans are, according to the rest of the country, relies heavily on near-caricatures of vivacious, big-haired, cowboy-boot-wearing women and taciturn, weathered men with Stetsons, Levis, and cowboy boots. Jeans, boots, and hats are functional clothing in rural West Texas. Since we didn't see any big hair, we can say that isn't true.

All of us, at one time or another, have been traveling down a highway at night, away from an interstate or freeway, and have seen small clusters of houses set away from the road with lights in the windows. We speculate on the lives of the people in those houses and why they have chosen to live in these isolated areas. We found answers in the Big Bend during our quest for the characteristic traits of authentic Texas—the Texas of long ago.

The people of Texas are indeed distinctive in certain ways. The people who settled this vast land came for a variety of reasons, some to escape the law in the United States, some to look for opportunities to better their lives. To make that leap of faith and overcome the hardship of coming to an unknown, harsh country, they had to be self-reliant and courageous and have an entrepreneurial spirit and the ability to forge lasting relationships as members of a community, all characteristics that we have come to identify with pioneer Texas.

Although this was a new, unknown land to these settlers, it is in fact an ancient land. It was home to tribes of Native Americans including the Jumano, Apache, and Comanche. The Texas War of Independence, ending in 1836, also brought Mexican residents, whose families had lived for generations in the area, into the new nation of Texas. Only nine years later, they suddenly changed nationalities again, becoming Americans with the addition of Texas to the Union.

In modern-day West Texas, the same distinctive traits are still apparent. In the larger Texas cities of Dallas, Houston, San Antonio, and Austin, corporations and other factors bring people to these cities from all over the world, and the urban environment often dilutes those characteristics. We have found in the Big Bend that the Texas character is still alive.

MARCIA HATFIELD DAUDISTEL AND BILL WRIGHT
El Paso, Texas, and Abilene, Texas

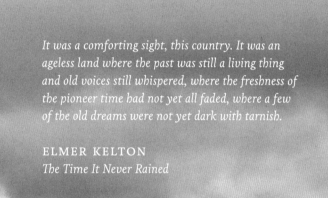

It was a comforting sight, this country. It was an ageless land where the past was still a living thing and old voices still whispered, where the freshness of the pioneer time had not yet all faded, where a few of the old dreams were not yet dark with tarnish.

ELMER KELTON
The Time It Never Rained

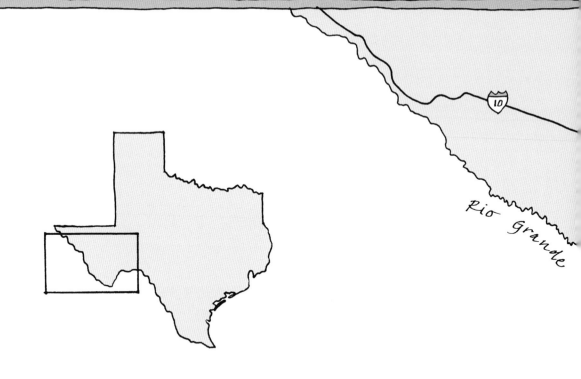

Rio Grande

Big Bend
★ TEXAS ★

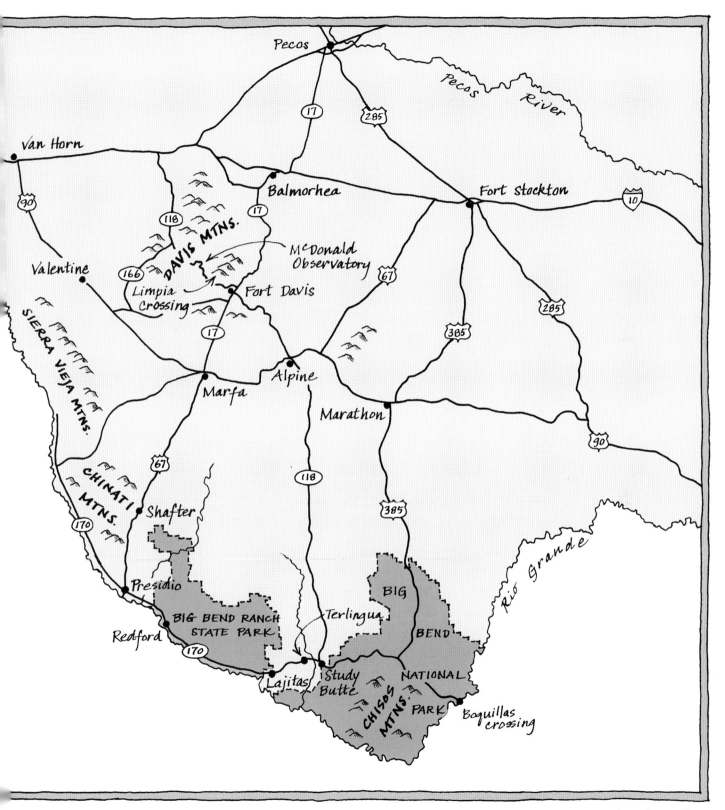

Pecos

Pecos River

17 285

Van Horn

Balmorhea

Fort Stockton

90

118

17

10

Valentine

DAVIS MTNS.

McDonald
Observatory

166

Limpia
Crossing

Fort Davis

67

17

285

SIERRA VIEJA MTNS.

385

Marfa

Alpine

Marathon

90

CHINATI
MTNS.

67

118

Shafter

385

170

Presidio

BIG

BEND

Redford

BIG BEND RANCH
STATE PARK

Terlingua

170

Lajitas

Study
Butte

NATIONAL

PARK

CHISOS
MTNS.

Boquillas
crossing

Rio Grande

Map by Molly O'Halloran

MARATHON

When brothers Solomon and Mayer Halff from San Antonio bought land in the Big Bend, they became two of the early settlers moving into the region during the nineteenth century. The brothers established the Circle Dot Ranch, only a few miles from the future town of Marathon, and leased land to the federal government for the establishment of Camp Peña Colorado, which served as the population center before the arrival of the railroad in 1882.

When the Galveston, Harrisburg & San Antonio Railway came to Presidio County, former sea captain and railroad surveyor Captain Albion E. Shepard bought land for his Iron Mountain Ranch, and more people settled in the area near the railroad. When a post office was established, Captain Shepard named the resulting community Marathon because its terrain reminded him of the plains of Marathon, Greece. Today Marathon, now part of Brewster County, is the county's second-largest city, with a population of nearly five hundred full-time residents.

The city has enjoyed a colorful history. Beginning as a shipping point for cattle from area ranches, it became the focal point for the U.S. military during the border problems resulting from the Mexican Revolution in 1910. The young captain Douglas MacArthur was the first to command troops there, soon followed by Lieutenant George S. Patton.

Over the years the community grew, seeing various commercial ventures come and go. For a while, it was the center for rubber produced from the guayule plant, and a large bee apiary was established. Later, fluorspar from mines in Mexico was processed and shipped. By 1914, Marathon had grown to a population of six hundred persons, with several stores, a bank, and a pool hall. Without a jail in this sometimes boisterous frontier town, drunks and minor offenders were chained to the legs of a windmill in the middle of town, and more serious perpetrators sent to a real jail in Alpine.

The beautiful landscape of Marathon, with its views of Iron Mountain to the north and Santiago Peak to the south, is typical of the scenery of the Big Bend. The spare high-desert landscape is uncluttered with billboards, and the roads wind through some of the most spectacular views in the Southwest. Part of the adventure of a trip to

Marathon is getting there. Whether flying, then driving, or going by train, travelers will see the spectacular scenery unfold along the way. The closest airports with scheduled service are Midland International, 170 miles away, and El Paso International, 215 miles west.

Marathon is the eastern gateway to Big Bend National Park, forty miles from the park entrance at Persimmon Gap. With nearly 350 days of sunshine per year and an altitude of 4,000 feet, Marathon also draws people year-round for camping and easy access to Big Bend National Park for day trips.

There is ample lodging for visitors to Marathon, including the historic Gage Hotel, designed by the well-known architectural firm Trost & Trost, which also designed El Paisano in Marfa,

El Capitan in Van Horn, and many other buildings in the Southwest. Owner J. P. Bryan restored the Gage in 1978. Bryan—financier, oil executive, and dedicated historian—in many respects did for Marathon what artist Donald Judd did for Marfa, and the remodeled Gage spawned bed-and-breakfasts, restaurants, galleries, and a bookstore.

Marathon received national attention in 1964 when the Marathon Chamber of Commerce was established. It was the only Chamber in the United States that was composed entirely of women. The Chamber of Commerce maintains an informative website and sponsors two annual fall events, a cabrito cook-off and dance, and the Marathon to Marathon Race between Alpine and Marathon, attracting runners and their families to the area.

The Utopians

★

CLYDE CURRY AND KATE THAYER

On Avenue C and North Third Street in Marathon, we encounter what at first glance appears to be a southwestern fairytale cottage called Eve's Garden. Despite its unique style, which borrows from southwestern architecture with characteristic arches and courtyards enhanced by eye-catching colors, this organic bed-and-breakfast is not a commercially inspired replica of Santa Fe and Taos, New Mexico, establishments but rather a well-crafted reflection of the taste, style, and unique vision of owners Kate Thayer and Clyde Curry. Kate and Clyde have sought to create an environment that stimulates thought and discussion and serves as an inviting setting for people to reflect on green architecture, ecology, and art. Their website, www.evesgarden.org, states: "Eve's Garden is a research level organic gardening demonstration site and an urban hacienda, combining to provide a comfortable Bed and Breakfast environment and a conversational forum to address issues regarding the ecology we live in."

Kate Thayer and Clyde Curry met and married in Marathon. Kate moved from Houston eleven years ago with a sense of relief at not having to lock her car while she filled it with gas. In Houston, she remembers, "it didn't matter where you lived or how much money you had, you were constantly worried about your stuff or yourself."

Eighteen years ago, Clyde came to Marathon from Virginia. Clyde's interest in building communities a different way began there. "In Reston, Virginia, where I came from, it was a progressive sixties town done by the oil companies. They brought twenty-eight architectural firms from all around the world to design the place. And the idea was to put lots of village centers, and then there'll be one little high-rise no higher than ten stories, a lake, a golf course, and then lots of condominium townhouses," he says.

Reston was a forerunner of the planned, gated communities that are commonplace today. These communities have strict regulations and covenants for the maintenance and building of homes in the development. Clyde began to chafe at the restrictions of the building code. Although the restrictions kept the community pristine and uniform, he rebelled at some of the more stringent rules. "You weren't allowed to paint your door, unless it was Reston Brown, and Reston Brown sucked. We spent a lot of time, about forty of us, painting our front doors red." Cited for this irregularity, the offender would repaint the door Reston Brown and bring a photograph to show the work was done before an appearing at the community's architectural board of review. During that hearing, others in the group would be painting their doors red.

He studied architecture and privately taught solar energy architecture, but he soon realized he would need millions of dollars to pursue this experimental work and build in Virginia. In Marathon, Clyde found the freedom to use different building materials. "For me, it's great. If you really want to answer problems, you've got to get way beyond the building code," he says.

Clyde was building a straw-bale house when

Kate moved to Marathon to work with a friend in starting a bed and breakfast. When the partnership dissolved, both Kate's house and the house that was meant to be the bed and breakfast were being renovated, and Kate owned both houses. Clyde started work on Kate's house midway during the renovation of the bed and breakfast, and Kate's home became Eve's Garden. Continuing the renovation of the other house, Kate and Clyde discovered their shared passion for the environment. Kate jokes she couldn't afford to pay Clyde anymore, so she married him.

There was the challenge of making a living, but doing so in accord with what they were most passionate about: the sustainability of the planet. Kate observed, "In a small town, there is no job unless you create one of any consequence. We were working on this project so we just started planning. We had enough land so we decided we would build it into a B&B. But it's changed a million times from the original plans," she says. Clyde completed his straw-bale house, so they rented it out and started adding a room at a time to Eve's Garden.

In remodeling their home and Eve's Garden, Clyde and Kate originally followed the standard southwest adobe-building method for the new construction, but Clyde soon discovered the value of papercrete. Mud, stones, and sticks are common building materials throughout the world, so using papercrete, which is made of portland cement and recycled paper, is essentially a modern adaptation of an ancient technology. The material is strong and highly insulating owing to the high density of the air pockets; the portland cement provides strength. Clyde explains that the modern process first gained popularity in New Mexico. Kate remembers their early efforts with papercrete. "We were making real adobe bricks, which are extremely heavy to drag around, and Clyde came in one day and said 'I found this papercrete stuff on the Internet, and for a little more money you can play around with this,'" she says. Clyde calls their efforts the Build It and Break It Center for Papercrete. They tested their materials to determine how far they could be stressed.

When Eve's Garden opened as a B&B, Kate and Clyde did not want it to be traditional or typical. "Usually, it's a creaky old house with somebody on the other side of the wall, so you're a little worried about that," Kate says. Another common perception of bed-and-breakfasts is a décor that is either country, with geese, rabbits, and kitsch, or Victorian, with lace and doilies. Clyde thinks everyone is getting tired of "Victoriana and froufrou."

We begin a tour of the building, going from the colorful and comfortable main house, passing through a doorway from the living room, and encounter an indoor lap pool, situated in a grotto like alcove. Blue-green light flickers and wavers on walls embedded with colored glass. As part of Clyde and Kate's plan, it is not just a stylistic feature but also an eye-catching part of their ongoing commitment to the environment. Clyde informs us that the pool acts as an energy-storage system with the greenhouse. They built the heat exchangers for $5.00. "We use the greenhouse, which produces an incredible amount of excess heat most of the time. We take that heat and change it into a different storage medium, the water in the pool, and put that energy away and then bring it out later when we need it," he explains.

Through another doorway, we find ourselves in a central roofed courtyard that is also the greenhouse, devoted to growing organic flowers. It is not a typical glass-enclosed greenhouse; it is fully incorporated into the building. The space is colorful, green, and lush, full of spectacular flowers: tall English rose bushes, bougainvillea, and other interesting varieties, including lilies that typically grow in South America and some very impressive amaryllis. There are too many varieties of flowers to name. The vivid colors and strong fragrance of the flowers make a convincing case for organic gardening. The garden is planted in soil only eight inches deep, with solid rock underneath.

Kate creates flower arrangements through her business Flowers by Kate for weddings in the area and has provided the flower arrangements for the Gage Hotel for three and a half years. She obtains seeds from different sources. We ask if all their vegetables are grown on the premises, and learn from Clyde that they buy nearly all their vegetables from a co-op in Alpine called Blue Waters, but they do grow some of their own and plan to grow more as a research project. Clyde explains that a book, *Gardening for the Future of the Earth* by Seeds of Change, led to their commitment to organic gardening and the use of organic seed. "They tell you how as geneticists, they went into Mexico and surveyed all the old varieties and tried to document them and save seed. They brought it back and started Seeds of Change to propagate organic seed and insure the biodiversity," he says.

The guest suites in Eve's Garden are off the greenhouse/atrium area and are completely private. Privacy is important to Kate, both for the guests and for herself and Clyde. Light streams in from the top of the domed ceilings in each room. The use of semi-transparent mineral rock, resembling isinglass, instead of window glass is perhaps one of the most extraordinary features

of the B&B. The light is filtered and soft, with a luminous quality.

On the back of the building is a large dome, called the "papercrete palace," which is the newest living quarters for Kate's son Noble and his wife Alaine. Noble and Alaine, who work with a nonprofit ecotourist conservation group, divide their time between Eve's Garden and Costa Rica. When they are in Marathon, they assist in the ongoing new construction projects.

A stay at Eve's Garden is an opportunity to participate in discussions about the environment, but a guest is free to engage in conversation as much or as little as they wish. More often than not, the discussions become lively, and frequently guests find that they stay a little longer than planned. In addition to hosting guests, Clyde and Kate conduct tours of the building for anyone who comes by, which leads to unexpected company. They estimate they conduct about two thousand walk-throughs and have six to seven hundred guests a year.

As committed environmentalists, Kate and Clyde wondered how they could affect the thinking of many people in the isolation of the Big Bend. "The whole world needs to understand this, so we decided to become the Hope Center. We purposely paint the radical colors for the excitability level and attract people," says Clyde. The architecture and colors inspire conversations about Eve's Garden and environmental issues.

Many times, guests find themselves still at the breakfast table talking when checkout time arrives. Clyde and Kate hope these conversations will motivate the guests to adopt at least one change in their lives at home and pass it on to inspire others to make a change that will benefit the environment. "Real change comes from people who step out beyond the rest and just decide to do it. They need leadership, and so you have two levels. What we need to do is train leaders," Clyde says.

Clyde and Kate tell us there were nearly four million visitors to Marathon in the past ten years. They have the opportunity to observe what sets the tourists apart from the ones who choose to live here. "Having been here twenty years, [I'd say] the ones who came here first couldn't make it elsewhere. They were coming because it was cheap and there was an alternative lifestyle," Clyde says. "In my case, I was so tired of the stupid Beltway scene. As a carpenter, even though I was a tradesman making twenty-eight bucks an hour, I could not afford a house. I came out here in order to have a life." Kate shares her feelings about their home at Eve's Garden: "This is our little oasis. When you live in a desert, most people build an oasis because that's how you survive."

Since the time of this interview, Kate and Clyde have divorced. Clyde is moving to Abiquiú, New Mexico, hoping to establish a holistic wellness center with a friend.

After twelve years, Eve's Garden is firmly established, and Kate will continue as the owner in partnership with her son Noble Baker and daughter-in-law Alaine Berg, who plan to spend more time in Marathon. Expansion plans have been made. "A new media and meeting room with a kitchen and a television room for guests, with a capacity of twenty, will be built," Kate says. The business is doing well, and Eve's Garden is still blooming.

The Book Man of Marathon

★

ADAM MUHLIG

Adam Muhlig was the most unlikely of persons to move to the Big Bend. Happily ensconced in an upscale Houston bookstore, Deterring Book Gallery, where he appraised and sold rare books, the dry and thorny reality of the northern Chihuahuan Desert would not seem a compelling destination. But then, Adam didn't know what it was like.

Born in lush Florence, South Carolina, he grew up in a very literary environment. His father, a teacher and Ezra Pound scholar with specialties in composition and rhetoric, introduced Adam to books and music early in his life, and there were always writers and musicians coming through their house. "As a kid, it really got me interested in books and music," he says.

Adam always worked in the book trade in some capacity. He did college work at the University of North Carolina, and when a number of his friends moved to Austin, Texas, he followed. Adam explains, "Some were interested in the music scene, and I was involved on the periphery and came to Austin a couple of times to visit. I found it was a great place to live. I packed up and headed west and that's how I ended up in Austin in 1999."

After a while, he moved to Houston and worked for Oscar Graham at Deterring Book Gallery in the rare book room, where he helped start the gallery's Internet book program for selling rare books and manuscripts. He also did some appraisals while he was there.

"Herman Deterring, who owned Deterring Book Gallery, was an artist and very interested in photography," Adam says. "He showed me several books on the Big Bend and then his own photographs," Adam remembers. Soon Adam found another connection to the Big Bend that was intriguing. When he joined his friends at their usual bar, the West Alabama Icehouse in Houston, he found out that several of his friends made camping trips to the area.

Adam was recovering from complications from a surgery for an earlier serious illness. "Going through that freaks you out. It changes you. I was twenty-five years old, and twenty-five-year-old males typically think they are invincible. So that was another thing that was hard to wrap your head around."

After the idea of visiting the Big Bend was planted in his mind, he began paying more attention when the area was mentioned. A friend and coworker named Jebbie told Adam that the Big Bend was a healing place for some people and was a great place to go and have time to figure

out what he wanted to do next. He also knew a woman with family there. "Her name was Carol Brown," he says. "I don't think she went out there much, but her mother lived in the Big Bend and she said she would introduce me around." So he decided to go and see what all the fuss was about.

His first trip to the Big Bend was to Marathon. He described the trip slowly, savoring the memory. "When I left Houston and I didn't understand how far it was, I said, 'Alright, I'm just going to drive out there.' It was early afternoon, and I drove the rest of the day into the evening! I still wasn't there, I just kept looking at the maps; I didn't have a GPS or anything. I kept going, 'It's really a long way out here!'"

When Adam took the Fort Stockton exit off I-10, he was dismayed and wondered what he had gotten himself into. By this time it was dark, and there was nothing there in the darkness but stars. Driving toward Marathon he began to listen to music. It was music, he believed, that connected him with the West Texas landscape.

Adam has a very eclectic taste in music and is a fan of Brian Eno, an ambient composer from England, and his band, Roxy Music. "When I listened to Brian Eno, that's what I thought about the landscape in West Texas," he says. "I was also thinking about an album called *Apollo*, which Eno did when they finally started editing the *Apollo* mission's tens of thousands of hours of film footage. NASA hired him to put music to all that film. I thought about that music when I was looking at the stars and the Milky Way on that long drive."

He finally arrived in Marathon and in the next few days investigated the town and surrounding territory. It was fascinating. However, he found that the Big Bend can be an acquired taste, and everyone who stays develops different reasons for being there. "Everyone has a different conversion experience," he says. "The landscape, that's what did it for me. It's just the stark contrast and the sheer remoteness of it. For a guy from the Carolinas, the drive on US 385 between Marathon and the Big Bend National Park completely blew my mind. I thought I had literally gone to the moon!" Afterward Adam found out that when the Apollo astronauts came back, they said the landscape most similar to the lunar landscape was the Big Bend landscape. He thought that was fascinating!

The remoteness of the area, the sparse population, and the uncluttered landscape invariably lend themselves to introspection for most people. It is in this vast solitude that Adam, recovering from surgery, made some profound life decisions. "The emptiness, the sky, the desert forced me to think about a lot of things about myself internally and how I approach things and how I saw my life view of myself. It made me more introspective than anything. And that's what I liked about it."

Adam hated living in Houston. "When you work in a rare-book store, you don't make a lot of money, especially when you are on the low end of the totem pole. I was poor and living in Houston, and poor and Houston just don't work. So I'm thinking I just want to get the hell out of here. I just decided screw it, I'm going to move out there."

He returned to Houston and quit his job at the bookstore and moved first to Marathon. He picked up a few miscellaneous jobs to keep him afloat. He did welding projects and erected fences with Mike Johnson on Iron Mountain Ranch and worked at the Chevron station behind the counter for the owner, Ernesto. "Marathon is tiny and everyone knows one another, but it's still very segregated. Many Hispanics don't really like white people, and in some ways understandably so, but I had a very interesting insight into all that because I befriended Ernesto as well as his brother, who owns the Shell station. He gave credit to essentially all the poorer people in town. He was more or less the 'company store.'"

Adam had been doing appraisal work in Houston, and he was able to continue because of Internet access. He was also working for a poet, William Jay Smith, poet laureate of the United States between 1968 and 1970. Smith lived in the Berkshires in Massachusetts, so Adam was going back and forth. "I was doing this project, appraising his archive, which took two years. . . . I would go to the Berkshires, then work for a month or two and catalog the stuff. Then I'd go back to Marathon, and I would do research."

He found that the money he earned on the appraisal project went much further in Marathon than in Houston or Austin. "I think in Marathon definitely you have to have an outside source of income—either [you're] an artist or a writer, or you made your money elsewhere and go there to retire."

Adam began to make friends in Marathon, including James Evans, E. Dan Klepper, and Alan Tennant, who encouraged him to make the move to the Big Bend. "Alan had just finished *On the Wing*, and it had just been published when I got there. I began working with Alan, and this was right before he was going on his book tour with Knopf for *On the Wing*. That was also during the time when they were negotiating the rights for a movie. I was helping him work on that, so I was going back and forth to Los Angeles. Robert Redford and Terrence Malick bought the rights for *On the Wing*."

Adam says that one of the most interesting people he met in Marathon was the artist Monte Schatz. Adam found Monte to be a very interesting character, as well as a good friend. "Monte was obsessed with amphibians and reptiles, he had Gila monsters, pit vipers, rattlesnakes, and he kept them all in his house in cages," Adam says. "He had this Vietnamese pit viper, which is one of the most venomous snakes in the world in his house. He actually slept with rattlesnakes, which was very creepy." Monte also had an albino king cobra that he would take to Adam's house. Monte was very attached to his reptiles, so when he had to go to Santa Fe for a few days for a big opening, he asked Adam to take care of the animals.

Adam thought about it and agreed but told him he was not feeding any of the really venomous snakes. Adam agreed to take care of the rattlesnakes but told Monte he would not touch the pit viper or the cobras. He went to Monte's house

a few days before the trip to be trained in the feeding procedures.

The first day he checked on the animals everything went well. "Monte had these two giant turtles in four hundred gallon tanks, the size of a bookcase, in the back of his house. They would swim around, and he had this one turtle, her name was Plumy Bum. I fed her the first day and she's swimming around in this big ole tank," Adam says. "The second day, I get over there and I feed all the snakes and I get to the back where he has the turtles. And Plumy Bum is floating. She is no longer with us—completely waterlogged and kind of half submerged. She had died." The turtle was fourteen or fifteen years old. Unsure of what to do next, Adam called a friend, Sue Roberts.

"He'd had her forever, so I freaked out, I think I may have called James Evans and a couple of other people, too. I said, 'What the hell am I going to do with this turtle?'" Adam says. "I don't remember who said this, but they said, 'You know what, Adam, drain all the water out of her and break her neck and break all of her legs, where they are just hanging, and stuff her in the freezer.'"

Adam did not want to call Monte while he was at his big opening, so he followed his friend's advice. The turtle was very large and waterlogged. "I don't know her diameter, it was eighteen to twenty inches. I drain her out, I break her neck, I break all of her arms, and I open the freezer in Monte's studio," Adam says. "There were probably fifty or one hundred lizards and snakes in there that had been his pets and friends in the past that he had frozen in there. I was thinking this is like Jeffrey Dahmer land here!" Adam placed the turtle in a big plastic bag, but the freezer was nearly full with the other reptile bodies. "I had to stuff Plumy Bum in there and literally stand on top of her. It was a chest freezer. I pushed the door back down and put weight on top of it so Plumy Bum would stay in there and stay frozen," Adam says. "I did all that and got out of there, because it did spook me. When he got back he was very sad, but he said, 'I appreciate you not calling me, and you did the right thing by sticking her in the freezer.'"

Living in Marathon, Adam also recognizes a darker side to living in a small town. Small-town life can breed grievances and grudges among such a small number of people, and Adam felt an undercurrent running through Marathon, sometimes resulting in drunken fights. Tourists to the area are unlikely to see much of that violence, but Adam recognizes that people in Marathon are tough. "Once you stay there and you are isolated in some way for some [time], [it can make] a lot of people a little crazy in Marathon and Terlingua," he says. "It's like those guys who live in the mine shafts in Terlingua. It's definitely an ascetic lifestyle if you choose to do that. I think it's great

if you want to do that, but it's something that you have to commit to 100 percent."

In Adam's three years of living in Marathon, he recovered completely from his illness and thought it was exactly what he needed at the right time in his life. Although he enjoyed living in Marathon for that time, he found it was necessary to leave. "I think everyone who goes out there is looking for something, or you might be running away from something," Adam says. "I think if you talk to people, those are a couple of themes that will come up. One of the reasons I left is because of what I do; it is impossible to live there, even with the Internet. I was both running and seeking when I went out there."

Today, Adam lives with his wife Ellie in Chicago, but they are keeping their home in Austin. He met Ellie in Marathon at the Marathon Coffee Shop, and they stayed in touch, and now they are married with a young daughter. Ellie's family ranches in South Texas, so the odds are Marathon will see them again.

The Cowboy and the Au Pair

★

IKE AND SUE ROBERTS

The Big Bend is a place known for good stories and good barbecue, and Ike Roberts is well known for both. He fits the Big Bend of Texas country like a foot fits a handmade boot. The day we went to his Z Bar Ranch to meet Ike and his wife Sue, it was cold, overcast, and windy, but like Ike and Sue themselves, their home is warm and comfortable. Also located on the working ranch is Z Bar Farms, the successful dairy owned and operated by their daughter Sally.

Ike and Sue are different in several ways, like two peas, but from different pods. Sue is a lively and vivacious woman with a charming English accent, but Ike has the watchful stillness of people who have spent most of their lives outdoors. He has a dry Bob Newhart kind of wit, and he was clearly unaccustomed to sitting in a chair indoors and answering questions.

Ike's family has a long history in ranching, mostly gained in working on the Gage Ranch. It was because of the Gage Ranch that Ike met his life partner.

Sue was employed in the City of Birmingham, England, as a dental assistant, working with children. One cold and rainy day she was waiting for the bus and made a decision. "I thought there's got to be somewhere else in the world that's not like this," she remembers. Sue was twenty and ready for a change of scene. "Lots of people my age then took jobs as an au pair, where you live with the family," she says. Most au pairs chose France or a country where they could use their second language, but Sue chose a country where English was spoken. She registered with a placement agency in London.

She had five offers but took a job with the Holland family, who were part of the Gage Ranch. She came to the ranch, twenty miles south of Marathon, in June 1966. "This was the wildest offer; it involved a lot of horseback riding. I rode in England and belonged to the South Staffordshire Pony Club, and I like horses. They had a cook and a houseboy, so all I had was the children," Sue says. She was in charge of three children, Dick, aged six, Ann, five, and Dorothy, two. "I'd get them up and dressed and we'd go ride. It was a pretty neat job, except we were miles from everywhere," she says. Sandra Holland, the mother of the children, began to worry that Sue was lonely. "I was not lonely. I had a boyfriend in England who called me while I was here, but I was fed up with him," Sue says.

Then she met Ike at a filling station and saw him later at a Fourth of July dance. Ike began working for the Hollands on the ranch and began

seeing Sue on a regular basis; however, he had to contend with a twelve-year-old boy as their chaperone, the son of the Hollands.

Sue had planned to stay six months as an au pair, then go to Australia where her uncle lived, but she never made it to Australia. After deciding to marry Ike, she left the ranch and returned to England, where the marriage was to take place. Sue is Catholic and Ike is not, so permission from the bishop was required for their marriage. Ike had to receive instruction from the parish priest, who was from Ireland. Sue says, "I'd walk up towards the church and meet him. Ike finally said, 'You know, this religion isn't half bad. We've been drinking paddy whiskey all morning.'"

Ike realized that his attire, which was rather exotic in London, drew attention when he noticed a man following and staring at him. He says, "When I was in England, I always had on my boots and hat. My God, I'd rather be caught without my drawers than my hat. I did enjoy seeing London; my sister-in-law used to send me books of the London Underground. I tell people that's the best way to see London, go under it."

Ike returned to the ranch the day after they married while Sue stayed behind in England to begin the legal residency paperwork for her to move back to the United States. She joined Ike only twenty-one days later, in spite of the fact that the paperwork could take up to six months to be approved. Ike went to his boss, who knew John Connally, the governor of Texas at the time, and asked if he could contact Connally to expedite the process. "He said, 'I can do better than that. I can talk to Lyndon Johnson in the White House,'" Sue says. It was a coincidence that our first meeting with Ike and Sue was on the anniversary of the day forty-five years before that Sue rejoined Ike in Marathon.

Ike was born in Alpine to a ranching family that owned a ranch west of Marathon. He has two brothers—John, who has their father's ranch sixteen miles southwest of Marathon, and Travis, who has their grandfather's ranch—and a sister Betty, who lives in Fort Stockton. His grandfather worked for Alfred Gage for over fifty years, and Ike worked for the Gage Ranch for fifty-two years, making Ike the third generation in his family with strong ties there. "My granddad was a foreman and manager up until he retired in 1950, and my dad was general manager up until 1970. I was manager and foreman up until 2005," Ike says.

Ike and Sue have three children: Joe, Tim, and Sally. When Sue was expecting Joe, the doctor was in Alpine, thirty-six miles away. Sue had an English friend in Alpine who had a book of exercises for pregnant women to make delivery easier.

"I told the doctor I was doing these exercises. He said 'You can do them if you want, but they're from England. In England there's a word poppycock, which means a bunch of bull. And that's what they are,'" Sue says. "I did them anyway, so when the baby was coming, Ike called for the doctor who said, 'Well, for a first baby, it's going to be hours, so just come along,'" Sue says. Ike laughs, "We had Joey on the road, so on his birth certificate it says, 'Hwy 90,' East of Alpine."

The two boys Joey and Tim were named after Sue's father and two grandfathers, but Ike named Sally. "It was the name of the first cow he ever had. So she was named after a cow and the boys were named after my family," says Sue.

All three of their children were educated in Marathon, but all spent time as exchange students. Ike and Sue wanted them to know more of the world outside the Big Bend. Sally was part of an exchange program through the San Antonio schools and spent a year in Venezuela, then in Germany and Australia as part of a farm exchange. Joey went to Switzerland, and Tim went to Costa Rica, also as part of an exchange program. On their return, they all attended and graduated from Sul Ross State University in Alpine, Sally with degrees in Spanish and chemistry, Joe with a degree in history and a master's degree in international trade, and Tim with a degree in political science.

It was through their children's experience with the student-exchange program that Ike and Sue became host parents for the program. "We hosted a total of thirty kids, not all at once, from all over the world for nine or ten years," Sue says. In addition to these students, children from La Linda, Mexico, attended the Marathon schools because their parents were employed at the fluorspar mine. "I used to substitute teach some of the time, teaching English as a Second Language. I had all these little Mexican girls and boys, but when the fluorspar mine closed down because it was cheaper to get it out of China, everyone went back to Chihuahua," Sue says. "There were two sisters, Hilda, who was fifteen and Zaira, who was fourteen. Their dad said: 'I wish my girls could finish, because they'll do so much better in Mexico if they have two languages.'" Sue asked if they could take the girls so they could finish their final school year, and their father agreed.

In addition to becoming proficient in English, Zaira also became Joey's wife. "Joey was eight years older than Zaira and was already at the university, so he was living in Alpine. It was years later when he started working at the Park, that he was taking the Diablos, the Mexican firefighters from Boquillas into the Park, and he had to speak Spanish to be able to take them out," Sue says. "I thought he was down in Chihuahua with the girls because he's learning Spanish. He wasn't. He was courting Zaira." Joey is now the district ranger for the east side region of Big Bend National Park, where he lives with Zaira and their three children, Larry, Michael, and George.

Their son Tim lives in Midland now, working in the oil fields, having returned to the area after living in Phoenix for ten years. "He was a tour guide in Washington, D.C., for the 4-H, and he worked for Paul Newman's Children's Ranch, for terminally ill kids. He was the horse wrangler," Sue says.

Sally worked for the Forest Service and lived in Douglas, Arizona, Portland, Oregon, and Swan Valley, Idaho, after working in Big Bend National Park. "You know, we can't get rid of them," Sue laughs. "So there's got to be something that draws them back."

Ike and Sue feel strongly that truly self-reliant children are raised in the country. "I worked with a lot of kids, even high school kids quite a number of years ago, and any kid that has some 'try' is great. All the kids that were raised in the country had some try. Even a lot of the Sul Ross kids I worked with didn't have any try," Ike says. "My son Joe had to repair a fence around Cottonwood Campground due to the flood. He wanted to know if I could come down and cook for the crew and help with the fence. Those young people didn't have any try. They didn't know how to start, even two big boys who were over six feet and 220–230 pounds!"

Ike knows that children raised in a rural environment see the source of their food and water, not just the end result. "If they didn't have water pipes in the house, they wouldn't know where to get a drink of water," Ike says. "There's a little girl, whose dad works in the park, who comes by and gets milk and eggs at least once a week. She's three years old and she went down with Sally to feed and put out hay for the cows. She said, 'You know, it's hay today and it's milk in the morning.' Three years old and she realized that."

When we were leaving, Ike showed us the sidewalk outside the house. The year 1926 is marked in the cement. "We got this place after we were married. This is an old place, and I'm sure the sidewalk wasn't built first, it says 1926, but the house was already built before they poured the sidewalk. The people who had this before dropped the ceiling. It was eight-foot. We took all that out and went back to the original. It's a little harder to heat, but put another jacket on. It's cool in the summer though," Ike says. When Ike and Sue said goodbye, they invited us back for the rare opportunity to ride around the A. S. Gage Ranch for a day.

When we came back in the spring, it was warm and sunny. Before we left for the ranch, we drove a short distance from the house to Sally's Z Bar Farms, the location of her dairy. The barn is home to the goats and sheep in pens, and the cows are outside the barn. It is a clean and bright place with chickens, cats, and dogs, as well. We watched as Sally brought out the goats to nurse, then went inside the adjacent building where she has a small office and her cheese-making room.

Sally has been licensed as a cheese maker for

over three years. "With the state of Texas, I have to have a cheese plant license. We have chèvre, plain, herb, and pepper. Then I press the chèvre and soak it in red wine so I can get rounds that have this beautiful color," Sally says. "I do burgundy and port. I do mozzarella, feta and pepper feta, all in goat's milk, then provolone in cow's milk, cottage cheese in cow's milk and asadero in cow's milk. I also do Greek yogurt in goat's milk." Sally packages and sells her cheese, and the farm also produces milk and eggs. She follows stringent guidelines in her cheese making and uses organic practices in her production. "To get the certified organic label, I would have to have organic feed sources. I can't find an organic feed source. That's why I have ticks on the dogs because I am using diatomaceous earth to get away from any sort of chemical. I think that is causing most of the problems that people have health wise," she says. Sally grows all the herbs and peppers that are incorporated into her cheese.

Sally worked for the Park Service for six years, then went to work for the Forest Service as a helicopter rapeller for eight years, rapelling into fires. "I was the liaison between the government and the private helicopter company. And so it was all contracts. I was responsible for the government's half of the money," Sally says.

She finally tired of the bureaucratic paperwork and decided to do something else, this time raising goats. "I started raising goats when I was fourteen with the 4-H project, and so I called Dad and said, 'What if I do something with my goats? You know, dairy goats or something?' He called back a week later and said, 'I got you six Alpine goats.' Now I've been in business for just over four years," Sally says. She is still on call for the Park Service as a firefighter.

Sally also makes goat's-milk soap and lotions and has heard from her customers with skin sensitivities that the products do not cause skin irritations. "One of my customers is a friend of mine and a cancer survivor. I send her my soap because it doesn't make her skin break out. To be able to grow and produce something that helps people is the most amazing thing," she says.

She is building a house on the property, and it is a work in progress. She acquired her building skills during the slow seasons of firefighting when the crews would refurbish sites in the Park, hanging doors and building small structures. She is using a lot of recycled material. "The concrete is new, the steel is new, and a friend of mine comes over and does framing for me. It's fun to see what I can come up with from other people's leftovers and what you can build without being a huge consumer," Sally says. The exterior is nearly complete, so Sally lives in the house while she finishes the interior. When complete, it will be a comfortable home with unusual and colorful touches.

It is her parents she credits for teaching her and her brothers to be self-reliant and independent. "They just persevere; they keep going, regardless. Drought, whatever happens, they stick together and keep plodding along. That is what they have given my brothers and I, you just keep going regardless of what you face," says Sally. "Don't sit there and whine about it. I think that's the greatest thing they've given us, not to be afraid to try anything."

We drove onto the Gage Ranch, and Ike was in his element, sharing his encyclopedic knowledge of the history of the area ranches. He can name every plant, animal, and rock formation on the Gage. He tells us that before the Gage was divided, it had over five hundred thousand acres, and after,

it had a little over four hundred thousand acres. "Right now there's two hundred thousand acres in each half. In the east half, they've sold a bunch of that into smaller tracts. This is the west side and it's still all in one piece," Ike says. He began working on the ranch at the age of twelve, when his father was foreman, so there is not one acre of the ranch that Ike does not know.

The Holland Gage Estate owns the east half of the ranch, which was divided four ways, between Bill and Roxina Donnell, Gage Holland, Ed Holland, and Kathleen Olsen. The Paisano Cattle Company owns the west half. There were two daughters in the Gage family. The oldest daughter had four children, two sons and two daughters, and the younger daughter, on the west half, had four children, a son and three daughters.

Although there are a few employees who live permanently on the ranch, none of the many Gage descendants live there. "They all live in San Antonio. Mr. Gage had a house in San Antonio, too. He lived there later on. He had a house here; in fact, he had several houses, but his first house was a dugout on the creek over there," Ike says. "The cattle business is where he made most of his money, but it's like a lot of those old-timers. They got here at the right time; it was all open range, so they ran a lot of cattle. My grandfather said that in 1909 they branded 10,000 calves and in 1910 wintered 500 cows due to the drought," Ike says.

In addition to the cattle, at one time there were goats and sheep on the ranch. "When the banks failed in '29, Mr. Gage had a lot of notes out for different people and wound up with a hell of a herd of goats, but he didn't know much about goats," Ike says. "You shear Angora goats twice a year, in the fall and again in the spring. My granddaddy had them sheared and the hair sold pretty quick. Mr. Gage sent him a note and said 'Jim, shear those goats again because they sure were good.'"

Ike pointed out a place he calls a "squat," where settlers established a home long ago. "I'm not exactly sure where the house was. Some people by the name of Hargus settled it. You could be approved to settle this land and get three sections, but you had to live on it and make a living from it for three years. They would stay there for three years and then sell out. That's how Mr. Gage and Mr. Combs wound up with so much acreage," Ike says.

We stopped to eat lunch amid the spectacular scenery of Chalk Canyon. Ike told us the story of a plane crash on Del Norte Mountain north of the ranch in 1944. "It was an army aircraft. There was a rock house, it's still there and they carried the injured man over ten miles and found that house," Ike says. "Mr. Neville had some registered Hereford bull yearlings in the pen. They took one of their pocketknives and butchered one of them for food. Some of the wreckage is still up there."

Ike had another memorable picnic in Chalk Canyon years ago, with Lady Bird and Lynda Johnson. "It was the year before I came to live here; Ike bought a new hat for Ladybird Johnson and my mom," Sue says. "We were at a bull sale in Marfa, and Alfred Negley, who married one of the Brown girls from Houston, was big with LBJ, and he asked us, 'Why don't you take Lady Bird on a picnic tomorrow with Mom and Pop [Mr. and Mrs. Catto]?'" Ike continued, "My Dad said they didn't have time to go on no damn picnic. Alfred said, 'Damn it, it's the president's wife!' So we had to go rent a Suburban and clear everything with the Secret Service," Ike says. "There were two vehicles to meet the airplane. Travis [Ike's Dad] rode with Mrs. Johnson and Mr. and Mrs. Catto and an archaeologist from UT, Curtis Tunnell. I drove Lynda and the two Secret Service agents. I think we were a little off course with a lot of the stuff [the agents] were supposed to do because one of them was supposed to be with Mrs. Johnson at all times, and she was in a separate vehicle."

We arrived in Chalk Valley, toured a pictograph site, and ate lunch. "At that time we still had screwworms. I carried a pair of tweezers in my pocket all the time for doctoring, especially little calves. They get worms in their navels when they're first born, then they dig at it with their teeth and get worms in their teeth," Ike says. "Lynda fell into a prickly pear and got some thorns in her hand. Theoretically, the Secret Service is supposed to have a first aid kit with them, which they did not. Anyway, I picked the stickers out of Lynda's hand."

On the ride back to Ike and Sue's ranch, we asked about their love for the area. Generations of Ike's family have lived here, and Ike could not imagine living anywhere else. "There wasn't anywhere to go, and I didn't want to leave," he says. Sue, coming from England, had a big adjustment in moving to the Big Bend but found that when she returned to Birmingham to visit her family she felt the pull of her new home. "I was three hours from the ocean in England, and I still missed it here," she says.

BIG BEND NATIONAL PARK

The Big Bend National Park was established by Congress on June 12, 1944, and, along with the Big Thicket in East Texas, designated an international biosphere reserve in 1976. It is one of only two such designations in Texas, one of forty in the United States. The reasons for the designation are apparent to any visitor to this rugged, isolated, and mysterious land: it is one of the most distinctive areas of the Great Chihuahuan Desert, which stretches from central Mexico, through the Trans-Pecos of western Texas and into New Mexico.

Bordered by the great horseshoe curve of the Rio Grande's international border, the national park occupies the inside tip of the curve, encompassing some 801,000 acres. The area was created during the Cretaceous period of the earth's history about 145 to 65 million years ago, when two ancient inland seas left layers of fossil-laden limestone, later punctuated by episodes of intense volcanic action. There are windswept hoodoos, impressive canyons, and majestic mountains. It is a photographer's delight.

Each year the national park hosts some 360,000 visitors from all over the world. It contains over 400 species of birds, 1,100 species of plants, and more tropical butterflies than any other national park. There are 200 miles of trails to walk, cabins to rent (some originally built by the Civilian Conservation Corps), and facilities for recreational vehicles and tent camping—and still most of the park is raw wilderness, accessible only by foot or horseback.

The unique landscape of the Big Bend National Park has an exciting cultural history, as well. There were prehistoric Indians and, later, Apache and Comanche, gold seekers, and early ranchers. In the early years of the twentieth century, cotton farmers established a presence in this intensely beautiful but unforgiving land. Only the hardiest and most rugged individualists could successfully live here, even for a short time. That is still true today.

★ *Big Bend Portfolio* ★

The Long Trail to the Park

★

MIKE BOREN

Mike Boren was a typical eighteen-year-old growing up in Abilene, chafing at what he and his friends perceived as the conservative, restrictive life in a small city. "Our hair was on fire to get out of there," Mike says, "We couldn't wait to get out."

Now the executive director of the Big Bend Natural History Association, he followed a long, adventurous path to make the Big Bend his home. Mike was born in Fort Worth, and his family lived in Breckenridge, Colorado, and Mineral Wells, Texas, before settling down in Abilene, where his father owned Boren Engineering. Mike began working for his father on weekends at the age of eight. On the weekends, when his father did not have to pay a survey crew and Mike and his brother were out of school, he and the boys were able to complete three surveys by Sunday night. "By the time we were teenagers, we were pretty fed up with West Texas. It seemed to me that everything bit you, stung you, or stuck you. We'd spent a lot of time working for dad. We had to go on strike to get paid. He finally started paying us five dollars a day when we were fourteen," Mike says. After graduation, Mike left for the University of Texas at Austin.

His year in Austin was quite a revelation.

In his first week he drove with his roommates to San Antonio to see a strip show at a club that admitted eighteen-year-olds. That evening, Mike was the designated driver of their 1958 convertible Impala. His roommates were asleep in the back seat. A few blocks from their dorm, Mike saw a beautiful, young naked woman running down the street.

Alarmed that she had been assaulted, Mike slammed on the brakes and pulled over to ask if she was all right. He pointed out she was naked. "She said, 'Yeah, I am a Communist.'" Mike thought, What a town! He asked: "What are you doing out jogging naked? She said, 'I was at a party and someone dared me to run to this other party naked and I took the dare. You wanna go to a party?'" Mike asked if she wanted a ride. "She came around and hopped in my roommate's car naked, and I'm trying to wake these guys up because I know nobody is ever going to believe this story. I've only been in Austin two days. And I couldn't wake them up; they were back there snoring," Mike says.

The party was in a garage apartment and was quite exotic. "They were all beatniks, and they were playing bongos and had berets on and were smoking pot. She walked in naked and it was like

it was normal," Mike says. This was heady stuff for a college freshman from Abilene.

By Thanksgiving, Mike realized that he had fallen hopelessly behind in his course work. He knew he would have to face the disappointment of his father and his half-brother, who were paying his private dorm room fees. His hometown girl-friend had recently ended their relationship. It was at this academic and personal low point that Mike became acquainted with a doctoral student from Europe who was conducting controlled experiments with the hallucinatory drug mescaline.

Mike had never even smoked marijuana when he was invited to eat peyote, from which mescaline is extracted. Peyote was legal in Texas and used for ritualistic and medicinal purposes, historically by Native Americans. The peyote buttons could be purchased from cactus gardens. "I was scared to death of any drug, but I finally agreed on the condition that they educate me first. They gave me a book, *Drugs and the Mind*, and a reading list," he says. Mike was intrigued, so he agreed to participate in the experiment.

Eating peyote induces severe nausea, so to avoid that, Mike and his friends made a paste of the peyote buttons, dried the mixture, and spread it on plywood outdoors. Once dried, this paste was ground into powder and put into capsules. "They would take the number of people participating, which in this case was four; the recommended dosage was three buds, and then we'd divide up the number of capsules into some god-awful number. I had to take twenty-six capsules or something, these big horse capsules, and you drank them with a Coke to settle your stomach," Mike says.

The experimental group met in Mike's off-campus private room. The other participants felt the effects much more quickly than Mike. "They had all done it before, they were all coming down, and I was just taking off," Mike says. The doctoral student in charge kept Mike there when he wanted to leave since he had not exhibited any effects yet. Soon, as everyone else was returning to normal, Mike suddenly realized that he was seeing unusual sights. "I looked over at my friend Nick who was dancing to Bo Diddley. He was doing this weird dance that was actually pretty cool, but he had his hands out and he was shaking them. I looked at his hands and they weren't hands. They were skeletal hands and the bones were rattling in rhythm to Bo Diddley," Mike says.

By 5 a.m., the others were ready to leave and were worried about leaving Mike behind, so they made Mike promise to stay in bed and sleep it off. Mike dutifully went to bed, but soon thought he saw Lothar—the comic strip character, Mandrake the Magician's assistant—standing in the closet. Lothar wore his comic-strip costume of leopard skin and carried a big spear. Mike was telling himself he knew this was a hallucination, but he needed Lothar to leave. Convinced that if Lothar were real and not a drug-induced hallucination, he would not be able to shake hands, Mike approached this apparition. "I said, 'Okay, if you are real, shake my hand.' I stuck out my hand and he stuck out his hand. I screamed and ran out the front door in my pajamas," he says.

Mike, running through the streets of Austin in the early morning, jumped into a basement excavation construction site so he could hide. When he hallucinated that a concrete pillar was bleeding, he started running again. Mike ran inside a deserted twenty-four-hour Laundromat. There was a lone pink pillowcase tumbling in a dryer: "I said 'Oh, my God, it's the Pink

Pillowcase of Truth.' It's been waiting for me. I ran over and snatched this pillowcase and ran back to my dorm room holding it, and it was warm and comforting," Mike says. "I put it on my pillow and slept like a baby knowing that when I awoke I would know the truth, because I had found the Pillowcase of Truth, which apparently was the purpose of this whole exercise. That was the Pillowcase of Truth. Because when I awoke I knew I didn't want to be a doctor. I knew I didn't want to stay at the University of Texas."

Mike held on to this magical pillowcase: "I carried it with me everywhere for several years after that incident and slept with my head on it every night. Then I joined the army, and I tried to smuggle it into the barracks of my basic training unit. It didn't work." His sergeant caught sight of it in his personal effects and demanded to know what it was. "I tried explaining that it was a gift from my mother that I'd just like to keep in my locker for sentimental purposes, but he wasn't buying," Mike says.

The sergeant threw it into the garbage. "He wadded it up and threw it into a container for contraband with everything else we were being stripped of, and I knew right there that it was going to be a long three years," he says. Mike still wonders what would have happened if he had been able to keep his personal talisman. "Such an ignominious end to such a priceless piece of personal juju that Mandrake the Magician's Lothar himself led me to! I can't tell you how many times I could have used its magical powers since then," Mike says.

He returned home to Abilene for the holidays, on academic probation, to face his family's anger and disappointment. He returned to UT Austin, but did not improve his grades much the second

semester. By then, his father was resigned to the fact that Mike was not returning to college.

Mike knew his father wanted him to become a physician, like his older half-brother in Fort Worth. "My Dad had my life planned for me. I didn't even like my half-brother that much and sure as hell didn't want to be a physician," Mike says. He wanted to see the world outside Abilene and experience the freedom of finding his own way. To please his father, Mike agreed to see a psychiatrist to prove that he was not delusional about his future: "I'll go see Dr. Ruben in Fort Worth. If he says I am crazy, then I will abide by your wishes. But you have to make a deal with me, if he says I am okay, you have to get off my back and cut me loose because I am ready to fly," he says.

The series of adventures that would become Mike's life began. He lived in Hawaii with his brother, at one point in the back of a Nash Rambler. Their eighteen- and nineteen-year-old dream of running an insurance agency fell through. Mike returned to school at the University of Hawaii. "I didn't know what I wanted to do, but I liked being in an academic environment. But the difference was, I had to pay for it now, and it was quite a different deal. After a couple of semesters there, I said it's not worth paying for it, when I don't know what I want to do, but as soon as I dropped out, I got a draft notice from the Abilene Draft Board."

Mike wanted to become a pilot, but his astigmatism kept him out of the Marine Corps Aviation Cadet Program, the only flight school that would take recruits without a college degree. It was 1964, before the situation in Vietnam became a war, so he enlisted in the army while in Hawaii. Mike served with the 3rd Infantry Division in

Europe as a military policeman. After his tour of duty, he was discharged in Europe.

He stayed in Europe, bought a BMW motorcycle, and set out on the road. "On a beach in Spain, three weeks after I got out of the army, I realized that I was finally free. I said, you know, by God, I am twenty-five years old. I have met my obligations to family, God, country, and the only thing longer than military service is the rest of my life," he says. "I'm going to do what the hell I want to do from here on out! I was just a wandering free spirit for the next twenty-five years. I lived in twenty-seven countries and thirty-five states."

While in Europe, he married a woman from Sweden he met in Venice. "I was traveling on my motorcycle, and we traveled around for a while. Sweden had really restrictive immigration policies. You couldn't stay longer than three months on a visa, and then you couldn't come back for a year. She suggested we get married," he says. "It wasn't a marriage of love, but I went back to stay with her. When I got to Stockholm, I found out her uncle was the prime minister, Olaf Palme." Mike worked as a mail carrier in Sweden but eventually wanted to return to Texas. The marriage failed, and Mike returned to traveling.

Mike had just returned to Denver after attending the first Gathering of the Tribes in Rocky Mountain National Park at Rainbow Lake, Colorado. Ken Kesey, author of *One Flew Over the Cuckoo's Nest*, was one of the organizers. Mike met his future wife Terry when he saw her walking down Denver's Colfax Avenue. Terry is from northern Wisconsin and had just recently moved to Denver. As he walked past Terry on the sidewalk, she smiled. "That smile did it. I thought, Wow!" he remembers. Mike followed her to the corner and asked if he could buy her a candy bar.

Ignoring the age-old advice to never accept candy from strangers, Terry and Mike went into the corner drugstore on East Colfax and Pearl Avenue. Mike bought her a Snickers bar. Their anniversaries still include a Snickers bar. Terry joined Mike on his adventures.

Along the way, Mike acquired skills he always wanted. "I would go to work for somebody and say, 'I'll work. I don't need a lot of money, but here's something I'd like to learn if you'd teach me as part of the payment. I'll work cheap, and I'll work hard,'" he says. As a result, Mike learned how to rebuild cars, then went to Key West and learned about sailing, leading to his degree in marine navigation from Florida Keys Community College. He sailed out of Key West for ten years.

But Texas beckoned again. On a visit home to Abilene to visit his widowed mother, Mike went to the grocery store wanting to cash an out-of-state check. The clerk immediately recognized his name and cashed the check. "I thought, This is Texas. This is what I've been missing. I went back home and told Terry I'd like to get back to Texas. She said, 'Why?' I said, 'I think I missed it the first time.'"

Mike and Terry moved to Abilene and worked, Terry in a restaurant and Mike as a car salesman. "It was the only job I could get. I did well at selling cars, but it was kind of a crooked racket. It made the drug smugglers look like princes," he says. It was when he was giving a test drive to an Abilene FBI agent that he heard about Angelo State University in San Angelo, Texas. They had a state-of-the-art computer science department. Mike was intrigued and ready to finish his education, now as a returning student in his forties. He enrolled and became their Vietnam era outreach counselor while he was attending school.

He also founded a literary magazine. He graduated with a 4.0 grade point average and won writing awards while he was completing his degree in English with a minor in Journalism. In addition, he earned a teaching certificate with an English as a Second Language endorsement.

Mike then became the West Texas bureau chief for the magazine *The Alert Texan*, which folded after one issue. It was at this point that Mike and Terry decided to take a trip to regroup. They took a poet friend with them to stay in the Cottonwood Campground in the Big Bend National Park. They saw an advertisement for the "Word Off" at the Starlight Theater in Terlingua. They went, fully expecting cowboy poetry. Instead, they found sophisticated readers and poets, reading Ferlinghetti, Ginsberg, and other beat poets of the 1950s, as well as others reading their original work.

Mike recalled a Bill Moyers interview with Carlos Fuentes, who, when asked where the Paris of the 1930s is now, immediately said he would go to the Texas/Mexico border. When asked why, Fuentes said: "It's because it's where the Third World meets the New World, and as we work out the problems of that frontier, so will the century go. And it's going to spawn hot literary voices." Mike felt he had just stumbled into the enclave of those voices. He had found a place where he could further develop his own literary voice.

The next day, Mike and Terry were eating lunch at the lodge at Big Bend National Park. Terry was working as a restaurant manager, which had become very stressful. She looked around the restaurant and said: "Look at this place! If I could manage a restaurant like this, it would be no stress at all." That lunch led to both Terry and Mike applying to National Park Concessions Inc. for jobs.

Mike was offered the position of assistant manager, and Terry was offered the job of head of food services for the concessions. The positions also came with a house and free meals. They moved to the park in May 1995. After a few years, the position of executive director of the Big Bend Natural History Association became available. Mike's educational background and his stellar references landed him the job.

The members of the board included ranchers, businessmen, longtime West Texas residents, exactly the sort of people Mike wanted to reconnect with and the reason for moving back he gave to Terry when they lived in Florida. "I wanted to go back to West Texas where I grew up and see how I fit in with these old gentlemen that I grew up with. We were young and wiseass guys, but in leaving that way we often overlooked some of the virtue. You come back in the back door and see that virtue. Then I wanted to know: How do I fit in? What kind of man have I become?"

Mike now closely listens to the World War II stories of the men he has known all his life when he visits Abilene and the ranchers and men of the Big Bend. "I thought about how much I have missed about these old men," he says. "I lived in places where there were really interesting people, but they're very driven, egocentric kind of people, and I wanted to know what kind of man I had become and whether my experiences qualified me to earn any respect back in this kind of world. I hope the answer is yes."

TERLINGUA AND STUDY BUTTE

The independent, self-reliant people who live in the communities of the Big Bend characterize Terlingua and Study Butte as communities apart. The residents are variously described as old hippies, renegades, eccentrics, and dreamers. Many of them choose to live off the grid. There are very few paved roads, and some residents happily live without electricity. The Brewster County Groundwater Conservation District oversees usage of the aquifers in Brewster County. The Study Butte Water Supply Corporation, a private company, is the water and sewage utility company. Many residents have wells to provide their water.

Although at first Terlingua seems semi-deserted when no festival or event is taking place, you can always find someone to talk to on the porch of the Terlingua Trading Company. Doug "Doc" Blackmon gives out a business card with his job title of director of "The Mental Health Clinic on the Porch." Tourists and locals alike sit on the benches along the porch drinking Lone Star Beer and visiting.

Terlingua is located in Brewster County, the largest county in Texas, a state known for counties larger than other states. The state of Connecticut is smaller than Brewster County by five hundred square miles. The county seat is Alpine, the only city in the county.

Terlingua was a mining town, settled following the discovery of cinnabar, from which mercury—quicksilver—is extracted. The Native Americans of the area were already familiar with the cinnabar, vivid red in color, and used it as body paint pigment. Miners came to the area in the mid-1880s, and soon a community of nearly two thousand was thriving. In 1903, Howard Perry of Chicago founded the Chisos Mining Company, which became the largest quicksilver producer in the United States.

The demand for cinnabar rose steadily during World War I and World War II for its usefulness in explosives. In the 1920s, 40 percent of the U.S. supply was produced in Terlingua. The Chisos Mining Company succeeded partly because Terlingua is located near the Rio Grande and the village of Santa Elena in Mexico, which provided cheap labor. At the end of World War II, countries such as Spain, impoverished by war, sold their mercury, glutting the market, and the demand for mercury plummeted. The company filed for bankruptcy in 1942. All that is left of the mining industry is the ghost town of the Chisos Mining Company in Terlingua and a few capped mines, including Study Butte, the Rainbow, and California Hill. The original Terlingua Trading Company is still in business, operated by the Ivey family. Drinks, books, and souvenirs are sold in the former mine's company store.

Today, Terlingua is a destination that draws tourists to annual events. Viva La Historia is a homecoming for the families whose ancestors lived in Terlingua and worked in the mines. There are tours of the mines, oral history presentations, food, and music.

The first of November is the Day of the Dead, when friends and families of the departed refurbish their graves. Townspeople clean and restore order in the cemetery, leaving food, flowers, dishes, candles, and altars decorated with photographs at the graves. That night, candles are lit, and a celebratory community potluck dinner is served.

The most well-known event is the annual Terlingua Chili Cook-Off. The Chili Appreciation Society named Terlingua the "Chili Capital of the World" in 1967. The chili-cooking competition began when Frank X. Tolbert, columnist at the

Dallas Morning News, challenged H. Allen Smith, a writer for *Holiday* magazine, to determine who was the expert on the subject of chili. A war of words was launched. Tolbert had written the book *A Bowl of Red*, published in 1962, which renewed interest in this most iconic Texas dish. A cook-off was planned in Terlingua, with Tolbert as referee. The cooks were Wick Fowler, representing Texas, and H. Allen Smith, the Yankee outsider. There were three judges: Hallie Stillwell, who voted for Smith, and Floyd Schneider, who voted for Wick Fowler; the third and deciding vote would be cast by Dave Witts, but after one bite, he claimed he was poisoned, his taste buds permanently maimed. There was no winner that first year, but the event is now in its forty-fifth year, held the first week of November.

Terlingua has an active nightlife. The Starlight Theater, built in 1931, was the original movie house and performance theater, and is now a popular bar, restaurant, and live-music venue. Another popular restaurant is la Kiva, a cave bar constructed by Gilbert Felts in the early 1980s. Felts died in 1989, and his nephew Glenn Felts has operated the establishment since 1991. It was named one of the "fifty best bars in America" by *Men's Journal* in January 2002. Live music as well as open mike and karaoke nights provide the entertainment.

Since the residents of Terlingua stand out as fiercely independent people, there is an accepting live-and-let-live attitude. Writers, artists, retirees, those with Ph.D.s, small business owners, people who resist technology, and people who embrace it live side by side. Finding out what draws people to live there is a simple matter: sit on the porch and talk it over.

Living in Simplicity

★

DICK AND BONNIE CAIN

The Agua Fria Ranch is located north of Terlingua and west of Highway 118. Even in the dry desert environment, this area is particularly barren. For two years there has not been a drop of rain, giving very little respite for the eyes in this landscape of brown and tan. This rugged environment is home for Dick and Bonnie Cain, where they raise tough longhorn cattle. We met Dick and Breezy, his son, at a small house located near a much larger structure, which is their church. In addition to their ranching duties, they provide a religious ministry to the immediate area. Dick and Bonnie are both pastors. After a short visit with Dick and Breezy, we agreed to come back and visit with both Dick and Bonnie since she was not there when we arrived.

"We aren't trying to have a big church. We are trying to have a good church," Bonnie tells us on our next visit. "You know, people that love and help each other. That is what we love."

Bonnie comes to greet us dressed in a long cotton dress with an apron, reminiscent of a much earlier time. She has a radiant smile in a face completely innocent of makeup. A young woman accompanies her, the beautiful daughter of friends from Houston, named Ashley Allen.

Ashley's parents brought her to Dick and Bonnie for a brief holiday from the stress of big-city life. "It's a full circle God thing. My Grandpa grew up with a man who knows Bonnie and Dick, and he grew up with my parents, so it is a full circle. I came out here for quiet time and inner healing," Ashley says.

Dick and Bonnie first came to the ranch fourteen years ago, when they visited friends in Alpine. They were living in Gonzales, Texas, where Dick leased a pasture for his cattle. When the owner decided not to lease the land anymore, it was time for them and their two sons and two daughters to move. "We came to the Cowboy Poetry Gathering in Alpine with some friends of ours. Dick had seen it advertised in *Western Horseman* magazine, so this friend was going to sing at the Cowboy Poetry Gathering, he was a cowboy also. We just loved this country, and loved the little town of Alpine because everybody was so friendly. We made the circle going to Marfa and Presidio and then the loop around to Terlingua," Bonnie says. "We went through the park and then around by Marathon. By then we were addicted to this country. It was like where Dick had been raised in Arizona, but it was totally different for me, but I loved it."

We follow Bonnie and Ashley to their main

home on the ranch, where Dick and Bonnie keep their longhorns and horses. The ride is over rugged roads, into a completely isolated section of the ranch. Along the way we encounter a small herd of feral burros. We were impressed when Bonnie told us that even though they were competitive eaters with their cattle, they chose not to eliminate them, feeling they had equal rights for the scarce food. "Yes, they are wild burros. When I first come here, they were wild and run up the hill," Dick says. "But I always carry a little cake and I throw a little cake out. They know me now.

They'll run up along side the road waiting for me, and I'll throw them a few pieces." "We like them because they're so tough," Bonnie adds.

When we arrive at the simple but well-kept cabin, several longhorns approach Bonnie's vehicle to be fed, which is the cattleman's technique for handling the animals. In addition to the cabin, there is a larger structure nearby, which is their bunkhouse, where visitors stay. The cabin does not have electricity or any of the modern conveniences that are considered essential. Bonnie does not have a kitchen sink, just a simple white enamel basin. Dick and Bonnie lease this part of the ranch, twenty-seven thousand acres. "No one had lived here for about twenty years. The place was so dilapidated no one was interested. The man who had it at the time said he was going broke out here. We met with the owners, and they were convinced that we would not be interested in it because there was nothing there," Bonnie says. "Nothing to live in, no modern conveniences, no telephones or anything, and very little grass, but we met with them and assured them that that was our lifestyle."

The owners made it clear that they would not be investing any money into making the cabin

habitable since they assumed anyone that leased the land would live in town and come out to tend to the cattle. Dick and Bonnie assured the owners that they preferred the lack of conveniences and would live on the land with their cattle.

The cabin is over one hundred years old, and when Dick and Bonnie first saw it, there were no roof, windows, or doors. There was a large hole in the floor. While they made the cabin habitable, they stayed in another cabin further up on the mountain that had a partial roof, sleeping in sleeping bags and cooking on a campfire until they could put a roof on the cabin. "There was no water there except from a spring, and we were

hauling water with an old pickup truck to different points where the cattle could get feed," Bonnie says. "It was a dry, thirsty, and barren land. We lost twenty head of cattle, and I had to stay here by myself while he was hauling cattle. I didn't know the land, but I was always a pioneer at heart. I always felt like I could make it."

The family who originally built the cabin were the Whistlers, who homesteaded the property at the turn of the twentieth century. Dick read the book, *Under the Escondido Rim*, by David Keller, a history of the famous O2 Ranch, which told the history of the area. "Most of this country wasn't settled until this time. Then, conditions were more favorable. They had lots of cattle in this country. Keller wrote about seeing one thousand head of cattle laying under the cottonwoods on Terlingua Creek," Dick says. He has developed an appreciation for the early residents of the land and admires the original rock fences on the ranch. "They build them out of rock, no mortar. And I marvel a lot at the staying power of the people that lived here and did this. There's places around here you can't even dig a hole; you have to make a rock pile to hold a fence post. I marvel at the patience," he says.

Dick and Bonnie bought adjacent property for convenience and easy access to the road, which is a necessity, particularly in the summer. "When it rains, you are locked in here. There's two creeks between here and our other place, and the creeks flash," Bonnie says. "We always have company, and if you have people back here when we have our rains in the summertime, they can't get out. We've been eight days at a time without being able to get out. Actually you are immobile. In the wintertime it isn't like that."

The ranch is also the site for annual camp meetings, where accommodations are provided by the bunkhouse and tents that visitors pitch on the grounds. "People come from different places, and they bring their Dutch ovens. We sing and we have preachers, it's really an old-time camp meeting. The people just love it," Bonnie says.

She was born and raised in the rural Ozarks of Missouri, in the Branson area. She has two sisters and remembers how they were raised in the country. "I was just a blonde-haired, blue-eyed girl with a dirty face. I hardly ever wore shoes because you saved your shoes for when you went to town. My feet were as tough as leather on the bottom," Bonnie says. "I was kind of a tomboy, and we wore little flour-sack dresses that Mama made. I just loved being that little country girl." Bonnie and her sisters learned how to survive with very few material comforts, becoming very self-reliant. Hog butchering and canning were a fact of life. "Every year, my mama killed three hundred chickens, and we canned a lot. Everything was pulled out of the garden. My mama canned three hundred quarts of peaches every year because my dad was addicted to them. There was a peach orchard in that area, and they sold the 'peach seconds' real cheap, so my mother would get them and we would can them," Bonnie says.

Her family was deeply religious. "We grew up knowing that God was real. It wasn't a religious thing, God is real," Bonnie says. "I grew up in the Bible Belt and God called me to preach when I was very young." Bonnie and her father were saved during a tent revival. The preacher was named Jim Honeyfield. "God comes in strange packages," she says. "Jim was a very different man. He had an old beat-up station wagon and an old patched-up army tent." He played the accordion every evening and attracted the attention of the people in the area. "He was a skinny little man with long hair, but he had the fire. Hill-country people are very curious. Everybody was watching this man, but they weren't having much to do with him," says Bonnie. "He started having this revival that was awesome and so powerful."

Every evening he sang one song, "In the City Where the Lamb Is the Light." The revival lasted seventy-two nights, and people were drawn from a wide area. "My daddy was one of them that were saved, and I was, too, at nine years old. That revival changed our lives. It changed our home," Bonnie says. "I felt the conviction of God, and I ran to the altar to give myself to the Lord, and everybody said there was a light shined on me. From that time of being chosen of the Lord, my life took that turn of following after the Lord."

Bonnie's father worked long hours at his saw-mill, and when the mill closed down, he worked at any job he could get. She remembers that, after he was saved, he spent time alone in the woods. "I saw him spend eight nights in the woods and never eat a bite of food. Slept on the leaves and took nothing for his comfort. He would fast and seek after God," Bonnie says. "God blessed him with a gift, that whoever he put his hands on the pain would leave them. His faith was to remove pain from your body. I don't care what you were suffering from, when my Daddy put his hands on you, that left. So in the community and around the area, people came for Daddy's prayers. Daddy was a very humble man. He never took any credit. God got the praise for everything that was ever done."

Bonnie soon heard the call to ministry and healing. "We grew up in a house of faith, but then it became my turn. It was different watching Daddy than when it was me to lay hands on

the sick. It was my faith and not Daddy's faith anymore," she says.

No one in her family ever went to a doctor because they believed that because of their faith, God would take care of them. Even now, Dick and Bonnie have not taken even an aspirin in over thirty years. "Faith will do anything. Whatever you believe in God for, it will happen," she says.

Dick was born and raised in Arizona. He had a cousin who moved to Missouri, and when that cousin came to a funeral in Arizona, he asked Dick if he wanted to come to Missouri. "Dick was kind of undecided, but then he said he was going to do that because he had never been to Missouri. I was just thrilled to meet a cowboy! It was love at first sight. We knew each other two weeks and got married and have been happy ever since," Bonnie says. "Dick always amazed me. I was not a cowgirl. I was more like a farm girl." "My little farm girl," Dick says. "He was my cowboy, and I aimed to have him," Bonnie laughs.

When Dick married Bonnie, he worked for her Dad logging in the woods but soon made the decision to move. "It just didn't fit me. I come out of desert country. We moved out of there and went to Louisiana. We spent eight years in Louisiana," Dick says. "Louisiana was a lot different than being in the desert, there was all that water," Bonnie says.

Dick began his herd in 1974. "The first cow I had came off a wildlife refuge—the government herd they started in 1927 in Valentine, Nebraska, and in Cache, Oklahoma. I got this one cow," Dick says. "She was a registered longhorn cow, and I bred her to a straight longhorn bull, and they had a cow. I called her Brownie. When I trailed cows from one place to another, she was always my lead cow."

Brownie died when she was twenty years old. Dick had the opportunity to see what he had only read about, a cow funeral. "When she died, she went to sleep in the cow pasture. The other cows mourned her because she had been with all of them. She was the oldest. They would go down there, and some of them would stay with her at all times," Bonnie says. "They stayed there until the bones were scattered," Dick added. "The others would go off and graze, and they would switch out and the noise they would make, it was something. They would circle her and look at her and mourn her and make that funny racket. We had never seen that. After the bones were scattered, they quit," says Bonnie.

Dick estimates his herd at about 150 cows. The drought has severely affected his operation. "It quit raining two years ago in July, and that's what hurt us so bad. We didn't get any feed last year. Then last year we didn't get a drop of rain except in that strip across there that put a little water in the tanks," he says. He does not raise his own feed, but would like to grow feed near the spring. It now costs two hundred dollars for a roll of hay, and it comes from South Dakota and Nebraska. In order to continue to feed his herd and the new calves, Dick will sell some of his roping cattle in El Paso. "They did real good the last time we were there, the price really jumped. They run about four hundred dollars for little lightweight roping steers," Dick says.

Dick and Bonnie's children are grown; three live in Alpine, and one daughter lives in Flatonia, near Houston. Three were born in Missouri, and one was born in Arizona. "We raised them with the old ways. They know the benefits of it. They have their own life as far as what they do, but they still keep it in simplicity. They try to stay out

of debt and live a simple lifestyle, but they don't have an outhouse. They still do try to live a simple life," says Bonnie.

They were raised without television or many conveniences. Bonnie would make cookies on a wood stove. She would send the children into the woods with gunnysacks to gather sticks and pine knots. "They would drag them in those old sacks up to the stove, and we'd make cookies. Our basic diet was pinto beans and homemade bread. I made ten loaves a week, and that would serve our family," says Bonnie. "We had a guy who

would come by and bring town bread, and that was pretty exciting for the kids. I just loved the kids being home because they were good kids and kids are exciting. They are always so full of energy and doing things." Without television, the family entertained themselves. Dick and Bonnie remember sitting on their porch in the evening while the children would reenact stories with Dick serving as the narrator.

Dick and Bonnie's grandchildren have been raised with television but know why their grandparents live the way they do. Their two great-granddaughters, age six and nine, are learning to sew from Bonnie on her treadle sewing machine. "Each of them made their little skirts. I'm teaching them to sew and to cook. I do Dutch-oven cooking, that's what I want to teach the other ones, the simplicity of having a portable oven to cook biscuits," she says.

Bonnie demonstrates her washday routine with a device that looks like a thick broomstick with a metal-flanged end. "You can use it in a bucket or a tub. We hardly ever wear something one time. For instance, if you have sheets to wash they're not that dirty, not like something you wore working in the garden," she says. Then Bonnie demonstrates the difference between a heavy-duty and gentle cycle by the speed of plunging the device. "You'd be shocked at how clean you can get your clothes with that," she adds. Everything they own is used and repurposed when it wears out. Bonnie makes her long aprons from the backs of dresses, which do not wear out as fast as the fronts. The quilts in the bunkhouse are made from discarded clothing.

In such a remote and isolated area, we assumed they would be concerned about emergencies and accidents on the ranch. As in every other aspect

of their lives, they trust in God. "We don't worry about that kind of stuff and we leave that in the hands of the Lord. He's blessed us all this time with good health," Dick says. "When I first come to the Lord, I had a tumor in my throat and Bonnie prayed for me and it shriveled up. I watched it every day when I shaved and it shrunk. That's been about twenty-eight years ago. We've got a live-in doctor. He's good to us, and He's kept us."

There have been occasions when their unwavering faith in God was needed. Bonnie had what she calls an "extreme miracle." Not long after Dick and Bonnie moved to the ranch, before the cabin was completed, they went to town to buy supplies. When they returned after the 150-mile round-trip just before dark, they began to unload two rolls of hay and a thousand-pound sack of feed from a lowboy trailer, with tandem axles attached to their half-ton pickup. The corral was on an incline. Dick unloaded the feed at the rear of the trailer first. Bonnie was helping unload what was in the front of the trailer, which required rocking it back and forth. "We just kept rocking it real hard," Bonnie remembers. "That old truck, the transmission kicks out of park, so I put a stick in front of it, and I thought that would hold it, but it didn't," Dick says.

The truck popped out of gear, and it went down the hill with Dick and Bonnie on the back of it. Dick jumped off the trailer from the passenger side. The cab of the truck was full of supplies so he could not jump in and over the seat.

"I did something I shouldn't have done. I stepped up on that rail on the trailer and jumped off. When I jumped, instead of falling forwards, I fell backwards," Bonnie says. "All this was happening in split seconds and instantly my head was under the first wheel and it was running over me.

He came around the truck just in time to see the first wheel running over my head."

"As I came around the front of the trailer, the truck was moving, but not real fast at first. It was just starting and so I could out run it. It was like I was watching a movie and I saw her fall and she was facing me. I could see her face," says Dick. "It was like slow-motion, but the thing that stuck in my mind was when that trailer went over her head, was that a lowboy will run over a big rock and jump. That trailer jumped high over her. There was no fear in me. The Lord was on me and I just watched this thing happen and I knew the trailer had to come off of her. There was nothing

that could be done. If I had stopped it, it would have dropped right on her."

The next wheel ran over Bonnie and the fender caught and rolled her. Her lungs were deflated, her ribs were broken, and her shoulder was dislocated. When Dick ran to Bonnie's side, he called on God. "The Word of God says, 'Call on me in time of trouble and I'll hear and I'll answer.' He didn't say call 911. He instantly started speaking life to me in the name of Jesus," Bonnie says. "I gathered her up in my arms," Dick remembers. "When he said that name, the name that has all power in Heaven and Earth, I felt the air go into my lungs, and then I felt fluid in my lungs. I was

51

gurgling and we prayed again in that marvelous name, and it was gone," Bonnie says.

Dick managed to get Bonnie home with her broken ribs and dislocated shoulder. She found when she looked in the mirror that she had tire tracks on her face. "I had a sac of fluid that had formed over my eye and was hanging down. When those tires were running over me, I could feel the burning sensation of the tires over my face, but I could not feel the weight of the trailer."

Soon, area neighbors came, forming a circle around her and praying. The sac of fluid that was over Bonnie's eye, sealing it shut, changed. "Instantly, the sac of fluid diminished, and my eye came open," Bonnie says. "It was just like an unseen arm jerked my arm, but there was nothing seen. My arm jerked back into place. Whenever that happened, they saw a miracle, and they fell on their faces. It shocked them." Her ribs healed rapidly. "People were just amazed, it was a miracle of God. We didn't think about going to the doctor, because we are people of faith," she adds.

The congregation at their church is small, drawn from the people of the area. In addition to serving as the pastor with Dick, Bonnie also provides music. "I play the harmonica and the guitar. There's a black lady in our congregation, and she plays tambourine, and we sing. We go down to the porch in Terlingua and sing the old-time gospel songs, and it's really surprising that people like it," she says. "They'll drink beer, but they like that. A lot of them have their roots in old-time gospel. Sometimes, some of them will throw us some gas money up there on the porch. We talk to them about God and meet some very wonderful people there."

Although Bonnie does not specify their religion as a particular denomination, she identifies more with the Pentecostals. Their congregation is devoutly Christian and is dedicated to serving God. "We just want people to be close and reach out to people around you. We have church at 10 o'clock on Sundays, and afterward we have lunch. I always cook the dinner. Sometimes we have potluck. Our children come and the other people, and we just like that time. We just sit and visit. That's very special to everybody."

Dick and Bonnie are happy living according to what Bonnie calls the "old ways," secure in their faith and their love of God. Even in this remote and isolated place, they have found their home. "This country is hard, and it's harsh, and you don't change it, it changes you. You have to change to adapt to it. It will toughen you and harden you just like it is," says Dick. "We've always lived in remote places. That's what I like. I'd love this ranch if it didn't have a road and I had to ride a horse into here."

Dreams Come True

★

INDIA AND WILLIAM WILSON

While India Wilson worked at the Terlingua Trading Company, she dreamed that one day she would own a tearoom and bakery. India is a hardworking, outgoing woman with a laid-back attitude, but she is also a sensitive, intuitive person who can occasionally see a person's aura. She is a writer, a poet, and a short-essayist, writing under the name "India Thomas" but using the name "India She" as her artist's name; she is also an accomplished painter. Perhaps because of her poet's sensibility, you soon realize when you meet her that she gives you more than cursory attention.

When we meet India, she shares her intention to someday open her business and says, "Sometime, when you come back out here, it will be there." We never doubted it would happen. Less than a year later, India's Café and Sweets, with its whimsical bandana-wearing skeleton riding a motorcycle marking the location was in business and has been a success for over two years.

India was born in El Paso and raised between Kermit and Odessa. She came to the Big Bend when her former husband, golf pro Terry Thomas, accepted the job of running the Lajitas Golf Course in 1983. India lived in Lajitas nearly ten years, but when the marriage ended, she left to

pursue other interests, including the cattle business, in Brock, Texas. "I always wanted to come back to Lajitas or Terlingua, so that's why I came back. My ancestors, the Comanches, were once here, so I always felt really at home," she says.

India started writing in earnest when she was thirty-five years old. She shared the experiences of her own life and also wrote about the common experiences shared by women. Her poems and short essays are sensitive observations that reflect her love of far West Texas against the backdrop of the desert landscape. "A friend had read some of my material and said, 'You really need to learn how to write poetry.' I had always written about my emotions as a woman, things I had gone through in life, but I had never really sat down and thought about writing poetry," India says.

Her friend directed her to a website, creative-poems.com, and this set her on the path of writing poetry. For many years, she wrote every day, sometimes producing several poems a day. India estimates she has written nearly 4,500 poems since that time.

It is through her writing that she met her future husband, William Wilson. William was born in Wiltshire, England, and raised in London. The majority of William's career was spent in the military, first in the British navy for six years, stationed in the Far East. He continued his military service after his discharge from the navy with a six-year stint in the army. "For the first twelve months I was out of the navy I couldn't settle. I think I had ten jobs in twelve months. I decided to reenlist, so I joined the army for six years," William says. "Then I was going to go six years in the air force—do the 'hat trick'—but at the end of six years in the army, I said, That is it. I am done."

William, who writes under the name William-goldenpen, is the author of two children's books, *Quacker's Bedtime Stories* and *Quacker's Bedtime Stories . . . Continued*, published by PublishAmerica in 2006 and 2007, respectively, and has just finished a novel, *Dark Star*.

William and India met when he became intrigued by her online name on a website for writers. "We're both writers, and she was on a poetry website. There's a list of who's online [on the website]. Her name was there, and it was INDIA, all in caps. I clicked her name and went to her website. She had a photo there, and I thought, 'Oh, that is nice!'" William says. They began to correspond, but three months later William's computer fell victim to two viruses. Nearly four months later, the problem was finally resolved. "I loaded my programs and got back online. The website that she was on came up, and I did not type in the address," he says.

For the next several months they continued communicating, then the relationship became serious. "I wrote a poem and she sent me an e-mail that said, 'I hope you don't mind me asking, but can you tell me who it was written for?' I sent back an e-mail that said, 'If you take the first letter of every line except the last line, you'll

find out who it's written for.' It spelled out 'India She,' which was her handle," William says.

"The title was only called 'She,'" India says. "A lot of people call me 'She'; it is my artist name, 'India She.' Tears started falling, and I thought, I really like this guy," India says. Soon after, William asked India an important question: "'What do you think about me coming to Texas?' About three days later, she sent an e-mail and said 'You're not here yet?'" William says. Six weeks later, William was on his way to join India in Weatherford, Texas. Then they made the move to Terlingua.

India was reluctant at first to pursue the relationship, since she had survived a very difficult one. "I had been married three times and divorced three times. It's just like baseball, three times, and you are out," says India. "I wasn't going to do that anymore, but he came along. I guess the good Lord just knew I needed a good man. I told him, 'I'll be really upfront, these are the things you won't do. If you do them, I won't stay married to you.'" William remembers that conversation. "She said 'I have this list. Here are the things you won't do.' Everybody thinks it was an 8 × 11 piece of paper. It was like a roll of toilet paper," William laughs.

"I am a very free-spirited, stubborn Texas woman. I am very independent, and I can be very aggressive when I have to be, but I can be very sensitive too," India says. "I needed a man as strong as me, but willing to drop a tear with emotion," India says. "I don't like men that fight the tears, because to me, a man has just as many emotions as a woman." They have been together now for ten years and married for five.

India was working at the Terlingua Trading Post while William worked at the Ghost Town

Café, but they both wanted to open a bakery. It seemed to be financially impossible, with the cost of fixtures and food. "Down here, if you manage to get minimum wage, you are one of the upper class. People I know are working for two dollars and three dollars an hour," William says.

The dream began to be a reality because of a birthday cake. When a local resident discovered that India had once worked in a Walmart bakery department decorating cakes, she asked if she could do a birthday cake. "Then somebody else heard about it and said, 'Can you do a cake for me?' Between Thanksgiving and Christmas we did just under 140 cakes and pies, and that was just for the locals," William says.

They now had a loyal customer base but still faced the financial reality of opening a business. When a space in a small shopping plaza, formerly occupied by the hair salon Hats Off, became vacant, the owner, who heard about the cakes and pies, asked if William and India wanted to see the space. "We came down and had a look purely out of curiosity; we had no intention of opening it up. We went in and looked and we thought there's a lot that has to be done in there," William says.

They thought about it seriously, and when they went back to look at the space again, they were greeted with a surprising sight. "There was stuff everywhere on the porch. There were boxes of plates, knives, and forks that friends and other community folks contributed. With that kind of support we decided we'd give it a try. We were down here every day, and every day there was more on the porch, including tables and chairs," William says. "I would say 80 percent of all this was donated by the community. We have no idea where most of it came from. If it hadn't been for the community, this place wouldn't be here.

It's as simple as that." It is this local support that sustains their business during the summer months, typically the slowest time of the year.

Their original plan to have a tearoom and bakery has expanded to serving breakfast and lunch, in addition to their cakes, pies, and pastries. "We've been here over two years now, and it just snowballed. I wanted a little sweet shop bakery and then everything changed," India says. "Everyone wanted a café, a place where they can get a good breakfast and good burgers. I do plate lunches as well as sweets. So they got a little bit of everything."

"We get a bunch of the locals here in the morning—it's come to be sort of a gathering place where they come and have coffee and shoot the breeze. It's good fun here from about six o'clock," William says. "They've supported us, and I think they'll support us again during the summer."

India's Place has also found a following among the judges, participants, and crowds of tourists who come to Terlingua for the annual Chili Cook-Off in the fall. Another group, who India calls the "Winter Texans," fill the RV Park and also have become regulars. "They've found this place and they like it. It's like a little bistro outdoors, and we've got a great view when you can see it past the cars. They enjoy the atmosphere," says India.

Since William has been in Terlingua for ten years, he has seen changes in the seasonal population. "You have people come here to work during the winter and spring. They usually work up on the river or in the park. They leave in the summer, but the basic nucleus of residents here stays pretty much the same," he says. Tourism is affected by economic and weather conditions, but it is now also affected by border issues. "The change that has happened here in the last year has been due to the economy and the fires that were up north. There was also a huge fire in Mexico, coming towards the park, and there were days you couldn't see the Chisos [Mountains] for smoke. It was that dense," William says.

There were also summer months of consecutive days of 115–124 degrees. "That's kept people away, and also having no water in the river for kayakers and rafters. The bad press from the governmental departments in Texas about the border has hurt us, too," he says. "But our border area is probably the safest along the Mexico border; we don't have a problem here."

William sees more retirees decide to live in Terlingua permanently instead of young families. Those moving to Terlingua, as is true in the rest of the Big Bend, adapt to the lack of big box stores and lack of instantly available medical care. The ones that can't adjust soon leave. "The majority can't live without it. When you come down here and find out Walmart is two hundred miles round-trip, or if you want to go to the doctor, you have a 160 mile drive, they just can't cope with it," he says. "Down here, if you haven't got it, you just do without it, or you wait until you can get it." William tells the story of a woman who came into the café and asked where the nearest Walmart was. When William told her it was a two hundred mile round-trip, she asked how they could live without a Walmart. William assured her it was no problem at all.

The stories of unprepared visitors to Terlingua are amusing because they highlight the expectations they bring from home. William remembers the day a woman drove up to the café, alighting from her expensive town car, dressed in high heels, expensive clothes, and lots of jewelry. She came to the door and without greeting William,

who was working, she asked directions to the mall. He told her if she looked outside, that was as close as she would get. The woman became very insistent, William remembers. "She said, 'I want a Sonic Burger.' I said, 'well, darling, we do burgers.' She said, 'No, I want a Sonic Burger.' I finally told her, 'You see that highway out there? Turn left, keep going until you come to the stop sign, and Sonic is on your left. Get a burger there.'" William says. "I didn't tell her it was eighty miles. She probably got up to the [Border Patrol] checkpoint and asked again."

Ironically, the limited medical services concerned India more when she was younger. "It was more a concern to my kids than to me. I had gone through so much in life that I look at it this way: I could get killed just as easily walking across a street in a big city as I can here. So I just leave it in God's hands, when it's time for me to go, I'll go," she says. But Terlingua does have helicopter service for transport to Midland/Odessa or El Paso in emergencies.

Although William is from England, he has not been back since he came to Terlingua and says he has no desire to return. "Robinson's Blackcurrant Jam and Marmite are the only things I miss," he says. Although the landscape in Terlingua could not be more different than England, William loves the desert. "This place has a peaceful beauty. We live on top of mountains, so our porch overlooks the Chisos. We watch the sunset in the Chisos every night," William says. "In the off-season, you could hear a pin drop on the highway it's so quiet. Sometimes it gets so quiet your ears ring."

India and William have strong family ties to Terlingua in addition to the restaurant, which is more than a full-time job. "You are tied to it all the time. When we go home we have things to get ready—I'm doing the books or the quarterly accounts, and she's getting ready for the next day—but it's fun. We have good laughs here, and we enjoy it," says William.

India has two daughters: Lisa Marie, who is the postmaster of Terlingua, and Donna Sue, who visits often from Fort Worth. Granddaughters Brittany Marie and Sierra Lowe also live in Terlingua.

While we were sitting on the patio of the café, India read the poem "Texas Woman" from her book *She Whispers*, published in 2007 by PublishAmerica. It is a collection of poems about love, loss, survival, nature, and observations from a woman living in the desert of Far West Texas.

TEXAS WOMAN

They are bold, independent, restless and free
they're full of wild passion with fire
And searching mystery

Tasting life like there is no tomorrow
she knows of hell and its sorrow

These women have powerful feelings
as big as their Texas sky

She can put a grown man down
on his trembling knee and his heart cries

Cold beer with western dance swing
long walks in painted autumn and spring

Thick juicy steaks and red warm wine
night time pleasure she blows your mind

India and William, living an ocean apart, found one another and made their life and home in Terlingua. We asked India if her feelings had changed about living in the Big Bend since she first came to Terlingua. "The way I felt about it when I first came is still the same. I am at home here, I am at peace here, I'm not fighting the big city; I'm older and I want a little peace and quiet in my life," she says. "Every afternoon when we get through here, we take a shower, pour ourselves a drink, go outside, and just enjoy the evening. I tell William all the time that I thank God every day that I have what I have in my life now."

Directing the Mental Health Clinic on the Porch

★

"DR. DOUG" BLACKMON

It is another hot summer day in the Ghost Town. In late afternoon, people gather on the front porch of the Terlingua Trading Company and sit on the benches. The drink of choice is Lone Star Beer. Doug "Doc" Blackmon is the unofficial director of the Mental Health Clinic on the Porch. "It's not a real thing. We made it up years ago for fun. Who got me started in this doctor thing was a photographer named Tracy Lynch and another lady. They took a picture of me in Study Butte and made a postcard out of it and called it 'Doctor Black,'" says Doug. "It was a picture of me in a three-piece suit with a lab coat, standing on top of a Cadillac with my cane and striking a pose. Everybody started calling me 'Doc' or 'Dr. Doug,' which is not true, but we play around with it." Doug compares the porch to a community center. The regulars come over after work and talk over the events of the day and the state of the world. Doug calls this happy hour "brewski time."

Doug Blackmon has lived in Terlingua since the 1970s. He was born in San Antonio but was raised in the country, so a sparsely populated area is familiar to him. His family moved to Houston where Doug graduated from high school in La Porte, in Harris County. A self-described jack-of-all-trades, Doug worked in Houston at a variety of jobs, including welding and electronics. Eventually, he tired of city life: "Why I like the country is because it's so peaceful and laid-back. Living in Houston was a shock, and it took a while to get used to that. Once I did I said, 'Well, no more of that, I want to get out in the country,' I've been here over thirty years. I first came here in '71 to look over some property my father bought, and I fell in love with the area and just stayed."

After Doug moved to the Big Bend, he held various jobs throughout the area, including working twenty-five years at the Study Butte general store. He settled in the Ghost Town, works at the Trading Post, El Dorado Hotel, and the Big Bend Family Crisis Center, also known as Casa de la Cultura in Terlingua, a non-profit agency specializing in providing support and counseling free of charge for families in need. Their services include assistance for victims of family violence and sexual assault. They also have fund-raising events to provide help. Their main office is located in Alpine, and offices and shelters are located in Presidio and Terlingua. The area they cover in the Big Bend is twenty thousand square miles. Lovika De Konick is the director, and Doug is listed as "Dr. Doug" Blackmon on their website. Doug's brother works at the center in computer support

and has designed thirty-two websites for businesses and individuals in Terlingua.

Doug recalls that, as more people moved to the Terlingua area, a demand for modern services developed: "Back around the eighties, people were wanting more things like water and electricity, air conditioning, and what you get in the city: telephone, satellite TV, computers, cell phones, that's all here now. We're part of the technological society now, we're high-tech. I have a computer; I have a cell phone," Doug says.

Although there are more than a few people in Terlingua who live completely off the grid, there still has to be a reliable back-up system for basic services. "We have a lot of power problems. We're trying to set up a system of routers that are

battery backup so when the power fails we still have the Wi-Fi signals; we're working on that to improve our community 100 percent." Some people in Terlingua, however, are resistant to the changes in the community, not just the long-term residents who have lived for years without these services, but some newcomers who moved to the area to completely live off the grid.

Doug sees this access to the Internet, which can facilitate self-education and research, as a bonus. The technological revolution brings links to library resources in the biggest cities to the country without anyone having to leave Terlingua to access them. Doug's friend Ken Barnes is an example of someone who uses this access: "Ken Barnes is self-educated as a geologist; he got interested in fossils, and he's a self-taught paleontologist, one of the best in the area. He's teaching teachers." Groups of high school students from Abilene make twice-yearly trips to learn from him, as do their teachers.

Doug has a website (www.drdougs.com) with links to community bulletins, the Mental Health Clinic on the Porch, Terlingua, and photographs of visitors to the Porch. "What I'm trying to do is promote the area, Terlingua and the Big Bend, and the businesses. It talks about going to the Leapin' Lizard art gallery or the Trading Post or Starlight's Restaurant and I'm talking about these businesses to bring more people in. We want their business." He is well aware of the impact tourism has on Terlingua.

The annual Terlingua International Chili Cook-Off boosts the local economy. When the judges and contestants arrive, they draw crowds to the cook-off that increase every year. "We survive on tourism, you know that's how we make our money, through these stores, through the little beer joints and restaurants. If we didn't have tourists, I wouldn't be here. We have to depend on these people, and we welcome them with open arms. I get to meet people, it's kind of a hobby, meeting people and talking to them and hearing what they think. It's an education just being around other people, and I enjoy it thoroughly."

Doug estimates the population of Terlingua at about one thousand, but the people are not concentrated in one area; the homes are spread out around Terlingua and the Ghost Town. The price of property rose with the development of the Lajitas Resort. "I think it was Lajitas getting built up so much that made the land go up to thousands of dollars per acre, not just a hundred or something like that, it skyrocketed. Certain

places out here, you can get a piece of property for a reasonable amount, but there's the water situation and the power issue and all that. Depends on what you want." Once property is purchased, because the inexpensive labor pool stream from across the border has been stopped, building on the land can take much longer and cost more.

He has found his home in Terlingua and won't ever leave. "This is one of the finest places I've ever been; there's the finest people you'll ever meet, and there's a lot of love in this community and a lot of sharing, more so than you would find in a big city. It's kind of like a family; everybody knows everybody, and we all get along, and if somebody gets hurt we all pitch in to try to help." When an older resident lost his home in a fire, the entire community came together and sponsored a benefit, raising $3,500.00. The help didn't stop there as volunteers rebuilt his house and the money put him back on his feet. "The community helped him out, and they had done that for several other people, too. It happens all the time, so that's the kind of situation we have here. Terlingua's a family thing, you know, we're like brothers and sisters, I guess you could say."

In addition to his love of the desert landscape and the people, Doug shares the experience of others who describe their attraction to the Big Bend: "When I first came out here, I thought this was a rough place. I was camping out with just a little tent and a sleeping bag, but I liked it," Doug says. "There was something here that just grabbed me, it was like something pulling at me, saying, 'This is where you want to be. You like being independent in a place that doesn't have a lot of people and a lot of traffic and a lot of chaos.' I thought about those things and, yeah, this is what I wanted, and I'm glad that I came here."

Life in the Cretaceous

★

KEN BARNES

Ken Barnes had no idea when his car broke down in Terlingua in 1969 that he would never leave. "I was working for an engineering company out of Corpus Christi when I came out here to do a land survey. I'm still waiting on parts," Ken laughs.

He was born in Mission, Texas, in the Rio Grande Valley. He was educated as an engineer. When he decided to remain in the Big Bend, he went to work as a boatman, on a rubber raft at the Villa de la Mina. Gil Felts and Glenn Pepper purchased the Waldron Mine in the 1960s and renovated the ruins, naming the property Casas de las Minas, now Villa de la Mina. Felts built and owned the well-known la Kiva Restaurant and Bar in Terlingua.

"I was a boatman off and on for a year or two doing mechanic work, then I became a county surveyor. First I was a deputy county surveyor, then I got elected county surveyor. I was county surveyor for eight years," Ken says. "In 1981, I got reelected, but the Surveyors Association took over all the surveying, including the licensed land surveyors and all the county surveyors. They wouldn't let me take the office. So that was a big mess."

Ken went from a career in engineering to becoming what he calls a "self-made" paleontologist. "It all started about 1987 or 1988. I went out to a friend's property to see some petrified stumps that he told me he found out there. I wanted to see them, and he told me they were still standing up in place," Ken says. "I never found them, but in the process I found a few fossils on another friend's property, so I called her and asked if I could collect those few fossils and put them on display around here as something to do. In the process of digging up those, I found about ten more, so then I had to go study and figure out what they were, and then it just grew from that." The fossil that drew Ken's attention was a large femur sticking up out of the ground. That bone started his quest to become a self-educated paleontologist.

Ken first displayed his fossils in part of a store in Study Butte, then in a school bus. "I had them in there for a long time, and then I went to Lajitas with it," says Ken. "Then they needed that space which was right next to their main office, and they wanted to give me a bigger space. And they couldn't find a bigger space, so they built this for me." The space is named the Mosasaur Ranch Museum. The website (www.mosasaurranchmuseum.com) calls the exhibit "Seas and

Shores of the Big Bend of Texas: From Mosasaurs to Dinosaurs." Ken is the founder and curator. The museum displays fossils of mosasaurs, dinosaurs, primeval clams, and ancient shark teeth.

The museum is also a laboratory for processing the fossils. The operation receives no outside funding, except small fees for groups, usually students, and donations. Since Ken supports the museum on his Social Security retirement money, with some rental property income, he also works part time on call to drive a bus for the fire crews in Big Bend National Park in the fall and spring. During mid-May to the first of August, Ken drives a shuttle for Far Flung Adventures in Taos, N.M., to continue to support the museum.

His interest in the terrain started immediately when he arrived. "The geology is fantastic out here, so I went studying it on my own, and a geologist worked for me for several years while I was surveying. You have to know the geology, so you know where to look and which geological formation," Ken says. "We don't just go out here and say, Let's dig over here, let's dig over there. We have to find something eroded out on the surface, and then we follow that up and find out where that eroded out from and see if we can find out where it came from." All the fossils come from private property with permission from the owners for the excavation; nothing comes from the parks or public land. Ken explains which periods the fossils came from: "There are not any Jurassic or Triassic here in this area. It's just Cretaceous, about one hundred million years to sixty-five million years old, and below that we've got three-hundred-million-year-old Paleozoic rocks."

The first time we visited Ken, we were given a tour of the impressive fossil collection in the museum. The displays are very informative, and more dinosaur bones line the shelves waiting to be displayed. During our visit, there were two faculty members from Southern Methodist University, working on computers. Now that Ken is seventy, he is making arrangements for his fossils. "Myself and the landowner made an agreement with Texas Memorial Museum to donate the dinosaur fossils to them, but I would stay in control of them as long as I was able," Ken says. "The problem is that they make me number them now, and I've got to do all that paperwork, and that's not to my liking."

"I am donating my marine fossils—the mosasaurs, the fish, and the sharks—to SMU for their final destination, and they're taking them," Ken says. "Most of them haven't been prepared yet, and they are preparing them. I've got one skull, there's a cast of it in that case. My high school teachers from Abilene and students made a cast of it." He will give the dinosaurs to the Texas Natural Science Center at the University of Texas. The Grace Museum in Abilene had an exhibition of Ken's fossils for fifteen months.

Ken has hosted groups from schools in Abilene and Austin. Larry Millar, an artist from Abilene, and Scott Clark, a teacher from Jim Ned School

in Tuscola, have accompanied the Abilene groups for years. Both members and officers of the West Texas Science Center, located in Abilene, they first met Ken in 1999, when all his files and fossils were in a school bus. "There was a group of students from Cooper High School," says Larry. "That became our first school because they were smart kids, and they wanted to go. We had fifteen, and we weren't sure how kids would react to Ken or how Ken would react to students. We'd talked to Ken a number of times, and he is a mellow kind of guy, and we figured this would be just great. Sure enough, it really was!"

The students and adults camped in the basin, then drove to Terlingua. "We met him at the Starlight, as we still do, and then drove out to the dig site and started working," Larry says. "We discovered he was very patient with the students, as he is with most people, I think, but he really likes kids." Since Ken's first career was not in education, he did not have much experience in working with students; however, they responded quite well to him. "In the dig pit," Larry remembers, "when we were working on bones, students were pretty tentative. He would always tell them, 'No, you've got to dig hard and if you break a fossil, we can usually repair it. We have to dig to find them.' His level of patience with students never really changed, and we have been doing that for fourteen years," says Larry.

Besides gaining invaluable hands-on experience, the students learned about the importance of paleontology from Ken. "Every time we went out with a new group," Larry continues, "he would always want to stop on the drive out to a couple of locations to talk about the paleoenvironment because this was part of the interior seaway," says Larry. "He talked to the kids a lot about what was going on with these bones and why the bones were important."

Larry first met Ken when he was on a UT dig in Big Bend Park. "He taught us everything we know about that place. We went in with absolutely zero knowledge. The first time we met him, he took us into the school bus. We had heard about him. One of the people on the dig mentioned there was this guy in Terlingua who's got these bones in a school bus. His name is Ken Barnes," says Larry. "He is the guy who surveyed the whole Terlingua Ranch, so he knows that place like the back of his hand. He took us over to the bus, and that was the first look. That was exciting! It really was, because it was just chock full. We have a lot more bones now because of thirteen years of digging."

The students came away from the trips with more than new knowledge about paleontology. "I think the kids all saw Ken doing something he loved and was passionate about. We've talked to our kids about doing what you want and doing something that you're passionate about, and they saw that in Ken," Larry says. "He came to that late in life, and I think that's a really good example that getting older is not the end of the world. There are things you can do."

Larry has read of other paleontologists who became interested in the subject later in life. He remembers the *Time* magazine cover of a dinosaur that older paleontologists cite as their inspiration to continue with the subject. "I always say to the students, 'I didn't do paleontology for the first time until I was forty-nine.' They all think that's old," Larry says.

Ken has found his experience with students very rewarding. "Since 1999, when I started working with those guys from Abilene, they get together high school groups and they bring them out here. We've got one school that's been coming out here for years and years now—St. Stephen's out of Austin. Close to half of the dinosaur bones out here were dug up by those kids under supervision," says Ken.

He finds all his discoveries exciting, but one that is drawing attention is a type of dinosaur. "We've got a little bitty dinosaur . . . actually a fellow from Yale is writing a paper on it, and we're going to name it after the Gaddis family. It's a little oviraptor. The beak is very bird-like, and we've only got the beak and one claw, but there's never been one found this far south," says Ken. "In Canada and Montana there's been about five of the species found up there. He claims this one is a new species. There's the sacrum and little femurs over there. We have to write papers on that."

That is why it is important that the fossils are identified by repository numbers since scientific papers cannot be written as long as the fossils are privately owned, Ken explained to us. He decided to get this done so he could assign numbers to them and start writing papers. "There's not anybody in Texas that has that much of one individual big duck-billed dinosaur like the ones we have out here, so they have to be identified with a correct repository."

He has been working with Mike Polcyn from SMU for years on the mosasaur fossils. "We've got papers we are going to be putting out on that pretty quick. I'll be involved with the papers we write," says Ken. Space in the museum has become an issue. "I've run out of space already. All of these shelves are full, mostly parts they are working on, but I could use a lot more space because I've got shelves full of stuff out here," he says.

He most enjoys unearthing the fossils and the research, rather than the paper writing. He has

twelve pages written on a recent find. "I've got a baby *Ceratops* skull parts and part of a full grown one that we are trying to describe, but it's getting complicated because it doesn't seem to match any of them that's been found in the Big Bend area so far. It's more like what they find all up in New Mexico. So it's getting complicated," Ken says. While he works in Taos during the summer, it is always an opportunity to continue his fossil work. "I can go out to Colorado and look at stuff in museums up there in Denver or maybe go down to Albuquerque or fly out of Albuquerque and go somewhere else to do some research work," he says. "While I'm there, I'll be doing paperwork on my computer all the time. I'll still be doing research."

Ken married and divorced while living in Terlingua. His thirty-two-year-old son, Charlie Barnes, his wife Julia, and his four-year-old granddaughter, Shauna, live nearby. Charlie works for Eco Minerals, a company that bags lignite and other materials. Although Ken likes Shauna being raised in Terlingua, since there are few young families, there are drawbacks. "There aren't enough kids for her to be associated with until she starts in school. She may start kindergarten next year," he says. Charlie has been building a house he started when he was fifteen years old.

"He's rebuilding an old ruin near my house and he's been working on it ever since. It's in Ghost Town, I've got a whole bunch of ruins down on that property," says Ken.

He does not characterize himself as antisocial, but he does not enjoy having a lot of people around. "There used to be not too many people here, but it's getting to where we have too many people again. We've got city water now and all that stuff, and people got houses built all over the place out there now where there weren't any before. They call it progress," he says. "I'm a real independent person that doesn't thrive on having a lot of people around me or anything like that. I just do my own thing. It's just a different way of life. I don't like the crowds. . . . I'm not very good at small talk for one thing, and I'm a bit of a narcissist for one thing, everything's got to go my way. I'm a hoarder."

Like many other longtime residents of the Big Bend, Ken is not concerned with the availability of medical care now that he is older. His philosophy is simple. "Whatever happens is going to happen. So no, that doesn't bother me right now," he says. Since the majority of new residents are retirees, he finds that many move away again because of limited health care.

The younger new residents also find it difficult to make Terlingua their permanent home. "They come down here and they are going to set the world on fire. Then it turns out it's not that easy getting a job and keeping a job around here. There's not that much work going on except for tourist business. There's a whole bunch of people that just do tourist things, like guides," he says. The annual event that draws the largest number of tourists at one time every year is the Terlingua Chili Cook-Off. "While they are here, it puts a cramp on a lot of us, because there's a highway patrolman every quarter mile up the highway, just about, stopping everybody for anything. Most of the people who come to the cook-off want to stay at the cook-off, so we don't have too much problem with that. It's only one week and it brings some money into town," Ken says.

We ask if he misses Walmart. "No, not at all. Of course when I leave here, the first place I go is a Walmart," Ken laughs. He usually travels to Midland/Odessa for bulk shopping, and can order his special glues and supplies through the Internet.

In comparison to the other communities of the Big Bend, Ken finds the people of Terlingua to be more independent. "They are all willing to live on a little less amenities and don't need to go to the store every day. It is tougher, but in some ways it is easier, though," Ken says.

Now that Ken is older, he does find that he does not explore as much as he once did. "I've gotten to where I don't get out as much as I used to. I used to hike around all over these hills looking for fossils and just hiking around looking at things and places, but as I got older and older I don't do that as much anymore," he says. He does some fly-fishing when he spends the summer in Taos, escaping the blistering heat of Terlingua.

Ken spends his time living in a long-ago past. He appreciates the breathtaking aboveground landscape that draws residents and tourists to the Big Bend but acknowledges that his landscape is underground: "Yes, mostly right now," Ken says. "But I like the landscape above, too. We still have the same sunsets every afternoon that everyone loves because they've never seen one like it. I have roots here."

The Healing Place

★

ROBERT AND
ELIZABETH HILL

Traveling north on dusty, unpaved roads outside the Terlingua Ghost Town, we find rugged terrain open to some of the most spectacular, unobstructed views in the Big Bend. There are solitary houses scattered around this area, and each one promises the sight of the beautiful landscape from every window. During one such visit, we meet with Robert and Elizabeth Hill, who live here six months of the year; the other six months they live outside San Angelo.

Elizabeth and Robert are both from North Carolina. Elizabeth grew up in the western part of the state, in Watauga County. Robert grew up thirty miles northwest of Winston-Salem, in Mount Airy. They met as students at Appalachian State University in Boone, North Carolina. They both pursued careers in education, Elizabeth in the public schools, and Robert at the college level.

In 1970 they moved to Asheville, North Carolina, to be near the small town of Flat Rock where Robert helped start a new community college. "I was the academic dean for twenty-one years at that school. Before that, I taught at several high schools in Maryland and North Carolina and taught geography at Appalachian State University," Robert says. The community college had an agreement with Appalachian State where students could receive an associate degree after two years, then finish a four-year degree at Appalachian State or transfer their credits to other four-year institutions. Robert was also an adjunct professor of geography at Appalachian State for ten years, in addition to holding the position of dean at Blue Ridge Community College. Elizabeth taught at several schools in North Carolina during this time and retired after thirty-three years in the Asheville area schools. Her work was primarily focused on first-grade students and teaching reading.

Robert retired from academia in 1991, and he and Elizabeth traveled extensively in the western United States. Robert was familiar with Texas, particularly Austin. "In the 1970s, I was coming to Austin quite often—about every other month—because our college received a sizeable federal grant and we were working with several universities in the country doing some upgrading with our faculty. We had a contract with the Department of Higher Education at the University of Texas in Austin, headed at that time by a former classmate of mine from graduate school, so I visited the campus often," Robert says.

When Robert returned home, he would tell Elizabeth how much he liked Austin. Then, one day over lunch in Austin, his friend, who knew

Robert was a hiker and enjoyed backpacking, asked if Robert had ever been to the Big Bend. He talked about the place in glowing terms and roused Robert's interest.

In 1984, tragedy struck. Robert and Elizabeth lost their twenty-three-year-old son, Patrick, to a debilitating disease. About two months after that, they were out having dinner one night, and Elizabeth says, "You know, one of the places you talk about when you come back is Austin. I'd like to go there with you sometime." Robert had a friend whose daughter had married a park ranger in Fort Davis, so Elizabeth and Robert flew to Austin and drove to Fort Davis.

After visiting several of the communities of the Big Bend, they rented a condo in Lajitas and were enchanted with the desert terrain, which was so different from their North Carolina environment. There were plants they had never seen before and skies that were vast and cloudless. They returned to the Big Bend every chance they had.

When Elizabeth retired, they returned to Lajitas and rented an apartment in the old Opera House. After two months, they bought land and built a house. "We lived several years in Lajitas and made a lot of friends with people in the area who were living off the grid and were catching or hauling water. So we just decided that if they could do it, we could do it," Robert says.

Elizabeth and Robert enrolled at Solar Energy

hunting lodge. They returned the next summer and took a class in advanced photovoltaics to learn troubleshooting and compliance with the national electrical code for solar systems. They came back for a third summer for the lab courses in wiring and installing different types of solar systems.

After their courses in solar energy systems, they came back and installed their completely off-the-grid system. "For example, all of our wall receptacles had switches to turn them off so we didn't have any phantom loads on anything; if you've got a television in your house or a cook stove contains a clock, you are using electricity all the time. We designed this house so we had no phantom loads," says Robert.

He did all the wiring inside the house, and together they did all the wiring and installation of their solar electrical system. The house is comfortable and filled with light. It is a work in progress. Elizabeth used wood left over from construction to design a mountain scene used for a headboard in their bedroom. One of the many projects they undertake is to make use of materials that may have been discarded.

There is a building behind the house that houses Elizabeth's weaving studio, a colorful and cheerful place stocked with her yarns. Elizabeth is an accomplished weaver, a relative of a weaver whose work has been displayed in the White House and later, the Smithsonian. The main house has a room used as a study and library. The mechanical systems for the house are located outdoors and in a utility room off the back porch.

Living off the grid for Robert and Elizabeth means they are not electronically dependent, either. "I spent four years in the navy as an electronics technician," Robert says. "During and after college, I worked for nine summers doing lighting

International in Carbondale, Colorado to learn how to design and install solar systems. They sold their home in Lajitas and built their new home outside Terlingua. The atmosphere of Lajitas was changing from a laid-back small town to a resort destination, exactly what Robert and Elizabeth wanted to avoid. In addition, the view from their front porch was a golf course with sprinklers running to keep them green, a waste of scarce water in the desert. "We bought this property, and we knew when we bought it there were no electric lines out here. People didn't want electric lines running across their land. We also knew there wasn't much possibility of water out here, either. Although I don't think anybody has really drilled trying to find water, if they went as deep as the water company in Terlingua has, they might find something," Robert says. "We knew we would need to install a water catchment system."

They acquired hands-on experience by helping to design and install an off-the-grid system for a and sound for the outdoor drama *Horn in the West*. So the electrical work was not new to me." When Elizabeth and Robert retired, they made the decision to banish television, computers, and cell phones from their lives. "We see people who come here in the wintertime and hike," Robert laughs. "They come to get away from the trappings of the city, then spend their holiday playing with a computer or cell phone and have to carry eighteen pounds of electronics when they hike."

The Hills come to Terlingua around the first of October and return to Christoval, a small rural town outside San Angelo, in April. They also continue to spend time in North Carolina. They were aware that access to medical care was crucial; Robert is seventy-seven and Elizabeth is a little younger, both at a time of life when more than basic medical care may be needed in the future. In Terlingua, they are over one hundred miles from the nearest hospital. San Angelo has the medical care they may need, but they also need their time in Terlingua.

When Robert and Elizabeth were looking for a home in San Angelo, they felt the town was too crowded and the traffic was heavier, creating more noise than they wanted. Elizabeth found their home in the small, unincorporated town of Christoval. Robert was attracted to the town because of the lack of city regulations governing housing renovations. "I had been through enough of that, so a town that didn't have any regulations appealed to me. The house we bought there was built in 1937. A local builder, who was considered to be one of the best in the area, ended up with it. Nobody had lived in it for fourteen years," Robert says. The builder rebuilt the house, so when the

Hills first saw it, it was very much like a new house, inside and out. They moved in and immediately added a back porch, patio, and a carport.

They have close friends in both communities but see San Angelo as much more conservative than Terlingua. Elizabeth observes the differences between her two homes: "I like Christoval, but you have lots of people in that town who have long distances to drive to work so you hear the traffic start moving in the morning about five o'clock," she says. It is the quiet and the slower pace they both enjoy. "One of the things we do religiously almost every day here in Terlingua is mix up a cocktail and go sit in the chairs out here and watch the sunsets. We are three miles from the paved road, so we don't have road noise," Robert added. "It would be hard to describe the thing that I really like most about coming back, but I do look forward to getting on the porch and just sitting down and not hearing anything at all and relaxing."

It is getting late. It has been an interesting visit. We walk outside the Hill's lovely home and gather on the porch, preparing to depart. Elizabeth's love for this place is very personal. Palpable. It's her connection with their son. His presence is in this home, with his photograph in a wall niche by the fireplace and a memorial located outside the house, lovingly constructed of native stone with small stone benches to sit on. We all stand quietly looking out across the desert toward the Chisos Mountains, bathed in the warm afternoon light. "When I hear a raven come around the corner of the house," Elizabeth says quietly, "I hear the air in its wings, before I even see him, and he speaks to me. It is a healing place for us."

REDFORD

Traveling eastward from Presidio on Texas's Road Farm to Market (FM) 170 toward Big Bend National Park, a traveler parallels the meanderings of the Rio Grande as it moves sluggishly through the Redford Valley toward the entrance of Colorado Canyon. The land is ancient, once populated by prehistoric Pescado Indians (*pescado* is Spanish for "fish"), and their habitations were thought to be in the area of present-day Redford.

In this location, the river serves as the border between the United States and Mexico and nourishes irrigated land in each country, where present occupants grow alfalfa, onions, and other crops. Those traveling along this beautiful scenic road at modern speeds find it easy to miss the town of Redford, and most never know they have either entered the village or left the sunbaked aggregation of mostly adobe structures strung along the sides of the highway. Buildings blend seamlessly into the earth from which they are made. Redford is a ghost town with only farm equipment and cactus-bordered yards to give evidence of current occupation. Certainly, the silent structures give no hint of the community's historic importance.

Redford was established in 1876 near the site of the old village of Polvo and originally bore the Spanish name "El Polvo," meaning "dust." Polvo probably became known to the Western world when Cabeza de Vaca and his three companions traveled there in 1535 in search of Spanish civilization after the disastrous end of the Narváez expedition.

By 1683, a mission was established in Polvo, the remains of which were still evident in the mid-1950s until the adobe walls were bulldozed by the county at the request of the property owner. A religious presence remained, however, when a Catholic church was constructed in 1913 to minister to the small population. By the 2010 Census, 132 persons were listed living in Redford/ Polvo, mostly centered around the former post office, which discontinued operations in 2012, and the new San José Catholic Church, which was built in 1970 on FM 170.

Despite difficult circumstances, Redford has survived. Historically one of the oldest communities in the United States, Redford is still home to remarkable people, who, like their community, endure.

The Fervent Philosopher

★

ENRIQUE MADRID

The area where the Rio Conchos joins the Rio Grande at Presidio is called La Junta de los Rios, a rich agricultural area with fertile soil and crops irrigated by the rivers. Sixteen miles southeast of Presidio is the village of Redford. The town of El Mulato, Mexico, is across the river. Surrounding this area, which extends nearly twenty-five miles in both directions along the rivers, is the Chihuahuan Desert. Redford once supported an elementary school and several businesses. It appears nearly deserted now.

All along this stretch of land were informal border crossings, now closed, where it was possible to cross into Mexico across shallows of the Rio Grande. In years of drought, it was a simple matter to walk across the dry riverbed. At Presidio's official crossing, the Presidio-Ojinaga International Bridge, residents cross into Mexico frequently, conducting business, shopping, receiving medical care, or dining out. For centuries, this area has blended seamlessly with Mexico. This ancient place, with human habitation dating from an estimated 8,000 B.C., had no natural boundaries, only manmade ones. Now, because of heightened border security, border patrol agents have increased in number in the entire Big Bend area and are now very visible here.

Redford is the home of Enrique Madrid, a member of one of the founding families of

Redford. His parents were Lucia Rede Madrid and Enrique Madrid. Lucia graduated from Sul Ross, married Enrique Sr., and moved back to Redford, where the couple then ran the family grocery store and she taught school. It is here that Enrique Madrid, Jr., was reared. He is a historian, translator, archeological steward, and independent scholar.

Much has been written about Enrique and his family. His mother received a "Thousand Points of Light" Award and the Ronald Reagan Award for Volunteer Excellence from President George H. W. Bush for her innovative idea of starting a small lending library where children could come to read and study in a part of her family's general store and gas station.

"It wasn't a public library," Enrique explained. "That was the interesting thing; it was a private library run for the public, and that idea so fascinated George H. W. Bush that you could educate people and the government didn't have to pay for it. She ended up receiving two presidential medals from President Bush for her library. It was a privately run library for the benefit of two nations. At that time, the border was open, so we had children coming to borrow books from both sides of the river, and as it was such a desolate area, it really caught the president's imagination. You can educate people even in a desert, reaching the children of two nations." The informal library eventually expanded from her home to nearly half the space in the family store. Enrique's mother also had a career as a teacher in Redford before the school was closed and the students transferred to Presidio.

Enrique's first cousin, nationally published novelist and writer Denise Chavez, has written about her emotional ties to Redford and the experience of spending summers there as a child, continuing her informal education at the side of this remarkable woman.

Enrique has also been interviewed and written about for his archeological and historical research of the area. Archeology students come to Redford to learn about the sites with Enrique as their guide. He also worked as an instructor with the Outward Bound program. He has grown up with archeology outside his front door. "You can see all the metates we have, and we have collections of arrowheads that my mother collected all her life. We're in one of the major occupation zones of humanity of North America here on the river. We walk out onto archeological sites; they're all over the place. We stumble over the metates. We still use the metates that my great-grandmother used. We grew up with archeology. If your mother's a schoolteacher, it's probably the worst luck to happen to a child because he never has a mother; he's always got a teacher. You can never go cry to her and say, 'I hurt my knee, I fell over something.' She'd give you a book, 'Here, get over it, read something. Read archeology.' I learned about archeology just from walking through the hills and then the formal studies in the books. It was just something you grew up with here if you're interested in the world." Enrique is one of the ten founding members of the Texas Archeological Stewardship Network of the Texas Historical Commission. His concentration is on Presidio and Brewster Counties.

Enrique and his wife Ruby met while they were students at the University of Texas at Austin. Ruby accompanied her roommate to a party in an apartment where Enrique and his two roommates lived. "He was sitting on the floor, and he had long hair, and he looked like an Indian. He was just sitting there, and I didn't think he had any interest whatsoever. But for a few weeks, we would go over there on weekends, and finally one day one of us left our purse there, so he and the roommate raced after us on our way back to the dorm. He was interested then. I guess we've been pretty much together ever since," says Ruby.

Born in the small town of Comanche, Texas, Ruby found Enrique quite exotic, particularly since there were no Hispanics, African Americans, Catholics, or Jews in Comanche. While at the university, Enrique majored in philosophy, and Ruby majored in sociology with a minor in history; she graduated in 1969 and became a teacher.

While in Austin, Enrique received his draft notice from the Alpine draft board. He rejected the card, and after returning it, he was immediately drafted. When he returned home he was arrested. "The FBI came and picked him up. He went to trial, and the judge threw it out because the draft board hadn't given him permission to apply for conscientious objector status. Then they redrafted him, but he failed the physical, so they quit bothering him," Ruby remembers.

Enrique adds: "The war had reached its height, the Tet Offensive was in '68. There were five Texans who fought the war in court. I was one of those. We tried, we literally tried to stop the war, we tried to get the draft declared unconstitutional, to pull the troops out. We tried to do as much damage as we could. We were hippies, we were flower children, we invented free love, and we tried to stop the war."

Another brief filed in court cited the draft as a form of involuntary servitude or slavery. Their legal efforts failed in court. Disillusioned, Enrique returned home to a mother who believed in the

American dream for immigrants and minorities and had spent her life educating the children of the area to enable them to achieve that dream. Enrique believed that this dream did not include Hispanics since the enrollment at UT Austin and the other universities in Texas was disproportionately Anglo. "So I came home literally to exile, like in Siberia. You know the America I saw at the university, the America I saw in the streets and overseas, it wasn't the America my mother had worked for; she didn't work to have her students shot by American troops or killed in a foreign war."

Ruby was teaching Texas history and Texas geography in a middle school in Houston. Enrique came to Houston in December 1969, and they married December 30. They returned to Redford and ran the family store while Ruby taught and Enrique worked part-time as a substitute Redford postmaster, while writing and conducting research.

Their quiet and introspective life was shattered on May 20, 1997, when Esequiel Hernandez, Jr., a high school student, was shot and killed by U.S. Marines patrolling the border in Redford. The eighteen-year-old was herding goats and allegedly shot his .22 rifle, used to deter predatory animals, in the direction of the marines, who were hidden from view; they returned fire, believing they were under attack. There was a congressional and grand-jury investigation. There were no indictments handed down, and Esequiel's family received compensation for the accidental death. Junie, as he was known in Redford, had been a student of Enrique's mother. This event changed Enrique's life and stirred him to join a Redford citizen's delegation to Washington, D.C., to secure the removal of military forces along the border. He has been interviewed and written about extensively on this subject.

His scholarly pursuits have led him to research a variety of subjects, including the making of a perfectly round tortilla. When Ruby and Enrique were teaching cooking classes, they traveled to Chihuahua to interview fifty women to find out how to make uniform tortillas. Enrique has diagrammed and explained the physics of the process of tortilla making in interviews and articles. He can also explain, with historical detail, the specific cooking methods used to create authentic Mexican food.

Enrique is currently involved in two causes: the process of having the Native American Jumano Apache Indians recognized as a tribe by the U.S. government, and to bring forward the cause for canonization of Sor María de Jesús de Ágreda of Spain, "the Lady in Blue," who was said to have appeared to the Jumano Indians in the 1600s.

Enrique is one historian of the Jumano Apache tribe and has been instrumental in the tedious and exacting work of identifying the Jumano descendants. He shows documentation: "This is a mitochondrial DNA analysis of the people of northern Mexico, of Ojinaga and Juárez, and there's the mitochondrial DNA from our mothers. This was done in the year 2000 in Ojinaga and Juárez, and the mitochondrial DNA from our mothers is 5 percent African heritage, 3 percent European, and 91 percent from Native American women. That's where my grandmother came from, that's where our girlfriends come from, from the people of Ojinaga. This DNA reached this area in the Big Bend twelve thousand years ago, the same DNA that crossed from Asia is still here,

and we're still here." The decision to recognize these descendants as a tribe is one that Enrique finds very politically driven.

"You're asking for recognition from a government that has all these moral issues in relation to the people who are actually a tribe whether the government recognizes them or not. We've always had this DNA, we've always been here, and we have our culture, and so we're still going to be a tribe even if the United States disappears. In 2095, we'll still be here, we'll still have the same DNA with a few changes here and there. We've been crossing the border for twelve thousand years."

The related cause for the canonization of Sor María de Jesús de Ágreda is equally laborious but is now at the point of verifying the three miracles in her name that will lead to her canonization. Sister María de Jesús, a cloistered Franciscan nun of the order of the Conceptionists, began reporting to her confessor in 1620 that, while in a trance-like state, she was interacting with Native Americans living in a desert in the New World who called themselves Jumano.

She was able to communicate with them by speaking to them in their language and was able to understand their speech as well. She gave them instruction in the Catholic faith and told them to seek out the Spanish missionaries for conversion and baptism. When the Spanish missionaries reached the Southwest, they were met by a large delegation of Jumano Indians carrying crosses and who were familiar with the Catholic faith, crediting the appearance of a Lady in Blue long before the missionaries had come to the New World. Native American tribes reported over five hundred sightings of the Lady in Blue across the southwest, including the Tigua of El Paso del

Norte and the Isleta Indians of Albuquerque, New Mexico. These tribes consistently reported the same story. They saw her blue habit and called her "the Lady in Blue." Enrique adds that she was also an advisor on theological matters to the king of Spain and was an accomplished scholar. In 2009, a celebration of the Lady in Blue was held in San Angelo, with Bishop Michael Pfeifer conducting a service at the Jumano marker located where two rivers meet, and the Lady in Blue was said to have appeared.

Enrique does not confine his scholarship to the past. He has a clear vision of the future and how the world could be a more peaceful and improved place. He defines himself as a "critical intellectual," a person not content to live within a society without trying to make it change to actualize its own societal ideals. In Enrique's case, the ideals are those embraced by the U.S. Constitution, including freedom, liberty, equality, and justice.

These beliefs have driven his demands for justice in the case of young Junie Hernandez and his belief that because of his heritage, he and others are due recognition as American Indians. He is also adamant that the time has come for women to claim their immense power and take an active and decisive role in world government and in the hierarchy of the Catholic Church, a view that is not common among men of his generation. When asked, Enrique can supply facts and historical precedents that support his contention that the time has come for this change.

It would be difficult to imagine Enrique and Ruby living anywhere else; they are firmly rooted in Redford. Enrique has a simple answer for why he stays: "This is my home, this is my family. I was a history major, philosophy major. There's no better thing to do in the desert than to read; this is where you go to read, this is where you come to think, to study."

The Missionary Poet

★

MELVIN WALKER
LA FOLLETTE

The long unpaved driveway to the home of the Reverend Canon Melvin Walker La Follette is lined with massive rosebushes covering the fences on the sides of the drive. In summer the roses are in full bloom. It is a colorful drive to his small home and office building. He has lived in Redford since 1984. He has retired from a career as an Episcopal regional missionary. His title was "Canon Missioner to the Big Bend," covering a very large but sparsely populated area; Redford is among the very smallest communities of the Big Bend. Melvin is also a published poet and writer.

Melvin was born in Evansville, Indiana, in 1930, during the Depression. "When I was six weeks old, my father became unemployed and moved back to Ridgeville, Indiana, which was his home; his father and mother lived there. I believe it was for $250, they paid back taxes on a house and lot, and that's where I grew up," he says. He lived there until he was seventeen, then began his academic career at Purdue for three semesters, then transferred to the University of Iowa for a year before he enlisted in the navy. "I was in the navy during the Korean War, and unlike some politicians I don't say, 'I was in Korea'; I say, 'I was in during Korea.' I believe there was one gentleman who stumbled over that."

He completed his undergraduate studies at the University of Washington at Seattle. He earned an M.A. at the University of Iowa, then taught at the university level, first at the University of British Columbia, and then he began work on an advanced degree at the University of California, Berkeley, as a James M. Phelan Scholar in Literature.

He continued to teach, accepting a position at Oregon State University in Corvallis while pursuing his graduate studies. "At the end of that time, I got married and moved to San Jose, where I continued graduate studies at Berkeley. After two years of full-time study, I took a job as an assistant professor at San Jose State University. I taught there two years and then went back to school for seminary at Berkeley Divinity School at Yale," he says. He graduated magna cum laude in 1967.

He found his voice as a poet and, at the age of twenty-two, was published in the December 6, 1952, issue of the *New Yorker*. He has subsequently published over one hundred poems and stories in periodicals and anthologies in the United States, Canada, the United Kingdom, Italy, and the Philippines and two books of poetry. The following poem was published in *A Controversy of*

Poets: An Anthology of Contemporary American Poetry, edited by Paris Leary and Robert Kelly (Garden City, N.Y.: Anchor Books, 1965), and is reprinted by permission of the author.

ARRIVALS AND DEPARTURES

I swim in darkness, swim
Because I am. Dim
Saline arcs my eyes,
No tears. I know him.

He is. I have understood
His secret fatherhood.
I live by quiet kicks;
Daily I earn my food.

When she cries, I hear her
And understand. They clothe her
With stars, she is all the stars
To me; she is my mother.

I come a foreigner
To things. I am a mourner
For all eld. I am wed
With one idea: to be born here.

I scream while torture
Attends my departure
Which they call arrival.
I am now a creature.

Already, the sudden sting
Of hands brings forgetting.
In joy, they hear me cry;
God knows, I sing!

—MELVIN WALKER LA FOLLETTE

After graduation from divinity school, he spent a year in Auburn, New York, at St. Peter's Episcopal Church as a curate. "Then I went back to St. Francis in San Jose, which was the parish that I had gone to seminary from. I came back to be the assistant of the rector, who had sent me to seminary in the first place. I was there three years, then I went to the Sonoma Valley, and for seven years I was the vicar of St. Patrick's, Kenwood, which was originally in Santa Rosa." In the Diocese of Northern California, he clashed with the bishop, who opposed the ordination of women, which Melvin had publically endorsed. Then, when he asked the bishop for permission to start a Spanish-language mass, in order to minister to the many Hispanic farmworkers in the area, the bishop said: "You stay away from those people; they don't have enough money."

He then changed career direction. "The upshot was, that I went to sea for five years teaching college classes on navy ships off the Pacific Coast. The navy has a tour that they call the WESTPAC cruise. The ships go in the Indian Ocean and Pacific Ocean for about seven months at a time, and I was on a number of those. I served on ten ships in five years." During that time, he traveled over a million nautical miles, crossed the equator twenty-four times, and visited nineteen different countries and twenty-nine ports. The courses Melvin taught were connected to Chapman College, now Chapman University.

Melvin traveled the world during those years, but when he returned to the Bay Area of northern California, his years at sea had changed his perceptions. He was also in the process of a divorce. "I had culture shock so badly that I couldn't stand it. It was terrible with all the fast traffic and the noise. My dad lived in Roswell, New Mexico, and

I got acquainted with El Paso. El Paso is the most like a non-American city, and that's a compliment, not an insult," he remembers.

He moved to El Paso and taught half-time in the English Department of the University of Texas at El Paso for a semester. When he became acquainted with the bishop of the Rio Grande diocese, some months later, he received the appointment to the Big Bend as a full-time missionary in March 1984. Melvin was doing volunteer work with the Hispanic congregation in El Paso, which prepared him for his new position in the Big Bend. "I had never been here before. I knew what it was like more or less because I had seen pictures. I knew that it was a Spanish-speaking area with a lot of poor people who needed ministering, and that sounded like what I was looking for, this was an area exactly to my taste."

Because of the vast area of the Big Bend, the territory was divided, and Melvin was to minister to the southern part of the area while

another Episcopal missionary would cover the north. Before his first year passed in his new appointment, the missionary covering the north died in an auto accident. For the next three years, Melvin covered Presidio, Lajitas, Terlingua, Terlingua Ranch, Alpine, Marfa, Van Horn, and Fort Stockton.

It was predictable that Melvin would find vast differences between his parishioners in Northern California and far West Texas, differences that were more than just geographic. "The people are nice in Northern California, but the difference in ministry is, presenting me a problem of making sure that each family has enough food and can buy a tank of gas, versus refereeing a feud between St. Martha's guild and St. Mary's guild over whether to paint the parish hall puce or periwinkle. You know, that's the difference. I like a challenge that has some more human significance to it," he says.

During his appointment in the Big Bend, Melvin was able to buy land and build a house and office on the grounds. In 1990, he was named Texas Rural Minister of the Year by *Progressive Farmer* magazine and Texas A&M. He retired in 1994, but he continues his ministry by conducting one Sunday service a month in Lajitas and continuing his work in feeding and clothing the poor. The people of the area still, in many ways, consider him their pastor. The next person appointed to the Big Bend was non–Spanish speaking, which was difficult. "She's gone now. About a year ago she went to Ruidoso, New Mexico, and we just elected a new bishop. He's going to be ordained on Saturday, and finally with somebody in charge we'll find out what happens to ministry in the Big Bend," Melvin says. As he promised, he does one mass every month but is still available to anyone who needs help. He characterizes his ministry as "needs based."

Melvin's retirement income is sufficient for living in Redford, but the cost of living in a major urban area would be prohibitive. An acquaintance that lives in New York City writes to Melvin about the cultural events she can enjoy. "She lives across from the Metropolitan Opera House, but that's something totally beyond a person who's retired on a missionary pension plus social security. I can have a nice place here and I can eat. I can eat anything I want and I still have some money left at the end of the month. My retirement income isn't enough to live in a packing box on Lakeshore Drive in Chicago."

Chicago is a favorite place that Melvin looks forward to visiting, usually once a year. He recalls, "I spent all day in the Art Institute, revisiting all my old favorites, because when I grew up, Chicago was the big town. So ever since I was fifteen, I thought the Art Institute was the center of the universe. We spent the day there, then crossed the street and heard Mahler's Fourth Symphony at the Chicago Symphony Hall. Going to the city once a year and doing the stuff I like to do is about the best I can expect, and it is probably more than I would get if I lived there all the time."

Although he certainly misses the cultural activities in larger cities, he does not miss the easy availability of shopping in chain stores. He only wishes Presidio had a larger grocery store. As most of the citizens do, he goes to Odessa or El Paso for major shopping, but he also goes several times a month to Ojinaga, Mexico, where there is a new, state-of-the-art supermarket. He provides transportation for people in need of medical care but without sufficient medical insurance to Ojinaga. "There's no decent universal health care in this country. Unlike civilized countries, this country can't provide health care for all its citizens. Unless we get rid of medicine for profit, there's never going to be any decent health care in this country. Medicine for profit is an abomination, just like religion for profit. But at least there are just a few churches for profit around, and everything's for profit in the medical field now," he says.

He does not share the concerns of other retirees in the Big Bend about the lack of extensive medical services. Either the retirees move away when they feel they will need more sophisticated medical care, or they feel that the lack of stress and infrequent doctor visits actually contribute to a longer life. "I think I've already lived eleven years more than the biblical life span, so I'm not worried about that," Melvin says.

He continues to write, characterizing himself as a poet but writing more prose now. Melvin is known in the Big Bend for his readings over the years. His poetry reading, with other writers in the area at the Starlight Theater in Terlingua, inspired Mike Boren of Big Bend National Park

to move to the area, recognizing kindred writer spirits in the Big Bend.

He has two completed unpublished novels and is at currently at work on a historical novel set during the time of the Texas Republic and is also finishing work on a novella with the working title *The Tragic End of Hipólito Arranda*, with a plot based on the story of Hippolytus, from Greek drama.

He has a sense of humor about the inevitable rejection letters. "I used to have a file of rejection letters, but I lost them somewhere. Probably the best one I ever had was a letter that I got from a small magazine in Canada, and it began, 'The poem that you sent us is probably the best poem we have ever received. Unfortunately, we will not be publishing it.'"

After his long career, Melvin is content living in Redford, lending his assistance to those in need and still providing ministry in the Big Bend. He reflects on his life: "I had no vision of where I would be, but many, many, many years ago after a very discontented youth and middle age, I saw a poster that showed a flower in a pot, and the caption was 'Bloom where you are planted.' And it changed my life."

PRESIDIO

The town of Presidio is located in southern Presidio County, directly across from Ojinaga, Chihuahua, Mexico. The history of Presidio, Texas, and Ojinaga, Mexico, are intertwined. Spanish explorers came to the area they named La Junta de las Cruces in the 1500s and celebrated the first Christmas in Texas around 1683.

The name of the village changed over the next two centuries from San Juan Evangelista to La Junta de los Rios because it was situated at the joining of the Rio Conchos and the Rio Grande. The Native American Jumano and Julime Indian tribes lived in the area in pueblos and raised crops on this fertile land, which featured plentiful water and game. When a member of the Jumano tribe described his sighting of a burning cross on the mountain, the village then became known as La Navidad en las Cruces.

In the mid-1700s, the village became a military garrison and penal colony. Presidio del Norte became the name of the settlement in the early 1800s, and the population changed with the Anglo settlers who arrived after the Mexican War of 1846–1848. The Treaty of Guadalupe Hidalgo, which set the boundary of Texas at the Rio Grande, in addition to the acquisition of land that became the western states, ended the war. With this annexation, settlers were drawn to this Trans-Pecos frontier and established large ranches, homes, and trading posts.

Although the Comanche raided Presidio in 1849 and subsequently drove away herds of cattle in the area, Presidio survived and in 1886–1887, residents opened a post office and a public school. Meanwhile, in the mid-1800s, Ojinaga, located on the Chihuahua Trail, the route from Chihuahua City, Mexico, to Missouri by way of the Red River, became a trading post. When Indian raids increased after the Civil War, the previously closed Fort Davis reopened. In 1875, the twelve-thousand-square-mile Presidio County was established with Fort Davis as its county seat. Later, when the railroad bypassed Fort Davis and came to Marfa, the citizens of Marfa voted to establish their city as the county seat. Fort Davis then became the county seat of the newly formed Jeff Davis County.

Presidio rancher John W. Spencer found silver in the Chinati Mountains, leading to the opening of the Presidio Mine in 1883. Nearly four hundred miners populated the small company town of Shafter, located twenty miles from Presidio. The mine closed and reopened several times by 1930, but it closed permanently in 1942. The mine closing in 1930 resulted in a population decline during a two-year drought. That same year, the Kansas City, Mexico & Orient Railway of Texas finished construction in Presidio of a railroad bridge into Ojinaga, connecting the two countries by rail. By 1936, the economic situation improved, and ranching and agriculture flourished in Presidio County. With the arrival of the railroad in the northeast corner of the county, livestock could be moved by rail instead of by cattle drives, so the cattlemen came and established large ranches throughout the county. Agricultural production changed from vegetables, grain, fruit, and hay to include a new crop: cotton. The construction of Elephant Butte Dam, located along the Rio Grande, provided a steady source of irrigation for the new crops.

The Mexican Revolution increased the population in Presidio from 1910–1917 owing to the migration of war refugees. Military posts, established by the U.S. Army, were located throughout Presidio County, with cavalry posts in Presidio and Redford, among other locations in the county.

Twice Pancho Villa captured Ojinaga, Mexico, adjacent to Presidio; in January 1914 he won the Battle of Ojinaga and was a familiar presence in Presidio.

During World War II, Presidio County was the location of two military bases: Fort Russell and the Marfa Army Air Field. When the war ended, Presidio County's population began a steady decline that lasted nearly thirty years.

Presidio's population, which was 3,072 in the late 1980s, has increased to over 7,800 residents, according to the 2010 U.S. Census figures. The amnesty program that in 1988 provided citizenship to previously undocumented citizens caused a population boom in the area. The population has grown again, owing, in part, to the increased tensions along the U.S.-Mexico border, which has resulted in additional law-enforcement, customs, and border-patrol agents being recently assigned to Presidio and nearby towns in the Big Bend and who have brought their families to the area. The population is projected to exceed 10,000 by 2013 at the present level of growth.

A Proud Legacy

★

DELFINA FRANCO ANDERSON

It is noon in Presidio, and we are having lunch at El Patio Restaurant with Enrique and Ruby Madrid, who are introducing us to Enrique's cousin, Delfina Franco Anderson. Delfina's sister-in-law Maria owns the Patio. Delfina is a member of the two oldest families in Presidio County, the Francos and the Redes. There are a large number of family members here in Presidio County with a long history.

Delfina was born in Marfa, grew up in Shafter, and then returned to Marfa where she graduated from high school at the age of sixteen. She then attended Sul Ross State University. "I started teaching at eighteen because they needed a first-grade teacher in Redford and I already had two years of college work and certificates. Then I went back to college and finished so I retired with forty-one years," Delfina says. After one year of teaching in Redford and another year in Presidio, Delfina moved to El Paso, where she taught at Burleson Elementary School, Clardy Elementary, and Jefferson High School during her twenty-seven-year El Paso teaching career. When her mother died, she returned to Presidio to care for her father. She began teaching again in Presidio, where she met her husband, Robert Anderson, who worked for U.S. Customs.

Delfina and Robert were married only twelve years when he became ill and passed away in 1991. Delfina then retired from the Presidio schools. "I decided to stay here in Presidio because I was very happy living here. Some people like Presidio because it's a small city and has a very good school system and is now busy with many construction projects. Presidio is a busy and good place to live."

Delfina has seen the Presidio schools increase their student population to over twelve hundred students in three campuses, which makes the Presidio school district larger than Marfa, Fort Davis, Marathon, and Valentine. This change in population over the years is an interesting mix of older residents and new, younger families moving to the community: "Young families that want their children to go to school here because of the good school system and also, they're able to keep close tabs on them; it's easier and safer. More people have moved into the district because the children have to live in the Presidio district to attend school, and the teachers also have to live here, so we have more students. Many of the husbands go to work out of town, but their families remain here. It is of great importance to keep families together."

She is one of eight children, who all went on

to make teaching their careers. All her siblings graduated from Marfa High School except the youngest in the family, her twin brothers, who graduated from high school in Presidio. Their oldest brother, a retired teacher, has passed away, and the rest are retired now, living in different areas of Texas. True to the family tradition of producing teachers, Delfina's uncle, Alberto Rede, taught for fifty-three years, and her mother taught for over thirty-three years.

Delfina reflects fondly on her career: "I really loved every year that I taught, but I felt like somebody younger had to take over." Her family also has a long history with Sul Ross, not only with all the degrees earned, but her mother, Lucy Rede, was the first Hispanic student at the university in the 1920s. Her experience was a very positive one; she encouraged Delfina to visit with her former professors when she enrolled as a student: "There was Mrs. Thomas, Miss Cowan, and Miss Britt, they were still there when I was a freshman in 1948. When I met each one, I told them: 'My mother wants me to meet you,' and of course they remembered her and were very nice and helpful."

Enrique says: "My mother added it up one time, with all the degrees that were from Sul Ross and how many years they have taught, and it was over seven hundred years of teaching just from when my mother was alive. It's a lot more now, probably double." These families of teachers have had a profound impact on the area. Delfina's grandmother, Mary Ann Rede, is acknowledged as the first person of Mexican descent to teach English in the Big Bend by tutoring Shafter residents at the age of seventeen in 1895. Lucy Rede Franco Middle School is named after Lucy, one of only a few Hispanic teachers in the 1930s.

In addition, Lucy was named Mother of the Year in 1960 and was inducted posthumously into the First Pioneers and Leaders of the State of Texas Hall of Honor by House Resolution 1675 of July 14, 2011. The House resolution also named May 6, 2011, as Lucy Rede Franco Day.

Typical of the communities of the Big Bend, there is a sense of shared ownership of the young people of Presidio. "The young people that are graduating look forward in continuing their education elsewhere, and many have been attending different universities, vocational schools, or two-year trade schools," Delfina says. "They usually get jobs wherever they graduated and come back to visit family. We're very, very proud of how well they are doing." Delfina is also proud of the large number of students who are the first in their families to attend and graduate from college.

When she returned to Presidio to live after so many years in El Paso, it was an adjustment, but an easy one. "When I first came, I had to get used to the small town again. Now I'm very happy here, and I go to El Paso to visit my family. Some wives of law-enforcement people find it very hard to adjust to life in a small town, but they are going to be here for so long, so they make the best of their stay."

Delfina has seen an increase in the population of Presidio with the arrival of more border security, road, and utility personnel; this has led to a growing business community. "Now we have several restaurants in town. We only have the Thriftway grocery store, but it's very big, and people from nearby places come and shop. We have various stores where you can buy shoes, clothing, and other needs. Paving city streets has created more work in the community and more businesses." The inevitable question has to be asked: Does Delfina miss the big box stores or the proximity of a Walmart? She answers that Odessa or El Paso are within driving distance for that sort of shopping, but she also feels that having a Walmart near Presidio would certainly be a savings for everyone.

As a retiree, Delfina is undaunted by limited access to sophisticated medical facilities. There is the Presidio County Clinic, serviced by a physician from Alpine who now works part-time in Marfa and part-time in Presidio. The clinic needs a full-time doctor, but at present has a licensed physician's assistant, and an El Paso doctor and his physician's assistant service another Presidio clinic. Anyone faced with an emergency requiring hospitalization would have to go by ambulance to Alpine or, if the condition were very serious, go to Odessa or El Paso. "I know some people have had to consult doctors in Ojinaga, Mexico, due to drastic emergencies. Some people go there for dental work since they have good dentists," Delfina says. "Lately, we take care on our trips to Ojinaga because of border security."

The option of crossing into Ojinaga is much more difficult with the tightening of border security, affecting both main entry points and informal crossings along the U.S.-Mexico border. "Living in Presidio, learn to really take care of yourself health-wise," Delfina says, "and be prepared with medical supplies. We're getting more and more needed facilities, which are good for the city, and we're looking forward to having a clinic and a hospital built in the near future. The city and county are trying to do as much as they can to get more facilities for the community. So I think we're progressing."

There are also part-time residents, snowbirds from up north who come to Presidio to stay for a few months every year at the Bishop RV Park. They are drawn to the climate and the close-knit community, where they enjoy life in Presidio. "Many of them keep coming every year because they love their stay. They spend so much time and then they go back, but we see them. After months here, they go to other places," she says. "While they are here, they make the best of their stay relaxing and enjoying life. As far as socializing, you have church, city, or school activities all year. We're always meeting different and interesting people, so it's nice."

When Delfina left Presidio to start her career in a much larger city, she did not foresee that decades later she would be living in her hometown again, but life circumstances and the pull of family and the landscape drew her back. "I never thought I was going to come back, but you never know. When I came back, I really appreciated the blue skies, the clouds, the desert plants, and the beauty of the mountains. Presidio is a peaceful city, and I love it."

The Family Store

★

EDMUNDO AND MARIO NIETO

On the main street of Presidio, stores are lined up on both sides, some still open with active businesses, but others vacant. The Nieto Department Store is still open. The interior of the store is reminiscent of an earlier time, with well-worn and beautiful wooden floors and display cabinets made of glass with wooden frames. The store offers a selection of appliances, veterinary supplies, jeans, shirts, work boots, kitchen utensils, the other items necessary for everyday life. Throughout the store, there are vintage signs advertising various brands of clothing and appliances. On the counter behind the cash register, there are family photographs and a candid photograph of Pancho Villa, taken when he was in Ojinaga, Mexico, and Presidio. The original location of the store was across

the street, but the business has been in Presidio since 1913.

Edmundo Nieto, the patriarch of the family, was born in Presidio on March 29, 1919. His father was from Ojinaga and, during the revolution, came over as a young man and started working for a man named Kleinman at his Presidio store. After a few years, he was approached by a customs broker in Ojinaga, who financed the opening of a store with Edmundo's father as the manager. When the backer sold his interest to Edmundo's father, he established the Nieto Department Store. The store changed location from the original adobe building with its high ceilings and no air conditioning to its current location.

Edmundo graduated from Presidio High School and then attended St. Edward's University in

Austin. The educational experience in Austin was something of a family tradition, as well: "It was through my mother's cousin, they were related to Kleinman's son, who went to St. Ed's, and she wanted me to go there because my mother went, my grandmother went, I think, in a wagon from here to St. Mary's Academy in Austin. Took them quite a while, I guess a month to get over there."

Edmundo majored in business at St. Edwards, then worked in San Antonio after graduation for a short time before he enlisted in the army in World War II. His basic training was at Camp Gruber in Oklahoma. Edmundo was selected for Officers Candidate School after taking the exam. He was able to return to Presidio for a weeklong furlough, then spent two months in Louisiana on maneuvers and field artillery. He was then sent to

New Jersey, and then embarked to North Africa. "In Oran, the war in Africa was nearly over when I got there," Edmundo remembers. "From Oran we went to Bizerte, but the battalion moved over there by land, it took us about three days, and from there we went to Italy. Most of the war was spent in Italy, it was a separate battalion; we were attached with the French forces in Italy. They had the center of the country, the French, the Americans, and British."

When Edmundo finished his military service, he returned to Presidio: "My dad was getting old, and I stayed to help him. In those days, we had a lot of business, most of our business, about 85 percent, was from Mexico. We used a lot of piece goods, remember?" Edmundo asks his son Mario. "People used to make their own dresses, it was full of piece goods and Levis. I remember when a little shirt cost a dollar, a blue shirt." The Nieto Department Store was one of the two biggest stores in Presidio, along with Spencer's, which closed recently. Spencer's was a clothing store, selling Western clothing for men, women, and children.

Edmundo and his wife raised a family of four sons in Presidio. Two sons live there. "My oldest son graduated from the University of Texas," says Edmundo. "He's an architect and works for the national parks up in Denver, and he's about to retire now. And my second, he's a doctor, he lives in Austin." Mario Nieto, one of the sons living in Presidio, has the most active role in the business. He graduated from the University of Denver but returned to Presidio in 1976 to help Edmundo run the family business. Mario married in 1981 and raised a family with his wife. They have two sons, and one of them graduated from Notre Dame and Vanderbilt Medical School. He is now a resident in anesthesiology at the Baylor

College of Medicine. Mario's other son works for an international company. He lives in Chicago but travels the world for his job. The education they received in the Presidio schools was obviously at least on a par with schools in much larger cities.

Over the years the business has changed in volume and customer base. According to Edmundo, "It has changed a lot, ever since NAFTA [the North American Free Trade Agreement] came over. Used to get a lot of trips from Mexico, Chihuahua, Camargo, people used to come and buy here. Now they have everything over there, and cheap. We don't get as many customers from over there now, only a few come here." Before, he used to sell a lot of Stetson hats and Nocona and Justin boots. "Now they get them cheaper over there and they don't come," Edmundo says. "But I remember those big ranchers in Mexico used to sport a good Stetson hat and a good pair of boots. But times have changed." Many customers who used to cross over to Presidio from Ojinaga to shop are now residents of Presidio. The new people are usually either former citizens of Mexico or government workers: border-patrol agents, customs agents, and immigration department employees.

The former residents of Mexico come to Presidio to work in agriculture, some at the tomato farms in Marfa and Fort Davis, and some at the ranches in the area. The border-patrol agents come in response to the need for increased security along the U.S.-Mexico border and to the communities in the Big Bend because of their relative proximity to the border and sparse population. Both groups frequently come with young families, which has increased the student population in the schools and boosted the price of real estate.

The schools in Presidio have the largest number of students, more than Marfa or Alpine.

The people of Presidio are rightfully proud of their schools. The Presidio Independent School District also serves the unincorporated towns of Candelaria, Chinati and Ruidosa. There are over fifteen hundred students in Presidio Elementary, Lucy Rede Franco Middle School, and Presidio High School. The Blue Devils of Presidio High School no longer have a football team; it was dropped from the athletic program in 2004. Now their high school sports program concentrates on baseball and softball. The Blue Devils have been in most state playoffs since 2000.

Edmundo and Mario agree that Presidio is a good place to raise children. Because of the size of the town, children are more visible: "You can see where your kids go or where they're at. In a big city they can go anywhere," Edmundo says. Mario agrees: "When I was raising my two boys here, we used to take them camping, hunting, they liked all those activities with the school, also. My wife didn't work back then until they left for college, they were raised with us always with them. On weekends we took them out camping and hunting. They enjoyed that." Mario thinks that, in an urban setting, you would see your children only at dinner and that their weekends would be filled with many activities with their friends. "Here when I was growing up, our biggest recreation was going to Ojinaga, that's where the action was. Not any more," he says.

Although Presidio fosters strong family ties, once the teenagers who are college bound graduate, they leave and do not return to live. There is a lack of employment opportunities for new college graduates in most of the Big Bend communities. "It's hard for any kid graduating from high school going to college and coming back," says Mario.

Reading and socializing with friends and family are the usual leisure-time activities in this close-knit community. When someone in the community needs help, the people of Presidio, like the other communities of the Big Bend, respond. There is a need to be self-reliant, as well. When something is broken, you get the parts and learn to fix it yourself, Mario says.

After their assignment to Presidio, most border-patrol agents and their families move away for a variety of reasons that Mario has observed. "I think most of them try to leave; I mean they miss their Walmarts, their big cities, so they're only here for a couple of years. I think mostly their biggest gripe is the heat; it's hot during the summer, and not many stores to go shopping in," he says. "They're not used to a small town, which I was. I lived in a big city, and I'd rather live in Presidio."

Mario admits that, had he been raised in a big city, he would feel differently about staying: "I guess if I were raised in a big city, probably not. Probably not. That's why the majority is border patrol. Most of them are from the El Paso area, so they want to go back, or their wives want to go. They don't want to stay here." There are also retired baby boomers moving to the area, looking for a less hectic way of life.

During the slow periods of business, Mario has had to rethink the stocking of the store. Their competition is two Dollar Stores and an Alco, which Mario describes: "They're a little Walmart. We used to sell more clothes, but our competition, like Alco, those big chain stores, we can't compete with the clothing anymore, but I'll be carrying some hats and work boots." The Nietos still have the market for the appliances and veterinary supplies that address the needs of the ranchers and the residents of Ojinaga, who buy appliances there.

When Mario returned to Presidio, the store

was incorporated under the name "Nieto M Department Store." The business was doing well. "Back then, when I came back, business was good here, the store was doing real good, of course there wasn't any NAFTA," Mario says. "We used to sell straw hats by the dozens, clothing, and everything wholesale. After NAFTA, you could go to Chihuahua, and everything up there was American made." When Mario is asked if NAFTA was negative for border businesses but positive for the Mexican people, he says: "The Mexican businesses are suffering also over this. It's the big businesses that are benefiting from NAFTA, the Walmarts, Sam's Club."

There may be hope for increased business for the Nieto Department Store. The Rio Grande Silver Mine in Shafter has recently reopened. Mario read that 140 people would be employed. Since Shafter appears to be a ghost town from the road, many of those employed would come from Presidio and the surrounding area.

The escalating violence along the U.S-Mexico Border that has warranted an increased border-patrol and law-enforcement presence along all border crossings is not as pressing an issue as it is in other cities and communities along the border. "No, I think it's still pretty safe. We haven't seen any problems here. Ojinaga is not as violent as other cities, like Carmargo, Chihuahua," Mario says. "I mean, there are killings in Juárez every-day, or kidnapping. Here it's not that bad, there is violence, but not like you would think the border would be."

Mario has found that his business is becoming seasonal: "We're barely just hanging in there. The bulk of our business is when we get cattle from Mexico, a lot of ranchers, we sell a lot of vet sup-plies and ranching supplies. So we depend on that business." The Nietos have weathered hard eco-nomic times before in their long business history. Presidio is Edmundo's and Mario's hometown; they are at home among the people they have known all their lives. Lively, engaging Edmundo says: "Time goes so fast, I didn't know I was this old." Father and son agree on their commitment to their family business. "We're hanging in there. It's kind of rough but . . ." Mario says. "We'll try to hang on as long as we can," says Edmundo.

ALPINE

Alpine, Texas, the county seat of Brewster County, began as a settlement named Osborne for railroad workers in 1882. Only one year later, when brothers Daniel and Thomas Murphy agreed to give the Southern Pacific Railroad rights to water on their property, the railroad named the town Murphyville, but five years after that, in 1888, the citizens of the town voted to change the name to Alpine.

With a population of nearly six thousand, Alpine is the largest town in the Big Bend. After a few days spent in the smaller communities of the Big Bend, we found a trip to Alpine is like a trip to the big city. Alpine is big enough to have its own university, Sul Ross State; its own medical center, established in 1999; its own professional baseball team, the Alpine Cowboys; and an art scene. Many of the historic buildings in downtown Alpine have been renovated as art galleries and restaurants. Alpine has the only McDonald's in the Big Bend. (Walmart, Starbucks, and big box stores are still distant. The closest stores of that kind are in Odessa, 128 miles away.)

In 1917, Sul Ross Normal College was founded in Alpine. Named for Lawrence Sullivan "Sul" Ross, who was governor of Texas from 1886 to 1891, and a Civil War general, it became Sul Ross State University, part of the Texas State University System, in 1969. Today, with a student body of over 2,000, the Center for Big Bend Studies, and the Museum of the Big Bend, the university has become a major contributor to the economy of the region.

In 1946, Herbert L. Kokernot, Jr., the son of a cattle rancher, transformed the Alpine Cats, a semi-professional baseball team, into the Alpine Cowboys. Kokernot built a beautiful new stadium, Kokernot Field, at the cost of $1.5 million, and, as part of his lavish plan, he brought in dirt by train from Georgia for the infield. The stadium was home to the Alpine Cowboys from 1947 to 1958, and during that time the team won many regional titles and placed as runners-up in the national championship. Kokernot supported athletics in the region by offering a place on the team and college scholarships for gifted athletes in the area. Today, Kokernot Field in Alpine is home again to the professional, independent-league Alpine Cowboys, as well as to the Sul Ross State University Lobos.

Visitors are drawn to Alpine for many annual events, such as the Art Walk on the Friday and

Saturday before Thanksgiving; the Texas Cowboy Poetry Gathering on the last weekend of February, which is the oldest such event in the United States; the Big Bend Balloon Bash on Labor Day Weekend; and the Way Out West Book Festival in August. Sul Ross has the outdoor Theatre of the Big Bend, host to many musicals and theater performances. The local drama group, called the Big Bend Players, schedule performances throughout the year. In addition to these activities, Alpine has the spectacular scenery and pleasant climate characteristic of the Big Bend. It has been listed in *The 100 Best Small Towns in America* by Norman Crampton (Arco Publications, 1996).

The Scotsman

★

JIM GLENDINNING

It is a long, long way from Scotland to Texas. "I was born on a farm near the town of Lockerbie, unfortunately known for Pan American Flight 103," says Jim Glendinning. The sheep farm is still in his family. Jim attended boarding school in Edinburgh, and shortly after finishing at Oxford University in 1961, he came to the United States and was naturalized in 1987. For thirty years he worked at a variety of jobs, usually self-employed, mostly in tourism, but he changed jobs every five years. "If the business wasn't going well, as in Houston, I had to move on. If the business was going well and I usually got lucky, I got bored with it."

Jim returned to England in the 1970s and owned two businesses in Oxford, the Pizza Cellar and St. Michael's Wine Bar. He came back to the United States in 1981 and started a business in Houston called Glendinning's of Scotland. It was a combination tearoom and Scottish import store located on Memorial Drive. By 1985, with the economy in rapid decline, Jim could see that his business would inevitably fail.

It was then that Jim saw a "Weekend Trip with the Sierra Club to the Big Bend" advertised in the Houston newspaper. The trip was mainly for foreign students at Rice University, but Jim signed up and left with the group on Thanksgiving weekend. The passengers would be sleeping on the bus.

The departure was on a noisy, foggy Houston day. When they arrived at Panther Junction in the Big Bend National Park, Jim was surprised: "The sun was blazing out of the skies, and I thought I'd woken up in Switzerland or something. I then thought, why, why have I just heard about this? Why aren't people talking about the Big Bend?"

Jim was already a seasoned traveler, but on this first visit to the Big Bend, the location, the connection with Mexico, the natural beauty, and the sparse population were irresistible. In 1986, Jim took a job with a tour operator in Alpine, living in Houston while he regrouped and thought about his future. Over the next three years his plan to stay in Alpine became a reality. When he realized there was not a comprehensive guidebook to the area, he decided to write one. "There was plenty of good stuff, historical reminiscences, flora and fauna, rocks, you know, but there was no general guide for the whole of the Big Bend region, by which I would say stretching up into the Davis Mountains and west of Valentine or further," Jim says. He went to a Houston Book Stop and found the names of six publishers producing books about the region to find a publisher and made inquiries. After ten days, he received a call from Texas A&M University Press, which published Jim's book, *From Big Bend to Carlsbad.*

Then Jim decided, in the days before the chain motels came to the Big Bend, that Alpine needed a bed-and-breakfast. "I was getting people as my guests who normally might have stayed in a new motel, people interviewing for Sul Ross, visiting Sul Ross to give talks, and so I was in the bed-and-breakfast business, opening in 1992, and in the guidebook business," Jim says. He bought a large house that was ideal, with the right number of bedrooms and common rooms,

centrally located in Alpine. *Texas Highways* wrote an article on the area and photographed Jim in his kilt with the Scottish flag flying outside the bed-and-breakfast.

The local community knew Jim since he opened the bed-and-breakfast to the public for lunch. Activities at the bed-and-breakfast included mystery weekends and Scottish nights with Jim wearing his kilt. So, in addition to people coming from other cities in Texas, the events at the bed-and-breakfast engaged the residents of Alpine and the surrounding communities. However, the 24/7 reality of operating a bed-and-breakfast was exhausting: "I was going to the door without a welcoming smile, gritting my teeth, 'You don't want a bed do you?'" Jim sold the business in 1999. "I met a lot of wonderful people whom I was able to introduce, and maybe sell my guidebook, to this amazing area," he says. Jim noticed that after a few days in the Big Bend, his guests underwent a change. "This area can work its calming, sometimes magical influence on people," he remembers. "People have come out here, and they were on edge, they were wound up, they weren't very happy, and I've seen the whole area work something on them to quiet them down, you know, bring out the better sides of them."

Alpine quickly became home for Jim, and he felt at ease in spite of his accent. "I remember talking to a waiter from Scotland in Houston during the boom years there when waiters could make a lot of money at a good restaurant, and I said, 'Do you go home, you know, back to Scotland?'" Jim asked. "He said, 'Well, I do, and I've got folks over there but I also go back to work on my accent so the vowels aren't changing too much and becoming 'Texanized.'"

Although Jim was very much at home in

Alpine when he began living there, he has seen the area change, offering opportunities—like yoga classes, or places to buy a cup of espresso, previously unobtainable in the mid-1990s—that are now commonplace. Jim sees a continuing new wave of people who are involved, starting new businesses and participating in the city council. Many writers, artists, and musicians provide a lively and vibrant artistic community. "That's one of the things that is neat about this part of the country; you've got a lot of educated people here. They make a joke about it down in Terlingua, you know. Someone sitting under a rock may well have a Ph.D.," Jim says. Telecommuting has made it possible to live in the Big Bend while working for a company elsewhere.

Jim owns Glendinning Tours, which advertises tours to Mexico, including Copper Canyon by train to Creel and El Fuerte, Copper Canyon, and Batopilas, traveling by bus, train, and van; Casas Grandes and Mata Ortiz; a hike on the Silver Route, where silver was transported from the Batopilas Mine, and a two-week stay in the Sierra Madre for the Sierra Children's Health Project. But the tours of Mexico have been suspended until further notice. He also conducts tours of Ireland and Scotland.

He has written another guidebook, *Adventures in the Big Bend*, which is now in its fourth edition, published by Iron Mountain Press. He had a radio program, "Voices of the Big Bend," on KRTS, Marfa Public Radio. He also writes articles based on his interviews for the *Cenzio Journal*, a quarterly publication in the Big Bend. Jim's interviews with the longtime residents of the area have been thought-provoking: "I've interviewed people time and again going back to the old days, and they've said, 'We left Ozona and came out here with our

goats,' and I would say, 'How long did that take?' thinking it was in some old jalopy. They came on foot," he says. Jim was struck by their modesty about their difficult pasts. "This is 180 degrees from your big-talking Texan of the caricature. They came on foot because that was the only way they were going to get here, and this place was the future to them, so if it took eight days, it took eight days," Jim says.

The landscape of the Big Bend is very different from Scotland, which gets nearly sixty inches of rain annually. Jim agrees that the desert landscape and mountains are a draw for new residents and a compelling reason to stay: "I think it's the beauty of the landscape and the power of the big sky, I think nature has got to be number one," he says. A concert pianist from Houston came to Marfa to perform, free of charge; at the end of the concert she engaged the audience by answering questions. Her first comment was: "You folks are really lucky out here, you've got something we haven't got in Houston anymore; you've got quiet." When Jim has trouble sleeping, he rides his bicycle up to the park in the middle of the night and makes several circuits, enjoying the absence of streetlights and the utter quiet.

Over the years, Jim has found that each of the communities of the Big Bend attract specific types of people. Marfa attracts a lot of writers and artists; Terlingua attracts people who are more reclusive and want to live off the grid; Fort Davis and Alpine are now attracting many new retirees. As a transplanted Scotsman, living for many years in Texas, Jim has found that Texans are set apart. "Texans are quite different and remarkable people. There's an image of Texans from other states and countries of being boastful and larger than life," he says. "But there's another side of them that

I've encountered talking with them, partly in my interviews, partly just neighborly, which is quite different, a quieter and more human sort of aspect to them, and I think that's nature having worked on them, they're at ease with their surroundings and with themselves."

When Jim left for a three-week trip to Borneo and the United Arab Emirates, he walked to the train station, twelve minutes away. Standing in the middle of the street was a big buck. "Usually the deer, and many more does than bucks, stay on the golf course because that is where the eating is, but this one must have gotten even more curious, so walking around a deer on the way to the station, I'm thinking: Man, we're still in nature here," he says. When he returned and stepped off the train, he was immediately offered a ride. Jim thinks of this as the human element of the Big Bend, that small-town quality: "He saw I was coming off the train, thought I might need a ride, was offering it. So nice, a feeling of belonging. Yeah, I thought, I'm back in Alpine."

The Defender

★

ELIZABETH ROGERS

Elizabeth Rogers is not a stranger to West Texas. Born in Uvalde County, approximately 250 miles from the Big Bend, her parents and grandparents were sheep and goat ranchers. Her maternal grandparents bought their ranch in Brewster County in the 1950s, but as they grew older and required more health care, they leased out the ranch. Liz explains, "My parents bought out my uncle's half (my mother's brother) of the Rosenow Rogers Ranch that we still have, and my paternal grandparents homesteaded north of Alpine. My paternal grandmother grew up in the Big Bend."

Liz earned an A.A. from Southwest Texas Junior College, a B.A. from Texas A&M University in 1975, and a J.D. from South Texas College of Law in 1978. She held several jobs before she joined the Office of the Federal Public Defender. She was an assistant city attorney for one year, an assistant U.S. Attorney for nearly a year, and then in private practice with the firm of Peticolas, Luscombe & Stephens for three years. "During my time in El Paso, we saw a dramatic increase in the El Paso and Pecos divisions, which we handled, but that was true all along the border, from San Diego to Brownsville. When they had the big buildup of border patrol and law enforcement along the border here, our caseload skyrocketed," Liz says. She estimates that her office handles 70 percent of the indigent defense cases.

Because of the increased workload, changes were made. "The assistant United States Attorney, Jim Blankinship, talked his bosses into letting him move to Alpine to be closer to the enforcement area," Liz says. "I was the head of the El Paso office since 1986 and stayed in charge of both divisions until I asked to be relieved because we were so busy in the Pecos Division, and the distance was too far for me to be a meaningful supervisor of both. Now I am the supervisory AFPD [assistant federal public defender] for the Pecos Division only."

Liz requested a transfer to Alpine because her boyfriend, Mike O'Connor, was in Marfa, and he did not enjoy leaving Marfa to go to El Paso, even for a visit. Since Liz loves the Big Bend, she feels fortunate to be in Alpine and continue her career.

The role of public defender is an emotionally draining one. Since most defendants tend to be found guilty, many cases are plea-bargained. Even so, there are strong and realistic concerns for clients because of their life circumstances. The case of Mauricio A. Martinez-Castillo was a particularly difficult one. Liz considers it one of the most heartbreaking situations she has encountered in her job.

In 1996, twenty-one-year-old Mauricio came to the United States. He stayed and worked for several years, then returned to Mexico in 2003. He opened a restaurant in Aldama, Chihuahua. After he sold the restaurant to his landlord, he opened another one in 2005. "He got into financial trouble, and like so many young people, he agreed to smuggle a load of drugs into the U.S.," Liz recalls. "He was arrested in El Paso at the port of entry in April 2007 and received a twelve-month, one-day sentence," Liz explains. "He was deported for life to Mexico in March 2008, and started working again in his family's restaurant."

He started receiving phone calls soliciting protection money in October 2008. He ignored the calls. Then, in November, he received yet another call but was told that this would be the last one he would receive. The caller demanded 5,000 pesos per week in order for the restaurant to stay open. Mauricio hung up. "On November 14, 2008, Mauricio and his friend, Luis Arrieta, were gunned down in front of the restaurant. Both survived, and I have the newspaper article with his picture on the ambulance stretcher along with the story. After he was released from the hospital in Chihuahua, they closed the restaurant, and it never reopened," Liz says.

Two weeks after the attempted assassination, Mauricio received another phone call. This time he was told that the next time he would be killed. "He now understands that he needs to take these people seriously. They demand 200,000 pesos; he tells them all he has is 50,000 pesos. He was instructed where to bring it, and he did," Liz says. A young man walked up to Mauricio, took the money, and never said a word.

By December 2008, Mauricio realized he had to leave Mexico. Through a friend in Montreal, Canada, he made the decision to seek political asylum. He sold his home and furniture for 250,000 pesos. The airfare to Montreal from Mexico cost nearly 80,000 pesos for himself, his wife, and two sons. "On December 24, 2008, they land in Montreal and immediately request political asylum. He is detained for two days, but his family is allowed to stay in the hotel, where they spend an additional 20,000 pesos for room and board. Canadian authorities deny his request due to his criminal record in the U.S. On December 26, he and his family return to Mexico and move to Monterrey. He wants to start over," says Liz.

He soon realized that he could not support his family in Monterey, so in April 2009, he made the difficult decision to return to Aldama. For the next year he bought and sold alfalfa in business with his uncle, but soon his peace was shattered. "In April 2010, he got another phone call, demanding immediate payment of a *cuota*, protection money. He starts paying what little he had to men who came around to his place of business about every three weeks," Liz says. Mauricio struggled to comply with the demands for the next four months, but now he was falling behind in paying his business expenses and the alfalfa suppliers. He was forced to close his business.

Until September 2010, he tried to support his family by doing odd jobs, but it was impossible. "His three-year term of supervised release ended in March 2010. He began planning to come back to the U.S. to find work. His two close friends had been kidnapped, Manuel Martinez, whose family owns gas stations and Javier Millan, whose family owns a large grocery store. Their families paid the ransom, but both men were killed," Liz says.

When Mauricio crossed the border into the United States illegally, he was arrested near Valentine in June 2011. "We filed a motion seeking a lower sentence because of these circumstances, but Judge Junell was not swayed. Mauricio is serving twenty-seven months in prison for illegal reentry after deportation," Liz says.

Mauricio impressed Liz because he never justified his previous drug conviction. He always accepted his actions and wished he had not acted as a courier. "The most poignant thing about our

discussions was his gratitude for our help, even though I was very negative on our chances of getting his sentence reduced," Liz remembers. "I asked him why he didn't go to Costa Rica or Argentina, and he answered, 'I am Mexican. We always look to the U.S. first and Canada, second. And I've tried them both. Now I've got to find a country where I can live and work.'" She suggested other countries such as Dubai or Singapore as possibilities, but Liz knew he would never have the resources to even get there. "His marriage of twenty-two years was over because, he said, 'I left her in the street with nothing. Do you understand me? Nothing,'" Liz says.

This case is one that has stayed with Liz, and she explains why: "I think Mauricio's case gripped me because I'd never seen someone who (1) survived an assassination attempt, (2) then flew his family to Canada to escape harm, and (3) understood the hopelessness of having a future for himself or his family in Mexico. I felt the bitter reality that these circumstances make absolutely no difference in our criminal justice system."

Because of the increase in border crossings, either from drug running or people seeking employment, there is a heightened presence of the Border Patrol and Homeland Security personnel. That can bring its own problems. Liz represented a man several months ago who was arrested and spent a night in jail because of a misunderstanding. There was a construction job going on in Big Bend National Park, and Liz's client and his boss both lived in Terlingua. Each morning at 5 a.m. they would leave to commute to the Park.

One morning, he was headed for work and became irritated by a car following his with undimmed ultra bright lights. To keep the lights

been making that trip for six months, along with his boss, who was stopped an average of three times a week. With the frequent change of agents assigned to the sector, it is a situation that occurs over and over again."

During her career, Liz has had the opportunity to observe the impact that current drug-enforcement and immigration policies have had on these problems. She has a compassionate view of both situations. Liz does not see that drug use has diminished over the past several decades. She recognizes that simply incarcerating drug users and smugglers has been ineffective. She believes it is necessary to change policy through a willingness to explore other options. "It seems to me that our policy needs to promote treatment if people are willing and just stay after it. Most people who are alcoholics don't quit drinking after their first AA meeting. Most people are not going to get clean on drugs if they're dependent just because a judge tells them not to," Liz says.

Her long experience in the courts has shown Liz what doesn't work. "We're clearly not a nation that's going to quit doing dope; we love it. If we're not going to quit doing it, decriminalization seems the most logical thing. I don't want to encourage drug use, it's not good for you. I don't want to encourage smoking, either, but people do it, and they ought not be locked up for long periods of time. Wasted lives," Liz observes.

Another source of frustration for Liz is the attitude that illegal immigrants somehow hit it big when they come to the United States. "It makes me furious because, if they would just follow me around for one day, I can tell you it isn't a jackpot, and they would be shocked at the time in prison you get." She suggests that, although we need to control our borders, work permits should

from blinding him, he changed the angle on his rear view mirrors. He endured this for about thirty miles but when eight cars pulled him over to the side of the road, he realized they were Border Patrol agents. "Since he had an out-of-state license, he was a 'person of interest,'" Liz says. "They took him to jail, and he hadn't done a thing in the world wrong, except not seeing that the Border Patrol wanted him to stop. The next day, I got him dismissed, but it was a real unfortunate incident," Liz recalls. "The Border Patrol claimed they did not know who he was, although he had be issued to people who will do the jobs that go unfilled. "If there were no jobs available, people wouldn't come. They might come out of violence, but they wouldn't come to work if there weren't any jobs. There are many jobs available because American employers never get their penalties, they just lose their worker who goes off to prison, and it's wrong and it's unfair," Liz says.

Liz shared two of the most interesting cases of her career with us. A Drug Enforcement Agency (DEA) special agent, Enrique Camarena, was murdered in Guadalajara. "Our government kidnapped a Mexican doctor, Dr. Alvarez-Machain, who was alleged to have participated in the torture of Agent Camarena by administering drugs to him during his interrogation," Liz says. She received a call on a Sunday afternoon while she was preparing for a drug trial from the assistant U.S. Attorney she was opposing in another case. "He said something big was happening, and he was going to dismiss my case, which he did early Monday morning," Liz began. "The something big was that the DEA had kidnapped Dr. Machain from his office in Guadalajara and driven him overland to León, Guanajuato, where the DEA plane was waiting, and flew him to El Paso for his initial appearance." Liz was appointed to represent him, not knowing how big this case would become.

She had to drive to La Tuna Federal Correctional Institution in Anthony, New Mexico, outside of El Paso, when ordinarily, Machain would have been held in downtown El Paso at the county jail. He was being transferred to Los Angeles to stand trial. "His case went all the way to the Supreme Court, but he was ultimately set free, I think exonerated might be too strong a word," Liz says. While Liz was attending a conference in New York City a few days later, Dr.

Machain was covered extensively in the national news. "I told my colleagues that he had been my client for a short time. They were astounded that I didn't call a press conference and hadn't made a big deal about it," Liz recalls.

Another case that Liz particularly remembers involved the perceived power of a *bruja* (witch) and a *curandera* (healer) in Mexico. The two are not the same but are sometimes confused. After Liz moved to Alpine, an assistant U.S. Attorney there indicted her client in a drug conspiracy case for being a *bruja/curandera* and casting spells over law enforcement on behalf of the drug cartel. "When you think about this for one second, it is just preposterous! If someone prays that their son won't get arrested, are they complicit with drug trafficking? Does the assistant U.S. Attorney have to show that her spells had power, or resulted in success?" Liz says. Her research and writing lawyer, Chris Carlin, filed the motion to dismiss. "I must say, it was such fun, I can find a copy of that motion, and I still tease Jay Miller, the assistant U.S. Attorney, about what in the world he was thinking. My lady was poor, poor, from the lower Valley of Texas, illiterate, and very happy to go free," she says.

Liz has a full and busy life in the Big Bend. She is an active participant in community social events and is a member of a book club that has been meeting for nearly fifteen years. She has also finished a Master Naturalist class. "I am a graduate of the Tierra Grande Master Naturalist program with two of my sisters, and we became Quail Masters last year. I am a member of West of the Pecos Cattlewomen; on the board of the Texas Nature Conservancy; and am a member of the Philosophical Society of Texas," Liz says. She is also very active professionally. "My biggest professional honor was being named Outstanding Assistant Federal Defender in 2000 by the Association of Federal Defenders. I previously served on the board of directors for the State Bar of Texas," Liz says.

She has seen the communities of the Big Bend settle into a self-selection process. She characterizes the people of Fort Davis as retirees in good health or people who want a second home in the mountains. She thinks Marathon attracts people from Austin, while Marfa attracts a large number of people from Houston, New York, and Los Angeles "It gets more of the young hipsters as well as the wealthy art patrons," she observes. "Many of the communities gain population from new law-enforcement agents who transfer to the region, and Alpine draws population from the presence of Sul Ross State University." She characterizes Presidio as having the largest group of native residents, while Lajitas and Terlingua have very few. "They really want to be away from everybody; they can stand the heat. They're really different and very interesting, very colorful, but they don't need to be around a lot of grocery stores or good restaurants," Liz says.

Liz is also known for her hospitality. She has a small casita behind her house and has been hostess to bicycle riders who pass through the Big Bend on their cross-country races. Many are from Europe, and it is well known that her home is a most welcome respite on their journeys. Her gregarious personality has always ensured that she has a large circle of friends wherever she lives, but she is struck by the longevity of her friends in the Big Bend. "I went to about three ninetieth birthday parties last year and an eightieth birthday right behind it. All of them are vibrant, easy, and wonderful to be around. They were dancing, they're not like old people, and they're my friends. Two of the ninety-year-olds can't drive because they can't see, but everybody takes care of them, they have huge social networks."

Liz can identify only one drawback to living in the Big Bend, one that is shared by many people who moved to the area, but it does not concern her very much right now. "The distance in going to the doctor. When people get in poor health it's a long way to medical care. I just think it's so unique because the freeway doesn't run right through us. I'm glad I-10 is a long way from us, but if I get old and frail, I bet I won't be so glad," she says. "The reason I love living here is that I'm a Texan, which means, of course, that I need and want to live in Texas, and this is the prettiest place in our state, bar none."

The Dean and the Dream

★

JIM CASE

Jim Case moved to Alpine when he accepted a teaching position in political science at Sul Ross State University in July 1981. Twenty-nine years later, he is the dean of arts and sciences. He was not a stranger to West Texas, having grown up in the Texas panhandle, north of Amarillo in the south plains of the state. "In 1977, I took a job teaching at Stephen F. Austin University in Nacogdoches, so most of my life I had actually been in the Panhandle/South Plains area," Jim says. "But I ended up in Nacogdoches for four years, and it was really lovely, but it didn't have that feel that I had grown to appreciate and really enjoy. It didn't have a sort of the high-desert sense about it."

Sul Ross is the smallest comprehensive four-year school in the Texas State University System. Since the population of Alpine is also small, Jim has not found a division between the university people and the townspeople. "The town is very protective of the university, and the university tries to serve the town. The university and the community, are, I feel, organically one," Jim says.

The university brings cultural activities to Alpine through their summer Big Bend Theatre program, in which Alpine residents participate. During the year, art exhibits, band programs, and the community concert choir provide arts events. The Center for Big Bend Studies, a research institute within Sul Ross, was established in 1987, and it states as part of its mission a commitment to public outreach and the promotion of educational activities in archaeology and history to students, researchers, and the public.

Although the climate and landscape of the Big Bend attract tourists and people who buy second homes, Jim has found that attracting new faculty can be a challenge. "It's not an easy sell because this is beyond small-town rural. The idea of a small town is attractive in some ways, but this is frontier," he says. "It's one thing to romanticize rural agrarian living; it's another to know you are 150 miles away from the nearest airport and Sam's, the big Walmart store. You're a long way off." He understood just how isolated the area is when he came to Alpine from Nacogdoches to interview for the job. "After you leave Austin and then get on I-10 going west and it takes you forever to get to Sonora and it takes you forever to get to Ozona and then it really takes you forever to get to Fort Stockton. . . " Jim remembers. "Ten miles out of Fort Stockton, you turn south and you think, What happens if I have my heart attack? You know, I'm in the middle of nowhere."

109

JIM CASE

Jim has also observed the movement into and out of Alpine, with the students moving away after graduation for job opportunities with higher salaries not available in the Big Bend. He sees Homeland Security employees moving into the area in response to U.S.-Mexico border issues and older residents leaving for more specialized medical care. Jim has always had an interest in health-care policy, and as a member of a rural health-care organization in 1981, he learned that the sparse population of the Big Bend qualified, according to the National Rural Health Care Association, as a frontier health-care service area.

The criteria were that the county served would have one person per square mile. He believes that category would still fit. "The other pattern I see, and I fall into this myself, is you're out here, you're older, you may not have family out here, or children, but you love the place, and you just ponder what happens if I'm fortunate enough to live to be eighty-five or ninety and really need more care than I can get out here," he says.

The realities of aging in an isolated area become apparent. "Someday you think it's time to leave, it's time to move closer to family, it's time to move to a facility that can give you the health care that you need. That's sad because, if I am fortunate, I will probably end up in that category,"

Jim says. "The other scenario is you fall dead, you trip over a cat and fall or something, and you don't have to worry about it."

Since Sul Ross is located in a sparsely populated area of the Big Bend, students must be recruited from other areas. Most universities have become regional institutions, drawing the majority of their students from nearby cities. "The growth of the university depends upon our bringing students in from outside the region. If you could take 100 percent of all the graduating classes of all the small towns in a five-county area around here, I don't know that you'd have 150 students," he says. Many Sul Ross students come from El Paso, and some from Odessa and Dallas. In recruiting faculty members, he has found the lack of a job that fits the skills of the partner of the person being recruited can be a problem. With the wide availability of Internet service in the Big Bend, that is changing since many people work remotely for companies located elsewhere.

For some, the adjustment to small-town living and the landscape is too difficult. "I lost one professor from New Jersey," he recalls. "I wish we could have kept her, but she said this place scared her. She would go down into Big Bend, and you see all the signs, saying don't do this and beware of this and that. It was like there were hordes of scorpions out to kill her, and she was frightened by that sense of the untamed. But we actually lose very few." Once faculty members are successfully recruited, they usually stay since they are initially drawn to the area.

At the time of the interview, Jim was preparing to deal with projected budget cuts for higher education in Texas, cuts that would be very deep, particularly for small universities without large endowments that enable larger institutions to

weather them. "I do think it's an important message for people in Texas to realize that in higher education, and at Sul Ross, the faculty will be taking cuts in income. Not salary; the public sees our income as being a nine-month contract, but faculty have always relied, especially at regional small universities, on summer employment," he explains. "The nine-month contract will be left intact, but we likely will be going to a different way of funding the summer school. Rather than doing it as a pro-ration of their salary, as we've done in the past, it's likely we'll be doing it as a flat course fee. So I'm unfortunately convinced that the income for our faculty will be less this next year, not because their nine-month contract was altered, but because they'll be getting less for teaching summer classes."

In the reception room outside Jim's office, there is a small sculpture of a black vulture and a painting on the wall featuring the bird. He is quick to explain that it isn't meant to metaphorically suggest the demise of teaching quality, only that his assistant, Carol, has a fascination with the bird.

Since Sul Ross is an institution with a strong teaching mission, rather than a heavy emphasis on research, faculty members will usually teach four classes per semester, rather than the typical two per semester in larger universities. "Their research, their performance, their creative activity comes on top of that, so that's a different ballgame," Jim says.

One of his areas of specialty is comparative politics. He has had the opportunity to observe the differences between the communities of the Big Bend politically. "When I came in 1981, I was told by locals that Jeff Davis County was the last county in Texas that you inherited your seat on the county commission's court," Jim says. "That's somewhat of an overstatement, but they had a pretty strong tradition of certain families having a prominent seat; for example, Jeff Davis County historically has more impact and significance in terms of ranching families and their role in the community."

Presidio County is interesting to Jim because of the very large Hispanic population with a different political culture. Because of the composition of their population, there are more Hispanic political office holders. "You don't see that in Jeff Davis County the same way, and then Alpine stands sort of in the middle. Brewster County is interesting because there's more parity between Hispanic and non-Hispanic white populations," he says. "In Presidio County you can almost always count on voting for the Democratic candidate, and Jeff Davis County is likely to go for the Republican candidate, so it is an interesting sort of political culture."

When Jim moved to Alpine, he fell in love with the mild winters, the rugged desert landscape, and the proximity to Mexico. Six weeks after Jim arrived, he received a sign that this is where he was supposed to be in a dream. In this dream, he was leaving Alpine to return to Nacogdoches, the move had not worked out. He dreamed of loading his truck and heading out toward Fort Stockton, full of grief. Suddenly he realized he didn't have to leave after all. "It was like a cheesy grade-B movie set you see in old westerns. The sunset was blazing oranges and blues and purples, and it was just like I was returning to paradise," Jim says. "There was a real sense of elation, and I woke up thinking I must have made the right choice in terms of taking the position out here because it really has been such a spectacular experience for me. I just took that as a sign that this was a good fit, and it has been."

A Native Heritage

★

MANUEL PAYNE

The circumstances responsible for where a particular person lives are a combination of genetics, social and political forces, and random luck, either good or bad. Such is the case of Manuel Payne, who came to live in the Big Bend because of an interesting family history.

Isaac Payne, Manuel's great-great-grandfather, a black Seminole Indian, was born in Florida. During the resettlement of the American Indian tribes, he was sent to Oklahoma with a group of black Seminoles. In 1849, at the invitation of the Mexican government, he and his family moved to Nacimiento, Coahuila, Mexico, with a group of his tribe. They were given land in return for their services to protect the border from Indian raiding parties. By 1870, during the Indian Wars in Texas, the U.S. Army was in need of scouts to aid soldiers protecting the border with Mexico. Isaac moved to Fort Clark, where he joined the U.S. Army as a scout and bugler. During a battle with Indians near the Pecos River, a small group of soldiers led by Lieutenant John L. Bullis was ambushed. All the soldiers made their escape but Bullis, who was thrown from his horse under heavy gunfire from the attacking Indians. Payne and two other scouts ran to his aid and brought him to safety. All three men were awarded the Medal of Honor for heroism for saving the life of the lieutenant. Isaac Payne is buried in the Black Seminole Cemetery in Brackettville with three other Medal of Honor recipients.

Isaac's son, Manuel's grandfather, was born in the Texas community of Las Moras, now Brackettville. He moved back to Nacimiento, where he married a Mexican woman from the prominent Vasquez family. Manuel's father, brothers, and sisters were born there.

During the Pancho Villa years, Manuel's grandfather fought for the Mexican government; when the war was over, according to family lore, the government took his horse, saddle, and rifle, promising to pay him fifty thousand pesos. Because the judge failed to sign the proper papers, he never received his money and was left with nothing. Manuel's grandfather decided to leave Mexico and move to Texas, where he established a ranch that was located in what is now the Big Bend National Park. "There's a house still there in Dog Canyon where he used to ranch, but I don't know if he built it or not. That's where he used to live, in Dog Canyon," Manuel says.

When the park was established, all the residents—at least ten additional families—were forced to sell their land and animals and relocate. Manuel's grandfather and his family moved to Marathon. His father married a woman from Terlingua and later moved to Alpine. The rest of the family scattered to various locations in Texas.

Manuel Payne was born in Alpine. He met his wife Luisa when she was a student at Sul Ross State from Kermit, Texas, and they married on November 21, 1972. They have a son, Eric, and a daughter, Cynthia.

Eric works in Alpine as a carpenter, welder, and handyman. Luisa worked for the Alpine Public Schools as a teacher's aide, at the Brewster County Courthouse, and at a doctor's office.

Briefly, as a young man, Manuel worked on several ranches but then joined the Texas Highway Department and settled down in Alpine. "Manuel's father did so much ranching himself that when Manuel got started doing the ranching, his father discouraged him from being a cowboy," Luisa says. "He didn't want him to go through all that. When he got the job at the highway department he was so happy that his son wasn't going to be doing any more cowboying."

During much of his life in Alpine, Manuel was a coach for the Alpine High School softball team. In recognition of his many years of service, the new high school football field was named Manuel Payne Park. He considers it the highest honor he has ever received.

Manuel is proud of his lineage, but he has not attempted to keep up with the black Seminole community or his various relatives. Luisa and he spend their time enjoying their retirement years. We ask Manuel to recount some of his most exciting experiences, and he declines. With a twinkle in his eye, he laughs and says, "That's private." Luisa likes the people, the scenery, and the community. "It's just a beautiful place to be," she says. "The rush in El Paso is too much." Luisa prefers a much smaller town. She can't imagine living in a place that doesn't have mountains, and she always felt Alpine was a great place to raise her children.

Manuel agrees they are not accustomed to the big city, so they don't miss an urban environment like El Paso. "We were there two or three weeks ago, and I didn't know how I was going to find my way out of there. I used to go to El Paso with the highway department and work around town, but since I have been retired for seventeen years now, it has changed a lot. I was scared,"

Manuel says. We ask if it's the drug violence in Juárez that makes him uncomfortable in El Paso. "We were talking to a corrections officer there in McDonald's over a month ago," he says. "They were coming in from Del Rio with a man who had gone AWOL, and they were taking him back to Fort Bliss. He said it wasn't the people from Juárez causing the problems or the cartels. It was the gangs that were causing all the problems in Juárez."

Manuel has developed health problems and now requires supplementary oxygen to ease his difficulty in breathing. He is happy at home where Luisa and he enjoy keeping their granddaughter from time to time. Manuel reflects: "I liked Alpine and never wanted to live anywhere else. Living here, I was comfortable. I have enjoyed living here."

The Work Ethic

★

TALGAR McCARTY

Talgar's, a colorful restaurant with an innovative menu, is next door to the Murphy Street Raspa Company in Alpine. Owned by Talgar McCarty, it has a devoted clientele. Her inspired cooking skills were developed at a young age, and the restaurant is a dream realized.

She was born in New Orleans, one of ten children, with six sisters and three brothers, several of whom were adopted by her parents. After her parents divorced, her mother, an artist, began spending hours on her paintings because her art paid the bills. She also worked decorating Mardi Gras floats. "After my parents divorced," Talgar explains, "I became that other person for my mom. While she was painting, I was by her side, helping her with the bills and doing what I could. I learned to bake bread and make fancy hamburgers. I would bring all my sisters together for dinner so we could all sit together. I felt very satisfied," she says.

When Talgar was eleven, she accompanied her father and two of her brothers to Mexico, where they were to work in a mining project. That trip changed her life. "I loved it so much down there. I think that I was probably one of those kids in the family that desired more, and I wanted to stay down there with my brothers," she says. "I was really young, but I had really good people around me. I've always connected with older people and tried to learn from them. I have had many mothers and fathers in my life."

She began spending her summers in Sonora and then attended school there when she was fourteen. While dropping off her brother's laundry, she observed the two women next door who made their living making tortillas. "They made tortillas by hand, grinding the corn, and I watched them. They cooked them on a rock, a *comal*. It was an amazing experience."

Talgar had a friend her age who would urge her to come out to the plaza, the traditional gathering place for the teenagers of the town, but she could not go until the tortillas were made. "I would go over and help speed up the process so we could go. I never knew that I would learn their way of cooking," Talgar says. "When they make their tortillas, they thinned them out like pizza. They're flour tortillas, but they're really thin. I learned those ways from a lot of the women. They make lunch for their husbands, and every morning I did the same thing for my family. If they have to get up at five in the morning, I packed them a nice little lunch. I learned a lot," she says.

When Talgar returned to the States, she worked as an au pair for a family in Vermont for nearly a year. Her opportunities to travel and work outside her native city of New Orleans taught her the value of work at an early age. She always had a weekend job from the time she was thirteen.

Tired of big-city life, the entire family moved from New Orleans to Terlingua, where her father built a house and started a construction company. The Hispanic crew lived on site, and many were not documented workers. Talgar remembers cooking for the crew: "We cooked for them a lot because back in that day they weren't accepted if they weren't legally in this area. We learned both sides of that world." During her time in Terlingua, in addition to working in the office of her father's company, Talgar also worked in several restaurants in the area, as a cashier in one, a cook in another, acquiring skills she would need later.

Talgar married when she was nearly twenty and lived in Florida for a time, then in Midland, and finally in Alpine. Six years later, she was divorced and the single mother of a young son, Izak. She found that her years as a stay-at-home mother had put her out of the loop in the job market. Faced with the economic necessity of earning an income to support herself and her son, she began cleaning houses. The flexible hours allowed her to pick up Izak after school.

It was a hard situation, but Talgar was determined that she would provide for her son. "They don't understand when you don't have milk in the refrigerator, they don't understand those things. You have to make that happen for them, and at the same time demand they do well in school, do all these things that they need to do in order to succeed in life," she says.

She needed to identify another source of income, and her culinary skills gave her that opportunity: innovative tamales. Not wanting to compete with the Mexican women in Alpine who made and sold traditional tamales, Talgar made tamales with different fillings, such as green chile, black beans, and corn. At first, she sold them door-to-door and at the hospital during lunch. "Nearly everyone bought, and I would smile even if they didn't buy. Something in the back of my head told me it's okay; if you encountered somebody who shot you down, go to the next person and keep going," she says. Soon she was taking orders for dozens of tamales for her customers.

The popularity of the tamales led to some

catering jobs that also required cooking several other dishes. The work was sporadic, but then grew to the point that she could not keep up with it alone. She wanted more regular hours, so Talgar went to work for Reata Restaurant in Alpine.

She thought she would have the job of waitress but was hired to be the dishwasher. "I took it, even though in the back of my mind I was thinking, What am I doing? I needed something to get me out of bed and keep me going. Sometimes it's not really the job. You may not like the job that you are doing, but it's the fact that you are getting up and trying to do something," she says. "Things come, eventually they will come. It was interesting working there. A lot of times people don't appreciate the person who washes the dishes, and I really learned to appreciate the dishwasher because I had been in that place."

An unexpected mentor, Betty Gaddis Yndo, made the next major step in Talgar's life possible. Betty and her physician husband moved to Fort Davis in 1950 and worked in a small hospital that is no longer there. They moved to Alpine when the Big Bend Regional Hospital opened. While Talgar worked for her father in the business office of the construction company, she met Betty. "Betty was always really happy and fun. I looked at Betty, and I said, some day when I'm older I'm going to be like this lady," she says.

When Talgar and Izak were returning from visiting a friend at Christmas, Betty was on the train, and they sat together. Betty asked what Talgar's plans for the future were. She had considered going to Guadalajara to take more cooking classes, but Betty had an idea. "A week later, she calls me and says: 'I have this project, and I think you're ready to open a restaurant,'" Talgar recalls.

"It was a little bit overwhelming. It was an old building. I had to design it. I mean there was nothing, just a shell. There was no patio, only one little bathroom in the back. You remember how bathrooms used to be back in that day, they were just tiny and you had to squeeze in there. I really put a lot of work into it. After I spent about a year during construction, I had to open. There was no more money," she says. "I was scared because I had been focused on construction and not on the creative side of selling food." Long, hard days of demolition and construction, tearing down walls, and installing plumbing left little time to plan for the opening.

When the charming restaurant opened, it was on Betty's birthday, and there were two items on the menu: tamales and fish tacos. Betty advertised the opening, and it drew a crowd; the opening was a success. Talgar plans to expand the selections with appetizers and a few more entrees. She is grateful for the support and encouragement she receives from her regular customers.

Many of her large extended family live nearby. They remember that Talgar always wanted more adventures and experiences in life. "I think they wonder sometimes about me. Why do you want so much more? I don't want to be rich, but I want to be successful enough that I can sit back, even if I only have a little casita, and be able to look at the things that I've done and be pleased," she explains. "I want to be able to be there for Izak when he needs me. Even when you go through high school and college, a parent needs to be there. I have to be there. You can't just put kids through school and think that everything's going to be okay. Your job is never-ending."

The restaurant is part of the revitalization of Murphy Street, originally a main street of Alpine, adjacent to the railroad tracks. Now the street is being transformed with the Murphy Street Raspa Company, Talgar's restaurant, an art gallery, and Patti Hildreth's beautiful boutique. Talgar's is also where a book signing and reception is being held at the time of the interview. The longtime residents of the neighborhood are asked to bring in photographs from long ago showing the Murphy Street of the past. Other city events, like Chamber of Commerce mixers, have been held at the restaurant.

When we see Talgar again, months later, she has made another major change in her life by leasing out the restaurant to a former restaurant employer from Terlingua. She is moving from the house she has rented for nine years and downsizing her possessions while she considers her next move. She is in a long-term relationship that could lead to a move to Midland, but she is not sure she is ready to become a wife.

In the meantime, she has more time to spend with Izak, who is now a teenager, a time that Talgar believes requires close parental attention. Besides her accomplishments as an entrepreneur, she has succeeded in the difficult role of single parent. "My biggest dream has always been that I would be able to take Izak on a vacation before he leaves home. Not because my boyfriend paid for it, or anyone else paid for it, but because it was me. No strings attached," she says.

"I see Izak moving forward. Now, at the end of the day when I go home, he has somebody to talk to. They grow up and they move on and I hope that he will do well. I'm praying. He's got his teachers who really love him; he's got the principal, who really loves him, and he also understands where I've come from," Talgar says. Izak is doing well academically and is interested in sports and science. Like his mother, he now has a weekend job, as she did at thirteen.

Talgar's response to adversity was always hard work and determination combined with creativity. "I think that if you have a dream, just try and jump into it, regardless," she says. "I've gotten to do some things that other people my age haven't. I've kind of worked against the grain, done everything the opposite, but partially because I had to," she explains. "Part of survival is just getting things done. It's changed me a lot. I think I wouldn't ever want to leave Alpine because this has become the heartbeat of part of my life. The beginning of something."

Since our last conversation with Talgar, she has relocated to Midland but still retains strong ties to Alpine. After this respite from the restaurant business, she is considering another project, utilizing her skills honed during her time owning Talgar's, perhaps back in Alpine.

An Adventure in Letters

★

JEAN HARDY PITTMAN

In 1956, twelve-year-old Jean Hardy Pittman fell in love at first sight. That love for the Big Bend has endured a lifetime. She grew up in Houston and Beaumont, and it was on a trip with her parents and younger siblings to Carlsbad Caverns, El Paso, then to the Big Bend, that her family stayed in the Gage Hotel in Marathon. "In 1956, the Gage Hotel was just a rundown, ordinary country hotel. There was a beer joint next door, and the music was playing all night with the sounds of people having fun on a Saturday night, but as we drove around Marathon the next morning, it struck me visually as extremely interesting, I don't know why," Jean says. "It was so plain, so authentic, so nothing like the Gulf Coast and the city. So I remembered that, I tucked it away."

Marathon stayed in Jean's memory until 1988, when, living in Houston, she finally came back. When plans to participate in an August hiking and bird watching trip in the Sierra Madres with the Armand Bayou Nature Center fell through, Jean and her husband Mike began a long camping trip across Texas, ending at the Gage Hotel. "We spent three days out here, and it changed my life. I knew right away I didn't want to leave." An avid gardener and gardening editor, Jean was overwhelmed by the beauty of the desert plants

and flowers, in full bloom because of the summer rains. She bought as many native plant books as she could find. When it came time to leave, it was very difficult. "I literally cried half the way back to Houston," she says.

Jean was a freelance editor and writer at the time, editing books for Shearer Publishing in Fredericksburg and writing stories for *Houston Home and Garden*, but her main focus was raising her three children. Then, in her forties, she began making frequent trips to the Big Bend: "I just kept inventing reasons to come out here and take pictures and write stories and did that for four years, and I was driving Mike crazy," Jean says. "I would go out and camp by myself, I'd go desert hiking by myself, and I felt this incredible freedom, a reconnection with nature and the earth. It was profound."

Jean wrote magazine articles during her trips such as "Houstonians in the Big Bend" to earn money while visiting the place she loved most. She learned the scientific names of the plants when she edited *Wildflowers of Texas* by Geyata Ajilvsgi for Shearer Publishing. She then decided to write a book on the plants of the Big Bend.

Soon, she realized that making trips to the Big Bend and then returning to Houston to write her

book didn't work. She wanted to be there longer. "I said I needed a place to go where I can write, and it was so lovely and we'll have a second place, second home out here, so we did. That was a mistake because I didn't ever want to go back to live in Houston."

In 1992, Jean and Mike bought a house in Marathon. With her children in college, Jean began commuting until she was accepted into the biology graduate program at Sul Ross State. Then her trips to Houston were planned around her academic schedule. "I just started really developing a life out here, and the marriage was

okay, Mike was going to move out here one day, there were tensions there, but I just couldn't help myself. I was happy here, and I was not happy in Houston," she says.

With the end of graduate school in sight, Jean planned to be a consulting field biologist for Texas Parks and Wildlife or for the ranchers of the area, but in February of 1994, Books Plus in Alpine, a small, mostly used-book store, came up for sale. Recognizing that Alpine was a university town without a store devoted exclusively to books, Jean and Mike, a fellow book lover, decided to buy it. Jean finished her thesis, "Flora and Vegetation of the Solitario Dome of Brewster and Presidio Counties," in the apartment in the back of the bookstore, now Front Street Books, in 1997.

Mike was the owner of a software firm, but when competition began to crowd out the smaller companies, he became interested in publishing. Jean and Mike established Iron Mountain Press of Marathon and republished Virginia Madison and Hallie Stillwell's classic *How Come It's Called That? Place Names in the Big Bend Country*. "He reprinted Ted Gray's books and then he did a couple of original things, and by 2002, we were well known as Iron Mountain Press," Jean recalls.

Suddenly, this small press became very visible when they published the sequel to *The Bridges of Madison County* (Warner Books, 1992), the novel *A Thousand Country Roads* by Robert James Waller. Waller was living close to Marathon, and in November 2001, he contacted Jean about the possibility of distributing his as-yet unpublished book through Front Street Books. Although Warner Books had also published *Slow Waltz in Cedar Bend* (in 1993), they did not accept the new manuscript for publication. When Jean met with Waller, he was unaware that Jean was an accomplished writer and editor and that she was co-owner of Iron Mountain Press: "So I said let us show you some of our books, and if there is one thing Mike does extremely well, he produces beautiful publications. His books are fine hardcovers, cloth, with quality paper, quality design, and typesetting because he loves the craft of the books as much as the content," Jean says.

Since Warner Books was not publishing the book, Waller did not want to circulate the manuscript among other New York publishers. "It was largely luck, Robert Waller just happened to be living here, and he had been in our store

a couple of times, and I guess he liked it, but he was really just going to distribute his own book and wanted us to help with sales and distribution," Jean continues. "Waller seemed to be a bit charmed with our operation and agreed to accept us as his publishers." That led to a very good working relationship between editor Jean and writer Robert Waller. "We had a solid working collaboration, and it resulted in the best book it could possibly be," says Jean.

A Thousand Country Roads was on the *New York Times* bestseller list for eleven weeks and was also optioned for film. Iron Mountain Press, incorporated as John M. Hardy Publishing, received national attention by publishing the book since there was much curiosity about why this small company in Texas was publishing the sequel to the blockbuster *The Bridges of Madison County*. "We had our pictures in *People* magazine; we had "Entertainment Hollywood" calling, which I hung up on. We did see some really nice articles written by pleasant journalists. The *Baltimore Sun* and others told the story of what happened, and it apparently captured the imagination of a lot of people."

Jean and Mike were then in a commuter marriage. Although they saw one another frequently and vacationed together in Europe to see their children and grandchildren, who lived there, Jean considered the Big Bend home, and Mike considered Houston home. Eventually, after many delays in Mike's move to the Big Bend, he decided he would not make that move. After forty-four years, three children, and several grandchildren, the marriage was over at the end of 2005.

After a year of emotional devastation, Jean reconnected with Blair Pittman, a photographer for the *Houston Chronicle* and *National Geographic* she had met in 1978 on a photo assignment. "He took my picture. I had an umbrella and I was trying to shield my camera from the rain and I got down to take the shot, so he took a picture of me," Jean says. "The next day he brought an eight-by-ten print and dropped it off for me at the desk of the *Houston Westside Reporter*, where I worked."

Although Blair was raised in Fort Worth and Pecos, it was when he camped out in the Big Bend at the age of seven with his family that he found a home. His visits became an important part of his life. When he developed serious health problems, Blair retired early and came to Terlingua to stay.

An accomplished writer, Blair had published several books with Texas A&M University Press, including *Texas Caves* (1999) and *The Natural World of the Texas Big Thicket* (1986). He called on Jean at Front Street Books: "He was selling me his little "Tales" book; we had a purely business relationship for a while," Jean says. His books *Tales from the Terlingua Porch* (Sun Country Publications, 2005) and *More Tales from the Terlingua Porch* (Sun Country Publications, 2009) found a distributor with Jean through Front Street Books, and Blair found a wife.

Front Street Books is a refreshing change from the generic chain bookstores. Although independent booksellers have been driven out by chain-store competition in other places, the Big Bend does not welcome corporate chain stores. Absent is the urban trinity: Walmart, Barnes & Noble, and Starbucks: "I think there's something else going on in the big-book chains and that is, people who work in them might be drawn to books and might like them, and they might be good readers, but they don't have the discretion to order what they want and to hand sell as much," Jean explains. "Chain stores are too impersonal and too large. When customers walk into an independent bookstore, they know those books

were personally selected, and they are inclined to establish friendships with the staff."

Jean has found that her own independence is characteristic of people in this area: "There are many more people out here who are honest about what they want to be. And they're not concerned about what somebody else thinks." There is a self-selection process that brings people to the Big Bend communities, a self-reliance and lifestyle "fit" that turns visitors into residents. "I hear people saying 'Gee, I wish I could live here. Oh, I love it here.' They come back and back and back, let's say somebody from Austin," she says. "But they're not willing to give up their income level; they're not willing to take the economic chance, yet some poorer people will take that chance."

With an increase in services and better selections of goods, the Big Bend is still far from a sophisticated, materialistic environment. "'What do you do for shopping?' people [who] visit here will ask," says Jean. I know of a woman who came out who said, 'I got off the train at Alpine and there was just nothing there.' We're so glad to see those kinds of people just get on the train and go away."

She is eloquent on the subject of what makes the Big Bend a wonderful place to live: "It is the desert environment that separates the Big Bend from any other rural, isolated area. The mountains, the terrain, and the sparse population also attract residents: the ratio of nature to people in this area is ideal because we have a world that is still largely untouched and not ruined. It's natural and it's beautiful. And it is a joy to drive through it."

Alpine attracts young families through faculty and staff hires at Sul Ross State University. It acts as a cultural resource. Alpine, as a community, besides being the only incorporated town in a county the size of Rhode Island and Connecticut combined, has the identity of being a university community. "Typically, beginning faculty are young, they come and bring spouses and children, so I think you probably have more new folks that have kids," Jean says. When she reflects on the different personalities of the communities of the Big Bend, she can clearly see the differences. "Marfa is a strictly different community, and it has evolved as an outré art community for the simple reason that Donald Judd settled there and invested so

heavily in that arena," Jean says. "I always point out that the other towns—Alpine, Marathon, and Fort Davis—have art for the rest of us." Terlingua, where Blair has a home in addition to Jean's home in Marathon, is steadily growing. "Interesting, interesting place, some really brilliant people down there. Many of them are there just because they love the harshness of the lower desert. You've got reliable, more or less, electricity," she says. "You've got a water system developing over a fairly large area, and so it's enabling more people to come down there and not have to live off the grid or live primitively."

The benefits of small-town living are evident when Jean is asked if she finds it necessary to lock her doors: "My front door's unlocked right now in Marathon. It's too much trouble to lock it and unlock it when I'm unloading an armload and it's a darn stubborn lock and hurts my arthritis and so I just make sure the thing is snapped so the wind doesn't blow the front door open."

Since we interviewed Jean, Mike Hardy died in April 2012 after a long bout with cancer. Blair has also confronted health problems that necessitated relocating to Alpine. Blair and Jean bought a house in town and Jean continues to run Front Street Books in Marathon and Alpine.

Jean has never wavered from her love of the Big Bend, discovered when she was twelve. The desert and the mountains have worked their magic. "One of the reasons I went out in the desert and hiked alone is because I wanted to experience being in Big Bend National Park, where no one knew where I was; nobody else was there and I could spend the whole day saying 'This is mine. This is my world.'"

The Visionary

★

GEORGE COVINGTON

George Covington is an author, photographer, and newspaper columnist. He was the special assistant for disability policy for former vice president Dan Quayle, a journalism professor, and holds a degree in law and a degree in communications from the University of Texas at Austin. He also has 20/400 vision. He is legally blind.

George was born in Texarkana, Texas. His vision problems were diagnosed while he was in grade school. "The family ophthalmologist said it was a combination of what we've come to know as astigmatism, nystagmus, eccentric fixation, and myopia—all of which were acute—and probably even further back, a degenerating retina. There

was no way of knowing then," George says. In addition, he was a self-described disciplinary problem: "From the first grade, the authorities kept saying, 'Send him to the school for the blind.' But they were saying that because I was a disciplinary problem, not because I couldn't see.'"

It was a time when there were no special arrangements or accommodations for anyone who was visually impaired. He played with his class-mates, and when he needed to write something down, he simply walked to the blackboard and wrote it down. While other children imagined futures as firemen or cowboys, George just wanted to leave town. When he did leave on a Greyhound bus in 1964, bound for the University

of Texas at Austin, he found his niche. "I discovered nirvana. I discovered, too, that people didn't judge you by your old man owning a shoe store or used-car lots, which was the pinnacle of social achievement in Texarkana, Texas," he says. "When I got to the University of Texas and realized that it was just my brains against everybody else's, I thought it was going to be great. And it was. I spent ten years there getting a journalism degree, and a law degree, and enjoying myself. I wasn't really held back that much by poor eyesight."

During law school, George was in a relation-ship with a woman who was doing postgraduate work in photography, and his view of the world changed. He carried the fifty-pound equipment around for her shoots but realized when he looked at the developed pictures with his pocket magnifying lens that what he had thought was a plant being photographed in the landscape was a rock. It was apparent that his memory or imagination was filling in the details of these shapes and he was wrong. He found the solution in *Popular Photography* magazine: scale-focusing cameras. The two best cameras for this were Rollei and Petri. George ordered the Rollei 35 mm scale-focusing camera and began taking pictures.

George particularly wanted to see faces. When he looked at the pictures of old friends, he remembered them because they were familiar. "But with new friends, I started seeing photographs of people I didn't know. I realized that my eyesight had closed down to a point where imagination had taken over," he says. By taking self-portraits, George was very surprised to find he did not look like he thought he did. "I expected to find that I was a young Robert Redford—and instead I found a young Groucho Marx!" he joked. He began filming his usual walking routes to the campus and found that he did not recognize any of his perceived landmarks, which meant that others with vision loss were also not seeing what they thought they were seeing.

After law school, George began teaching at West Virginia University School of Journalism. Soon he attracted media attention with his photography. The publicity always emphasized George as a "blind photographer." This characterization was useful. "I have used the concept of blind photographer to correct the media's image of what a blind person is. Most people don't realize that 90 percent of people who are legally blind have some usable vision," George says.

George was not interested in selling his photographs; instead, he wanted to use photography as a tool to see. He frequently uses the statement "Most people see to photograph; I photograph to see." George sets shutter speed and aperture by clicks and then uses a magnifying lens to set the distance. Since information on photographic techniques for the visually impaired did not exist, George wrote the photography manual *Let Your Camera Do the Seeing: The World's First Photography Guide for the Legally Blind* (1981).

He then signed a contract with the Association of Flight Attendants in Washington, D.C., to establish their first communications department, then went to work for the Department of the Interior working on the staff of both Jim Wright and former vice president Dan Quayle, where he served as special assistant for disability policy. It was during his time as the first full-time White House aide for disability issues that the Americans With Disabilities Act was signed in 1990.

During his Washington years, George was the subject of a chapter in the book *Chronicles of Courage: Very Special Artists* by Jean Kennedy Smith and George Plimpton (1993).

He also became close friends with Charlie Wilson, the subject of the recent movie *Charlie Wilson's War* (2007). Looking back on the politicians he knew, George remembers: "I would have to say that the two most honest men I ever met were Dan Quayle, a Republican, and Charlie Wilson, a Democrat. Quayle's honesty got him ridiculed by the media, and Wilson's honesty got him a Hollywood movie." He has fond memories of attending Washington social events. "When I'd show up at these receptions I'd always show up with an incredibly beautiful woman, and most people didn't know that nearly every time, it was one of Charlie Wilson's staffers," he laughs.

In his newspaper column, George bid a fond farewell to his old friend when Charlie Wilson died: "Charlie will be remembered by history for the role he played in bringing the Soviet Union's war machine to its knees, but to the people of the second congressional district of Texas, he'll be remembered as the congressman who put his people first," he wrote.

George relocated to New York City, busy at work on two projects, one a PBS mini-series, which aired in 1996, in which he was featured and helped produce, the other a book, co-authored with Bruce Hannah, titled *Access by Design* and published by Van Nostrand Reinhold in 1996. The book introduced the concept of designing consumer products in a way that enabled them to be used by the widest range of people. "We usually use the example of a seven-year-old girl and a seventy-year-old woman. If they can use it, then most people with disabilities can use it," he explained. George also conducted photography workshops for the Smithsonian, the Harlem Independent Living Center, the Hirshhorn Museum, and the National Museum of American Art and taught a digital photography workshop for the Korean Association of the Blind.

When those projects were completed, a friend called George and told him she was going to Alpine, Texas, to find a home to buy for retirement. She reminded George that he said he wanted to live in a small college town. Since George was returning to Texas on family business, he flew to Houston and then came to Alpine. "We drove out here, drove in one afternoon, drove up

to Mountainside Dorm parking lot, and you get a whole view of the western rim of the Alpine Valley and the mountains and the mesas, and I could see a little bit better then, well enough to see the rims, so I rented an apartment the next day, went back to New York, and closed everything down and moved out here and haven't regretted it for a minute," he says. George has made a place for himself in Alpine and has a wide circle of friends. He has been on the local radio talk show and is a very popular guest.

He continues his creative interests in writing and photography. His article "Vegetarians and Pedestrians—The Loneliest people in West Texas" and his photograph "Desert Stonehenge" are in the book *Beyond Boundaries* (2006), published under a grant to VSA Arts of Texas, the State Organization on Arts and Disability. 1st Books Library published his novel, *Photo Hero: A Satire of Photography*, in 2001.

A master storyteller, George's love for the people, climate, and life in the Big Bend is reflected in his popular newspaper column "High Desert Sketches," published in the *Alpine Avalanche*. His columns are funny and acerbic and cover a wide variety of subjects. Recent titles include "Purses and Bags in the Big Bend," "Are There Girlie-Men in the Big Bend?" and "Javelina: Creature of Myth and Legend."

When he moved to Alpine, George discovered the beauty of the desert landscape through his photography. He frequently says: "As long as I can see to photograph, I will never be blind."

Back to the Future

★

VICTOR AND
CRISTINA NORIEGA

At the Murphy Street Raspa Company, the shelves are lined with bright Mexican pottery and mirrors with handmade tin borders mounted on the wall. Ranchero music plays in the background. The Raspa Company advertises that they have snowcones, gifts, *dulces* (sweets), art, ice cream, and *refrescos* (refreshments) and features an impressive candy counter.

The evening of our visit, the tables and chairs were nearly all occupied. An older couple—the man dressed in jeans, boots, and western shirt, his Stetson on the table—were sitting with their young grandsons, dressed identically to their grandfather. When asked if they came here often, the grandparents said it was one of their favorite places. It is the last night of their grandsons' visit, so there was time for one more treat before they left in the morning. One of the boys said he ordered a Dragon's Blood *raspa*; he wasn't sure of the flavors used in making it, but he really liked the name.

The owners, Victor and Cristina Noriega, are in their early thirties. We were intrigued that a young couple would decide to leave the urban environment of San Antonio and commit to a simpler life in Alpine. Victor explains that what led them to Alpine were the climate and

the environment. They began visiting Alpine in 2005 and kept returning to visit and fell in love with it. Victor was in advertising, and Cristina was in marketing, so they realized that would not be how they would make a living in Alpine. At first they thought of opening a gallery, but they wanted something Victor refers to as "more tactile," so it became a store.

They bought a building on Murphy Street, which was historically the Hispanic part of Alpine. They saw a need to have this type of store in Alpine, one that would serve not only the community at large but also the sizeable Hispanic community. The Noriegas bought the building, rather than leasing it, and began the long renovation process, leaving the original butcher block, vegetable bins, and other elements of the original grocery store, mindful of the history associated with the location. Their vision was to make the Raspa Company a true neighborhood store.

Victor makes it clear that he is not an activist, nor is the Raspa Company a political statement of any kind; Cristina and he simply realized that Alpine lacked many things familiar in the Hispanic community that were easily found in San Antonio. In addressing the scarcity of familiar Mexican products, they were filling a need. There

is also a revolving collection of Mexican folk art at the Raspa Company. Victor calls them "cultural commodities" because, in addition to being tangible objects for sale, they serve to reconnect the local Hispanics to their culture and introduce others to this type of art.

The Noriegas' decision to move to Alpine is unusual since it is counter to the accepted notion that couples in their twenties and thirties are attracted to the bigger cities and work up the corporate ladder while raising a young family. Victor and Cristina had a different idea when they moved to Alpine in 2008. Much of the renovation was done in three-day weekends commuting from San Antonio. Soon after, they were expecting their first baby as they opened their new business in their new hometown. "It was all kind of crazy, but it was still all part of the adventure that we sought coming out here," Victor says.

While making the decision to relocate, they were frequently told that Alpine was a place to go to retire. The Noriegas felt differently; they were well aware that they would not want to be renovating the store or shoveling gravel and mopping floors at retirement age. "I think the sentiment was, Let's do it now, and if it doesn't work out, we can always bounce back, why not take the chance, why not do it now?" Victor remembers.

A major benefit in their lives is the opportunity to spend more time with their baby daughter, nearly impossible in San Antonio with two demanding careers. "We've found our friends, and I guess it was a helpful coincidence, they were all pregnant around the same time, so we had that close-knit community. We essentially became our own family. So that was something that made us step back and say, this is a really special place," Victor says. Nearly half of their new friends have strong family ties to Alpine; the other half come from even further away than San Antonio, drawn here for the same reasons that attracted the Noriegas. We ask if Victor thinks that more and more people of their age are starting to realize the value of this less-complicated life, free of urban stress: "I think that more and more people are appreciating it even if they can't necessarily have it because we've got a lot of friends who say the same thing: 'Oh you're living the dream. I wish I could do it,'" he says.

Victor realizes that, as a small business owner, he has long workdays and that the financial rewards aren't always great. He remembers that his coworkers in San Antonio did not have the luxury of enough time with their families. Those who do make this leap of faith cannot be so entrenched in our consumer culture that the idea of moving into an area where the nearest Walmart is many miles away would make them uncomfortable. These newcomers would have to rely on their own resources; they would have the luxury of more family time, but without the urban activity and distractions, that can present a challenge.

Victor misses some aspects of big city life: "If I get a toothache at 3:30 in the morning and I need some Anbesol [a topical pain reliever] and there's

none here, then I miss Walmart a little bit," he says. "When I want some Greek food there's not twenty places to go to. But, for the most part, I don't." Since their family in San Antonio is only six hours away, they visit often and see the concrete, office buildings, and buses that are not

part of the landscape of the Big Bend. They are ready to come back after two days. "It's nice to get some different food, to go into a bigger store or boutique or something we don't have here, or doesn't belong here, but we're very ready to come back after that," Victor says.

He brought over a small replica of the Raspa Company that has pride of place on the counter. A second grader made it for a class project. She brought it in with her dad because this is her favorite place. "It's just one of the many things that remind us it's a bigger picture than what we see from day to day. We just get stuck behind the counter or out here sweeping and things like this remind us, this is a lot bigger than us, this is not ours anymore really, it belongs to the community," he observes.

Victor and Cristina did not want to look back in twenty or thirty years and ask themselves why they chose not to make this move and change their lives. Alpine has become their home. Victor reflects on their future: "We want to really be part of this community. It was not just open a store and make money. We're not making a lot of money, we're scraping by, but we're loved and we're respected, and it's a valuable part of the community."

Since we last saw the Noriegas, they have returned to San Antonio to live. At that time, Cristina was expecting their second child,

Paloma, who was born in May 2012. Since both Cristina and Victor were raised with large extended families, it was an experience they wanted their own children to have.

The business was doing well, but it took a staggering amount of time and effort from both Victor and Cristina. "When it was just the two of us, it was perfect since we could do all the back-breaking labor and work very hard to survive," Victor says. With a growing family, the time that was necessary to take the business to the next level would dramatically curtail their time as a family. "It was really taxing as a business owner. With the second child, it was no longer an experiment with just us; it was so busy. To be able to grow the business, it would detract from our new family," he says. The Noriegas still own the Raspa Company, but they have hired managers to run the business. Their families in San Antonio are delighted they have returned and that they will have a major role in the children's lives.

Victor misses some of what he calls "the joys of small-town living" and the close friends they left behind in Alpine, but the transition to San Antonio was not difficult. They moved back into their previous home there, and Victor's new job in advertising is only a block from his previous job. "It was very bittersweet," Victor says. "It was a difficult decision to make and took a lot of thought."

THE JAVELINA CHRONICLES

According to the U.S. Census, there is approximately one person per square mile in the Big Bend. The animals greatly outnumber the human population, so the residents co-exist with such animals as coyote, elk, deer, the occasional mountain lion, bobcat, weasel, fox, skunk, raccoon, and the ever-present javelina. The shorthorn lizard, band-tailed pigeon, the silver-haired bat, and Steller's jay, all endangered species in Texas, are also residents. The ferociously countenanced, fast, and wily javelinas are the subjects of many stories, usually comical.

Javelinas are sometimes mistaken for feral pigs, but they are not. Alpine resident George Covington wrote in his newspaper column "High Desert Sketches" for the *Alpine Avalanche*, "We have an estimated six million feral pigs. There are wild pigs in Texas and I don't mean Aggies on a Saturday night." One look at a javelina usually sends anyone unaccustomed to them running in the opposite direction. "Most people in West Texas have a javelina story. The stories range from tales of a cute and cuddly little orphan to a vicious and dangerous wild animal. Sometimes the stories start with the first and end with the latter," he said.

Javelinas are usually anti-social, but drought conditions will force them to make forays into civilization, and they can be found eating in the home gardens of the Big Bend. Their packs can be seen most often after dark.

Ruth Abel of Limpia Crossing had two small javelinas as regular visitors to drink from the water dishes set out for the deer. "They always came as a couple, I always called them the mister and the missus. They came by themselves and ate whatever was left from the deer," she says. "They waited until the deer were gone, and then the missus jumped in the water dish and sat like you would take a sitz bath, just having a ball there, and the mister stood by with his tail up."

Ruth has another pair of javelinas that visit regularly; since she isn't sure of their sex, she calls them both "Wilbur." "When they come, they stick their nose through the wire fence, and I have some corn inside, and I dump it on the outside of the fence, and they go down there and eat, and then I can feed the rest of the animals. They wait until I leave, then they jump into the deer feeder. They say javelinas don't jump, my foot," she laughs.

Ruth was feeding a neighbor's cat when she encountered a large herd of javelina. "Here came a whole herd around Tip's house, all ages, teenagers, babies, and old ones, and, you know, when there are mommas and babies, they are dangerous; you better watch what you're doing," she says. The smallest of the herd attracted Ruth's attention because of his size, but she heard him before she saw him. When she encountered him under the house, "I heard this [clicking sound], you know, they click, they give you fair warning, and I bent under the porch to get the dish for the cat, and there was that javelina, clicking." Her husband Don had succinct advice: "Get your ass out of there." Because of the large herds of javelina, he also carries a pistol. But Ruth found that firing the pistol did not intimidate the javelinas: "They don't run, they are just like statues. They stand still," Ruth says. "But don't be fooled; when they run they come slowly but get up to speed immediately. Immediately. So I walked sideways, but they stayed there until I came to my property, and they just stayed over there and ate the cat food."

When historian and writer Lonn Taylor and his wife Dedie made Fort Davis their home, they found their own javelina story. "When we first moved here, the Presbyterian minister was a young man named Joe Gosset, who was new to West Texas. He and his wife had two miniature dachshunds, little dogs that were bred as hors

d'oeuvres," Lonn jokes. "The Presbyterian manse was on the street that is just at the foot of Sleeping Lion Mountain. When he walked the dogs in the pre-dawn darkness, he carried a pistol in case he encountered a javelina on the prowl. He was the only armed preacher in Fort Davis."

Sul Ross graduate student Matt Walter told Alpine writer and photographer George Covington, "One night I came out of class a little late and walked through the center of campus. There were javelinas everywhere. Only a couple of weeks ago I noticed a pack of about thirty coming down Ave A toward North Harrison. They are regular visitors to this area and don't seem frightened of people or cars."

George's friend Bill Ivey told the story of being called one morning because a film crew working in Terlingua were cornered by his two pet javelinas. Most of the crew were having breakfast in the restaurant and were prevented from leaving by the javelinas. A few of the crew were in a truck but wouldn't come out, so Bill had to come retrieve his pets.

One night a man heard his dog fighting in the front yard. He went out to separate the two dogs but soon realized one of the combatants was a javelina, who then took off part of his calf, which was sewn back on at the hospital.

Javelinas will bond with humans. "I've held a baby javelina, they're very affectionate, they're very bright little creatures, and I put it in my lap and petted it, it was just cooing like any baby animal would," George Covington says. People who have raised orphan javelina have found them to be very intelligent and protective of the person they bond with. One orphan javelina lived with a family in Alpine until he was grown, and then, as young males are wont to do, ran away with a pack of wild females. As their alpha male, he would make occasional visits to the family, leaving his pack in the front yard while he went to the back to be petted and fed. Years later, he returned alone, having lost his alpha male status. He had come home to die.

"Most people who have raised orphan javelinas have learned to expect that they will eventually return to the wild. However, 'wild' does not necessarily mean the rugged existence of the barren waste of West Texas," George says. Javelina will press their noses against patio doors to be fed, and if the door is not secured, they will use their flat noses to push open the door, leading to unexpected, hungry visitors.

Bryce Milligan, publisher of Wings Press in San Antonio, has a javelina story from a time he took his family camping. "We'd camp at Davis Mountains State Park and hike when we weren't on top of Mount Locke watching the sunsets (best place in Texas for it) or going to the star parties," he says. "Coming back late from a star party, it's not unusual to hear the javelinas rooting about in the mast." The javelinas would run through the campsites late at night, followed by skunks. "But this one time, something spooked them out of their normal course, and up came a dozen javelinas at top speed, right through our campsite and into the open door of the tent. Pretty soon we were chasing our tent as it zigzagged through the woods, caught on the nose of a very ticked-off javelina," Bryce says. They tried to retrieve their gear in the pitch darkness and encountered a gang of skunks. "And thereby hangs a tale as to why we showed up that midnight at Indian Lodge with no reservations, a bit disheveled and with more than a bit of an odor," he recalls.

The strangest javelina story told to George was by Gus Lines, who grew up during the Depression. His father shot a javelina. "While preparing the animal for taxidermy he discovered that the animal's teeth were gold coated. "It looked like that javelina had just come from the dentist office," Lines said. This javelina experience is the only one to have ever made it into *Ripley's Believe It or Not* in January 1936.

MARFA

Between the Davis Mountains and Big Bend National Park in the high desert is the town of Marfa, with a population of 1,981 as of the 2010 U.S. Census. It is the county seat of present-day Presidio County, which has 3,857 square miles of varied landscape, from some of the highest mountain ranges in Texas, to the plains of the Marfa Plateau. The county has canyons and springs, as well as Capote Falls in the western part of the county.

Marfa began as a railroad water stop; the depot was built in 1882, and the post office followed in 1883. According to the *Handbook of Texas*, the town was named after a character in the novel *The Brothers Karamazov* by Fyodor Dostoevsky, which was suggested by a railroad executive's wife. Marfa became the county seat when the boundaries of the county were changed to retain Fort Davis as the county seat of a newly formed Jeff Davis County. Three other counties—Brewster, Foley, and Buchel—were established from original Presidio county lands.

The Marfa Lights—or Mystery Lights—were certainly seen by the Native Americans of the Big Bend long before 1883, when Robert Reed Ellison saw them while passing through Paisano Pass and reported his observation. The lights can be seen on most clear nights. They are changeable and sometimes appear as twinkling colored lights that dance along the ground, appearing and disappearing. Over time, the scientific reason for this naturally occurring phenomenon, which also appears in a few other places in the world, has been explained. However, most people prefer to enjoy the light show, which draws tourists to Marfa, without an explanation that would dispel the mystery.

Marfa established churches and schools as the town grew, and the U.S. Army made Marfa the headquarters for the Big Bend Military District. In 1917, Camp Marfa, later renamed Fort D. A. Russell, was one of the army outposts in Presidio County created to monitor the U.S. Mexico border.

The economy of Marfa continued to grow, as the cattle ranchers could buy and sell cattle as well as ship their cattle by rail in Marfa or Valentine. By 1930, when the grand El Paisano Hotel opened, Marfa was a thriving town. Renowned architect Henry Trost of El Paso, whose buildings are still well known throughout the Southwest, designed the hotel. Another El Pasoan, Charles N. Bassett, was the builder. The Spanish Revival style hotel is still drawing tourists to Marfa. The Crews Hotel was also in downtown Marfa; the Judd Foundation now owns the building.

A period of prosperity came to Marfa during World War II when Marfa Army Air Field was established. According to *Big Bend Sentinel* columnist and historian Lonn Taylor, this pilot-training base and airfield covered 2,750 acres, with 6 runways and 250 buildings. "At its peak in April 1944, it had a total compliment of 575 officers and 2,144 enlisted men, and it employed 604 civilians," Lonn says. Because of this sudden increase in Marfa's population, townspeople would rent out rooms and garage apartments during the resulting housing shortage. Some families found residences in Alpine, on the Sul Ross campus or at the Davis Mountains State Park Indian Lodge. The Officers' Club and the USO Club, with live entertainment, as well as local bars and dance clubs, provided Marfa with lively wartime nightlife. The base closed in 1945.

Marfa will always be known as the place where director George Stevens made the 1956 movie *Giant*, based on the 1952 novel by Edna Ferber. The book was not popular with many Texans because it contained characters that were stereotypes. The filming was a two-month shoot in the summer of 1955 at the Ryan Ranch, owned by Worth Evans, outside Marfa. The ranch has been in the Evans family for generations, and the rugged terrain, the working cowboys, and the cattle herds made it the perfect location for the movie.

No one who lived in Marfa at that time will forget when the cast, which included Elizabeth Taylor, Rock Hudson, Sal Mineo, Mercedes McCambridge, James Dean, Chill Wills, Jane Withers, Earl Holliman, and Dennis Hopper, came and filled the El Paisano with the rest of the cast

and crew in the Crews Hotel. Clay Evans, the son of Worth Evans, remembers working as an extra, along with his brother, in the movie on their weekends home from college. Most of the town, indeed a large percentage of the population of the Big Bend, were either extras or came to observe the filming. Every night, Stevens would screen the day's rushes at the Palace Theater in Marfa. Everyone was welcome to see them.

These famous actors became familiar with the people of Marfa and the Big Bend as they ate in the restaurants, drank in the bars, and made trips to Ojinaga for margaritas. When the cast and crew left, the three-story façade of the fictional Reata ranch house was left behind. After windstorms and the punishing desert heat, only a few timbers remain on the ranch Clay Evans owns and operates. The movie *Giant*, released in 1956, appealed to Texans in a way the book did not; it presented Texas and Texans as powerful, expansive, and wealthy, but it did not shy away from the issue of racism in the state. *Giant* became a movie classic. Since then, two recent (2007) movies—*There Will Be Blood*, based on the 1927 Upton Sinclair book *Oil*, and *No Country for Old Men*, from the 2005 Cormac McCarthy novel of the same name—have been filmed in Marfa and the surrounding area.

The population of Marfa steadily declined over a thirty-year period, then artist Donald Judd came to Marfa. He had his first glimpse of Marfa as a soldier in transit to Los Angeles to be shipped out to the Korean War. On his return, he became a painter in New York City, eventually abandoning painting for an art form of constructions. He is associated with the minimalist movement, but he rejected that label.

In 1972, after renting a house for two summers in Marfa, Judd became disenchanted with the

New York galleries and museums. Although he kept his five-story building at 101 Spring Street in New York City, where he was able to mount large-scale works, his own and others, he wanted vast outdoor space, which he found in Marfa. With low land prices in Presidio County, he bought ranches, land, and buildings, buying the former Fort Russell and its buildings as a large-scale permanent exhibition space both outside and in hangar-like structures. It is the home of the Chinati Foundation, with artists-in-residence programs and internships.

He also established the Judd Foundation, dedicated to the preservation of his work, both in Marfa and New York. Donald Judd died in 1994 at the age of sixty-five. The Chinati Foundation brings a steady stream of artists to Marfa to live and work temporarily and draws tourists from around the world for their annual open house, sponsored by both the Chinati and Judd Foundations.

The Lannan Foundation, founded by Patrick Lannan, Sr., a collector of modern and contemporary art, was founded in 1960. The mission of the foundation is to encourage innovative artists and writers and social activists. After Lannan's death in 1983, the foundation expanded its grant programs, with the foundation offices in Santa Fe, New Mexico, administering the fellowships. The sought-after Lannan Residency Fellowship usually provides one or two months of writing time in Marfa in a residence owned by the foundation.

Marfa residents reject a comparison to Santa Fe as a writer and artist colony. Marfa, they believe, is a unique blend of environment, traditional ranching, and, now, art and music. The community is the home of the only public radio station in the area. Longtime residents have seen the face of Marfa change but know that the vast high-desert landscape and the people who have made this part of West Texas their home for generations will remain unchanged.

Home to Stay

★

JOHNNY CALDERON

When Johnny Calderon finished his military service, he was stationed in Denver. "Living in Denver, you're in a crowd, in a big crowd, and you feel so lonely because you really don't know anybody," he says. "That's what I missed about Marfa, that sense of people, everybody knows you, everybody you know is friendly, and you get to know people." It was also the day-to-day activities he once enjoyed in Marfa that he missed: "I like to work with wood, and I like to have a little shop where I could work with wood and do whatever I wanted to do. I didn't have that in Denver, and that was one of the things I missed," Johnny says.

After his military discharge, he married a woman from Valentine and attended Sul Ross State University for two years, then transferred to Baylor, majoring in physical therapy. It was difficult to support his family, even with his wife working as well as himself, and by this time he had two children. After two years in Waco, they returned to Denver, where he had made friends while he was stationed there. "We used to go out, the wife and I and the kids, but we never knew anybody really, just the people that were in the service when I got out, so that's when we talked about moving back to Marfa," he says. "We wound up getting divorced, and I moved back to Marfa by myself in 1983." Leaving his wife and children behind was difficult, even to return to where he was most at home. "I loved Denver because it was so big and so clean and there's a lot to do, but then again there's nothing like leaving the house and not having to lock the doors," Johnny says.

Born and raised in Marfa, he has never regretted coming home. "I have been promoting Marfa for a long time. I was executive director for the Chamber of Commerce for two and a half years, and I promoted Marfa very, very well. I went to work for a company that sold insurance, and I worked for them for seventeen years, and then after I retired I started the *Marfa Magazine*," he says.

Marfa had changed dramatically since his childhood. "There was a problem a long time ago, the Mexicans went to a Mexican school, it was called Blackwell School, and they kept us there," he remembers. "At one point, if you spoke Spanish, you were paddled, but we didn't speak English in the house, we spoke Spanish. The school district finally integrated, and Blackwell closed down in 1965."

He was the first and only person in his family to graduate from high school, then was the first to attend college. Later, a cousin earned an

undergraduate degree. "In those days, we had nothing but Anglo teachers, and even though there was a lot of prejudice, they were the ones that taught us, they stayed here. They could have gone somewhere else, but they stayed," Johnny says. "They were probably criticized by their own people in town because they were teaching Mexicans, but that changed, that changed a lot. You just have to let bygones be bygones and see

what it is today. I think Hispanics have more opportunity than they've ever had before."

Since his time with the Marfa Chamber of Commerce, promoting the town, and with the perspective of growing up in Marfa, Johnny has seen immense change, not only in West Texas, but throughout the country. "Right now I think that Mexicans throughout the United States—and I can't speak for all of them, but I'm going to—are doing better now than they've ever done before," he says. "In my growing up days, very few Mexicans had a business of their own, you always worked for a white man. In fact, I was in high school, and I used to think that all the white people were rich. I know now they're not."

Johnny attended a seminar through the Marfa Chamber of Commerce about how to bring young people back to their hometown after they graduated from college and start a business. One business opportunity was in movie production, which was no longer restricted to California. Location shoots offered business opportunities. Returning from a family vacation in Ohio, Johnny stopped overnight in Chicago. "We stayed at the Day's Inn, and when we went to the bar, the place was right next to the Civic Center and it was full of Mexicans! I said 'Wow! What's going on here?'" Actor Edward James Olmos was at the convention encouraging Hispanics to become involved in the movie industry because of the expanded opportunities outside of Hollywood.

It is ironic that Johnny missed one of the biggest events that ever took place in his hometown, the filming of *Giant* in 1954. "I had gone with my father's parents, my grandparents, to Idaho, and we went out there to pick vegetables, vegetable beets," Johnny remembered. "My uncle was in charge of this migration camp in Wendell, Idaho, so I missed the movie *Giant*, but ever since then, I've really liked the idea of actors coming to Marfa."

After the filming of *Giant*, the temporary boom in Marfa died, but Johnny saw remarkable changes in his hometown because of the Marfa Lights and the artist Donald Judd. Judd's Chinati Foundation attracted artists from all over the world, and the Marfa Lights started attracting tourists. "Then all

of a sudden, it all came alive again. It was mainly because of the attention Marfa was getting with the Marfa Lights, the Mystery Lights," he says. "It was getting world attention, and Marfa was [at that time] just a gateway to the Big Bend or the gateway into Mexico. Then all of a sudden, with all the people coming into town, it became a destination."

Soon, tourists from Europe were coming to Marfa as a cultural destination because of the art. Then, because of the vibrant cultural life in Marfa, people from the big cities of Texas, Dallas, Houston, and Austin were buying second homes there. They bought adobe houses and then transformed them into much more expensive homes, increasing the value of the real estate of Marfa.

There is a significant population of New Yorkers in Marfa, coming to work at the Chinati Foundation or opening businesses in Marfa and staying there. Marfa has a disproportionate number of art galleries for a town of about two thousand people, with fifteen galleries, adding to its reputation as a cultural destination.

As part of his ongoing passion in promoting Marfa, Johnny is the publisher of *Marfa Magazine*. It is an annual publication, full of information on the activities of the communities of the Big Bend and ads promoting the businesses in the region. "This year I'm going into Santa Fe, doing the international Indian festival that they do. I have a writer over there that's going to do that," he says. "Then I went to Sweetwater, Texas, because they have the rattlesnake roundup, and I took pictures, I'm also a photographer, I took all those pictures out there that you see." Johnny loves his work because it brings him into contact with a wide range of people. "I love people, I talk to people all the time. That's probably why I have the magazine because I'm constantly talking to people," Johnny says.

In addition to his magazine, Johnny also has a band, called Johnny and the Cadillacs. The members of the band vary, depending on the availability of the area musicians. His former band was called the Tejano Music Band, but he has renamed it. "I took a picture of a Cadillac that was in Marfa from Austin sometime in May, and I said, I'm going to put the Cadillac in my poster, we'll be Johnny and the Cadillacs because I'm Johnny and I play and I always wanted a Cadillac," he says. "I play the saxophone. The players that I'm playing with, they're all professional; they've all done really good stuff, and they're joining me because we want to have money for the Rotary to give scholarships." The band plays rock and roll, doo-wop, blues, and country and western music.

Another side benefit of returning to his hometown, where Johnny knew nearly everyone, was meeting his second wife, Gloria. "There was a neighborhood grocery store in Marfa, and she worked there for her cousin, the owner. One day I walked in there, and she was there, and she looked really nice, and I didn't know who she was, and she didn't know me, and of course I asked her, 'Do you want to go on a date?' She told me no," Johnny recalls. "I said okay. And she didn't speak to me anymore, she walked off." Undaunted, Johnny returned, and after talking to her cousin Joe, found out that he knew her father. "My uncle used to have a place called 'The Little Red Barn' where the gringos would go out and have a beer," Johnny says. "Since there was no other place in town for them to drink, they would go there. Domingo, Gloria's dad, would play the guitar there." That connection helped Johnny get acquainted.

Johnny has been witness to the transformation of Marfa. In addition to the artists and writers who come to Marfa through the Chinati and Lannan Foundations, who are temporary residents, part of the increased permanent population of the Big Bend are the retiring baby boomers. Many of the new residents cite the breathtaking scenery and temperate climate as a reason to move to the desert. Johnny, long accustomed to the landscape, thinks it is the people who draw new residents to the Big Bend. "Life is so simple in a small town. You know, you don't have to worry about anything. I love Marfa."

143

Benefit for Fort Davis

★

JOHNNY AND THE CADILLACS

On April 9, 2011, a catastrophic fire swept the Big Bend, affecting the small town of Fort Davis more than any other community. Beginning about 1:30 p.m. in an abandoned stone structure, and driven by winds above fifty miles per hour, it swept across the drought-stricken grassland with lightning speed. When it was finally controlled, it had consumed hundreds of miles of expensive ranch fencing, 340,000 acres of grazing land for thousands of cattle and wildlife, and up to thirty homes in Fort Davis. Known as the "Rock House Fire," it ranks as one of the most economically devastating events to occur in West Texas history. In the spirit of helping one another, money was raised to help the victims of the fire who lost their homes in the disaster.

On Friday, June 3, 2011, Johnny and the Cadillacs performed at Padre's, a popular bar and restaurant in Marfa that features live music. Johnny Calderon organized and publicized the event, not only donating his time but also the money for printing posters and placing newspaper ads in the *Big Bend Sentinel*.

That evening, the performers in Johnny and the Cadillacs were Johnny Calderon, Robert Halpern, publisher of the *Big Bend Sentinel*, and Mark Pollock and J. R. Harrell, of the group the Border Blasters. The music was a lively mix of country and western, blues, and rock and roll.

The crowd began gathering at 7 p.m. for the 8 p.m. performance. By 9 p.m. it was standing room only. Between sets, money was collected for the Fort Davis Relief Fund. At the end of the evening, $755.00 was collected.

The Big Apple in the Rearview Mirror

★

TOM RAPP AND TOSHI SAKIHARA

It is over 3,000 miles from New York City to most of the communities in the Big Bend country of West Texas, but in Marfa, it is only a few steps from the curb to a gate that is the entrance to the Cochineal Restaurant, located at 107 West San Antonio Street. Guests will immediately be reminded of the beautiful micro gardens in New York City's Museum of Modern Art as they enter the courtyard, floored with crushed stone and bordered by trees shading the area. At the south end of the exterior space are clustered tables and chairs that attract the outdoor dining local patrons. The restored adobe building contains forty seats and an intimate bar with an open kitchen and a garden in the rear providing homegrown fresh herbs and vegetables.

Cochineal is owned by Tom Rapp and Toshifumi Sakihara, who made their way to Marfa and opened the restaurant on May 22, 2008. The idea for this delightful oasis in the northern Chihuahuan Desert began many years before when Tom and his son Jonathan decided to enter the restaurant business in New York City. They graduated from cooking at home to becoming exceptional chefs by studying Julia Childs's two-volume set, *Mastering the Art of French Cooking.*

Tom and Jonathan opened the Etats-Unis restaurant in New York City in 1992 after joining forces with Toshi, an experienced baker and accountant. "With a talented team in place, in both the kitchen and in the dining room, our first restaurant was ready to expand. The *New York Times* review of October 1, 1993, written by Ruth Reichl in her second restaurant review since joining the *Times*, was spectacular, awarding our new Etats-Unis restaurant two stars and putting it squarely on the culinary map," Tom says. "This quote summarizes just how clearly she understood the restaurant: 'The food is unlike that found in other restaurants. The Rapps have no professional training, and their food has the appealingly rustic character of the best home cooking. . . . The food is astonishingly exuberant, accepting no limits and recognizing no boundaries.' The restaurant thrived, garnered more positive publicity than a thirty-seat restaurant deserves, and was awarded a Michelin star in 2004."

In 2005, Jonathan decided to open his own hugely successful restaurant, River Tavern, in Chester, Connecticut. Tom and Toshi had developed the itch to find a new challenge and decided to look for a new location to establish a restaurant. "New York is a very expensive place to live," Tom says. "We were experiencing less and less of the culture the city had to offer. To go to the theater and have dinner was becoming a $600 affair." Since Tom's roots were in Connecticut and Toshi had made New York City his home for ten years, it was a cause for concern. "The fact that we were using the city less produced a kind of guilt, because we weren't utilizing its full potential," Tom says. They sold the restaurant in 2006 and began to search for their new home. A warmer climate was at the top of the list.

Their search for a new location took them across North America. They made forays into San Miguel de Allende, Mexico; Key West, Florida; Santa Barbara, California; and Ojai, California. Marfa appeared on their radar in an interesting way. Toshi, from Okinawa, Japan, came to the United States in 1980 and attended college in San Antonio. He then moved to New York City in 1989, where he was employed at a Japanese accounting firm and met Tom. A possible move to Texas for Toshi was not the stretch it would be for Tom, since he was already familiar with Texas. But when Toshi and Tom came to Marfa for a three-day weekend, Tom was sold. "We got here, and this expansive, incredible Texas landscape seemed just right somehow. We discovered it was Donald Judd country, so we spent the weekend looking at Donald Judd works and bought a house," Tom says. "In 2004, one could buy a house for, from a New Yorker's point of view, [what one could charge] on a credit card: 'I'll take that and two pairs of socks,'" Tom says. "We bought a falling-down adobe and were very pleased with our purchase. It was a great old two-story house in town, right smack on the railroad tracks." The ownership of the house anchored them in the Marfa community and insured their return.

Although they thought the purchase price of the house was a bargain, restoration and remodeling would prove to be very expensive. They soon found out that the house was a historic place. "There was a long period where we where trying to explain to others where this house sat. People had no memory of it. Suddenly this light bulb would go off, 'Oh, the old Calley house.' Instantly it became in memory their favorite house in all of Marfa," says Tom. "We decided not to be the guys who came from New York and tore down everyone's favorite house." They decided to sell it.

Before the house was even put back on the market, Tom and Toshi accepted an offer of nearly two times what they originally paid. For a year, Tom and Toshi rented a house. "We started doing dinner parties and meeting people and fell in love with the idea of living in Marfa. Our current house came on the market, and we bought it, thinking it was ready to move into. It was . . . $700,000 later," says Tom. Once the renovations were done to accommodate a restaurant, Cochineal was born.

Marfa has seventeen restaurants with a broad spectrum of food choices. When Cochineal opened, Tom and Toshi decided not to offer entirely traditional Tex-Mex style dishes. They found, through their experience in New York, a different Mexican cuisine. "In New York, most of the cooking is done by people from Pueblo, Mexico, regardless of whether it's Chinese, Indian, Mexican, American, French, or Italian. The guys in the kitchen doing the cooking, except for the very high-end French restaurants and maybe high-end Italian restaurants, are all Puebloans. To a man, they're really good cooks. Pueblan food has an incredible heritage and a sense of place," Tom observes.

The isolated location of Marfa makes twice-monthly trips to Austin or El Paso necessary to

shop for the restaurant. Tom has found that Costco fills their needs for meat and rivals what was available in New York. They also shop locally for the vegetables that aren't grown out back in their garden. Although they draw customers from the other communities of the Big Bend, the large numbers of national and international tourists to the area make Cochineal a viable business.

Tom and Toshi have seen Marfa change dramatically since they moved to the Big Bend. Toshi finds the biggest change to be in the composition of the town's population. "After a couple of years working here, I saw people coming from Austin, Dallas, and Houston often buying second

homes. Lately, many young families are moving in," he says.

Tom sees the changes in Marfa as waves of new people, with Donald Judd largely responsible for the first wave. Judd established the Chinati Foundation museum and the Judd Foundation and attracted an international audience to Marfa. A second wave came when Houstonites bought large parcels of land, which attracted people from across Texas to Marfa to build in the area. "This group left the town with a wonderful theater building, known as the Crowley Theater, a great bookstore, and several more civic buildings," says Tom. It was this second wave of people who brought Maiya's Restaurant to town. Chef Maiya Keck, whose restaurant experience includes the Bluepoint Oyster Bar and Al Forno, in Providence, Rhode Island, came and opened her popular restaurant in 2002.

Tom and Toshi see themselves as part of a third wave, opening Cochineal and observing the arrival of a population of young families: "We now have a Montessori school and a proposed private intermediate school. It is an exciting place to be a part of," says Tom.

Tom and Toshi have not changed their basic approach to food preparation. Cochineal continues to offer much the same type of food that they offered in New York with a menu that changes daily, providing fresh ingredients. Patrons love the palette they provide. The formula is very successful.

The young writers, artists, and musicians of Marfa crowd the Cochineal bar, and tourists as well as other locals enjoy the high-end-level dining experience. They maintain a wine list of some 250 bottles in a wide range of prices to complement their meals. Tom and Toshi place a lot of emphasis on staff training. They are proud to see young Marfans learn to appreciate well-prepared food and discover how skilled and competent they can become, perhaps becoming chefs themselves in the future.

Publishing Marfa

★

ROBERT HALPERN

When Robert Halpern's mother was asked how she came to Alpine, she always responded: "By boat." Born in New York City to German immigrant Louis Forchheimer and his wife Matilda Winkler Forchheimer, she traveled by ship at the age of two from Manhattan to New Orleans, then by train to Alpine, Texas. Matilda's parents, the Winklers, had already made West Texas their home and had established Winkler's Department Stores in Fort Stockton and Alpine. "My grandfather, Louie Forchheimer, started to work for his in-laws, the Winkler's, and he soon purchased the store in Alpine and changed the name to Forchheimer's," Robert says. "It's interesting because it's a double "h," F-O-R-C-H-H-E-I-M-E-R. There's a town in Germany called Forchheim. You see it on the map, so if you're from Forchheim you're a Forchheimer."

Robert was born in Alpine in 1954 and grew up in the family business. "It's a family business, so everybody worked in the store. I started out at ten cents an hour like my cousin David, and you swept and you took out the trash. It was an old-timey store. The morning guy had to take a ratchet and roll the awnings down. That was one of the drills in the morning. We worked in the back, sold and did inventory," Robert remembers. One weekly duty that appealed to him was helping to compose the weekly ad for the Alpine newspaper. Robert's parents strongly believed in advertising for the store, not only in print, but also on the radio. "We would get books, the manufacturers would give you books to cut, whatever clothing line you bought or something descriptive, so it was all done with the ad books by paste-up and clip art. That's how I started; that's how I got interested in print," he says.

Robert attended Sul Ross State for two years, finishing the basics, then left Alpine, moved to Luling, Texas, and joined Joe Bob's Bar and Grill Band, the popular country rock group, as their drummer. Robert had been playing drums since grade school. The band, founded by Joe Bob Burris and his sister Cindy Bob, was well known in central Texas. They played venues such as the Split Rail and clubs in Boerne, Kingsville, and the Cheatham Street Warehouse in San Marcos, where George Strait came to national attention.

After a year with the band, Robert returned to West Texas and finished his degree in journalism at the University of Texas at El Paso in 1980. Robert married Rosario Salgado, whose family came from Presidio. They met at an Alpine drugstore while he was working in the family business.

In the fall of 1980, Robert was hired at the *Odessa American*: "It was still a p.m. newspaper, the *Midland Reporter Telegram* was the a.m. paper, but the *OA* was the working man's paper, typical of the Permian Basin, where the white-collar town, the geologists and the land men, are Midland and Odessa are the roughnecks, the hot shots, the welders, and those kind of folks," Robert says. "It was still a p.m., which meant that, when you went to press, you had to have your stories by eleven, and I got up real early and would make the rounds at the cop shop. You had to check at the E.R. and see who was admitted overnight because of shootings, stabbings, or oil-field accidents, then write up your stuff."

When the paper became a morning paper, Robert stayed for five years and was promoted to city editor. "At one point I was a regional editor, so I came out to West Texas and did stories. So I went from cub reporter to city editor, and then we moved back to El Paso for about three or four years where I became an assistant city editor of the *El Paso Times*," he says.

Previously, Robert worked at the *Times* as a copy person and he found the border issues and the Judge Woods murder story, which reverberated in El Paso, exciting. His job was in the Teletype room, retrieving copy from the sports wire, the arts wire, and national news.

The information churning out from the machines was then delivered to the corresponding news desks, where the stories were written and sent by pneumatic tube to the press floor. When Robert returned to El Paso, the technology had changed greatly since his employment there as a copy person. "When I became an editor, it was union, and this was new to me because there's not much union in Texas. The guild owned the production floors," he says. Union rules specified

that non-union editors had to put their hands behind their backs. "There are all these rules the union spelled out. The editors who weren't union couldn't touch the pages; they could proof them and just say what needed to be fixed."

After a few years, with a two-career family and two children, Robert and Rosario decided it was time to move. Robert's friends Bob Dillard and Bill Brooks owned the *Alpine Avalanche* in the 1970s. When they sold the paper, Dillard launched the Fort Davis newspaper but also had some ownership of the *Big Bend Sentinel*, which was struggling to survive at the time.

Robert and Rosario bought the *Big Bend Sentinel* in 1993 and returned to Marfa at a challenging time. "It was really the low time for Marfa in the late eighties, the savings and loan had closed, things were closing, and ranching never fully recovered from the drought of the fifties," Robert explained. "Marfa took a hit everywhere; after World War II, the Marfa Army Air Field Base and Fort D. A. Russell closed, and this town of 5,000 became a much smaller town. There were many things besides the drought and the closing of the bases."

Even with a changed Marfa, Robert and Rosario wanted to come back to the area. There were more reasons than their strong family ties and a better quality of life that drew them back to Marfa. "Donald Judd was first attracted to the landscape. What he saw is what he emulated in his work, and it's site specific and permanently installed. I'm site specific to Brewster and Presidio Counties; it's really a sense of place," Robert says.

As the publisher of the weekly newspaper, he has the opportunity to find out why new people move to the area. He has found that there is a particular sort of person attracted to the Big Bend. "You have to love the land and you have to be

resilient, have a can-do attitude, and maybe that's true for everyplace in the world, but you've got to want to live here to put up with some non-urban things, but that's a good quality of life," Robert observed. "I ask people what brings you out here, and they might say the art, but mainly people will say 'Well, we've been coming to Big Bend National Park for twenty-five years, and we just decided to buy something out here.' They may buy something in Fort Davis, Marfa, Alpine, or Terlingua; so I think it's the old frontier spirit."

That frontier spirit is part of the identity of Texans. We think of ourselves as Texans first of all, but in West Texas, there is strong identity of being West Texans, set apart but within the state. The sparse population of the Big Bend and

the necessity of relying upon one another instead of an urban infrastructure is part of the strong attraction to the area. "What other place is still where you wave at each other and that you help people because all we've got out here is each other? If you see someone stuck on the highway you stop because you would want the same thing to be done for you," he says.

Robert sees the difference between the communities, with Alpine, having a university and hospital; Marfa, with the reputation as an arts community and the center of the Border Patrol; Presidio, and its relationship with Ojinaga, Mexico; Terlingua, as a community of iconoclasts; and Marathon, attracting runners, bikers, hunters, and visitors to the Big Bend National Park. It is the Marfa Sector of the Border Patrol that has increased the population in the area. Not only have agents and their families been transferred to the Big Bend, but so have civilian government positions.

"For every five or ten agents, you have to add another mechanic, I suppose, because you've added rolling stock, and I suppose the paperwork is incredible, so for every ten or twelve agents there's another clerical position," Robert says. "How many civil servant jobs did it bring? We have a housing issue here we're trying to address; there are more housing opportunities in Alpine."

Another factor that may have a positive impact on the economics of the Big Bend is the reopening of the Shafter Mine. "This company has the price of silver where it needs to be for them to make a twenty-, thirty-, forty-million dollar investment or whatever it is, and they're opening it for the first time since the end of World War II," he says.

Robert and Rosario have found Marfa to be a wonderful place to raise their three children, all graduates and valedictorians of Marfa High School. Their daughter lives in Spain and works as a translator. Their son Alberto, a graduate of American University, has come home to work on the newspaper. The youngest son is a sophomore at American University. They still have a large extended family in the area. Robert's ninety-one-year-old mother lives in Alpine.

Robert appreciates the unique qualities of the Big Bend, an area that will never have a cookie-cutter look or feel. "If you live in the suburbs of San Antonio, they look like the suburbs of Dallas, and they look like the suburbs of Houston. The downtowns still maintain some of their originality, but it's a gentrification and urbanization of the state," he says. Every time census figures are compiled, the population of rural areas continues to shrink, but it is not a mystery to Robert why people come to the Big Bend to live. "For the environment and the quality of life, a quality of life you can't put a price on. Clean air, clean water, and it's safe."

The Chinati Intern Who Stayed

★

TIM JOHNSON

The Marfa Book Company is located on the main street of Marfa. It is not a bookstore with narrow aisles from floor to ceiling but an uncluttered space with books arranged on shelves along the walls and tables in the center of the room. Flyers advertising upcoming events are at the counter, not only events that are centered on authors and readings or signings but activities the entire community would enjoy as well. The books themselves are a mix of regular bookstore fare and unusual art and Texana books. The space has an urban feel not usually found in small-town bookstores.

Tim Johnson, a Houston native, became familiar with far West Texas as a child. His uncle, Michael Gallagher, a Jesuit priest and attorney, lived in El Paso in the Segundo Barrio downtown neighborhood. He worked with the organization Las Americas Immigrant Advocacy Center, assisting people seeking citizenship and asylum in the United States. Tim would frequently visit his uncle in El Paso. "That was my introduction to the general landscape of the High Chihuahuan Desert. I fell in love simultaneously with the hybrid nature of the culture and with the look of the land and sky," Tim says.

He was a regular visitor to El Paso and the Big Bend, and after college he lived in El Paso for a time, then returned to Houston. Living in the suburbs, he soon tired of a long commute to work, and he felt displaced. "I really felt distanced from the cultures that I really wanted to be a part of in Houston. It was just so much effort to be part of the art and music scene there because everything was in the town, but it was difficult to connect to them," Tim says. When a four-year relationship ended, Tim was ready to leave Houston again.

While Tim lived in El Paso, he visited Marfa and saw the art at the Chinati Foundation, which had a profound effect on him. He was impressed with art that was integrated into the town. "I was just looking for a place to be on my own for a short period of time while I rethought my life," Tim says. "I didn't know what would come next, but I wanted a place away from what I was doing and where I was, so that I could clear my mind, and that would also be stimulating."

Tim contacted the Chinati Foundation for possible employment. Two months later a position was available, a three-month internship. The internships are not just for artists, but young people from a broad range of backgrounds. Some interns are college students, and some are recent graduates. At the end of the three months, Tim's

time was extended. "Marianne Stockebrand, the director, asked me to stay on and help her work through a small portion of their catalog, which Yale University Press had just published," Tim explained. "They asked me to work on the timeline and also to continue to give tours if I wanted, because it was a pretty good match. I'd developed friendships with those people." Tim received another three-month extension, then needed to find a way to stay in Marfa, which he had grown to love. Tim is a poet, and he found inspiration in the landscape of the Big Bend.

One day when Tim was browsing in the Marfa Book Company, the owner, Lynn Crowley, asked if he would like to work there part-time. He was unsure if his hours in the bookstore would bring in enough money to rent a place to live, but R. C. Bradshaw, who was also employed at the bookstore, offered Tim a place to live very cheaply. After only a few days, everything changed. "Lynn left Marfa for Houston, beginning what would become her divorce from her husband, Tim Crowley, co-owner of the store. Then suddenly out of the blue, Tim asked me if I wanted to take over the store. I agreed and said that I was willing to give that a try," Tim says.

He was well aware that independent bookstores were struggling to exist in competition with the large chain stores. "It seemed like a precarious kind of adventure at the time, obviously, a bookstore anywhere in the world has a tough go of it now, especially a bookstore in a town of two thousand people. To be honest, I wasn't entirely confident, but the idea of the experiment or the adventure was appealing. So I agreed, and I said, Let's give it a try," Tim recalls.

He was determined that the bookstore should do more than sell books; he wanted it to become

a sort of cultural hub for Marfa. He has brought musicians, both local and visiting groups, to perform in the store. Visiting filmmakers show films. "We have a regular film-screening program here that I do with my friend Ralph McKay, who's a programmer for the International Film Festival of Rotterdam. He's been in the film world for many years, and he knows a lot of people, so we write e-mails to ask filmmakers for permission to show their films," Tim says.

The bookstore also hosts political candidate forums for local and county elections. These activities are particularly important during the slowest months for tourism in Marfa, January and February. "I want this store to be a place that's both interesting for people who are interested in art and people who are interested in West Texas, and I try to share that with people," Tim says.

When he became the owner of the bookstore, he was already a familiar face in Marfa, but he felt the need to demonstrate that he was in Marfa to stay. Since Marfa is a town with a strong tourist base and a fluctuating population of young people who come as interns for the foundations, the permanent residents can be wary at first. "I did feel initially there was a sense of some people wanting to figure me out, but it didn't feel like it was coldness, and I actually really admire that," Tim says. "I can understand why people would do that, especially living in Marfa. Sometimes people really want to capitalize on a kind of cachet without really wanting to be a participant."

Visitors frequently characterize Marfa as the most sophisticated of the towns in the Big Bend because of its reputation nationally and internationally as an artists' and writers' destination. Tim, along with the other permanent residents of Marfa, rejects the sophisticated reputation that Marfa has acquired. "I think that the work at the Chinati Foundation is very serious and thoughtful, but I don't think it's unapproachable. It's actually a very open and democratic form of art," Tim explains. "There's a kind of mystique that surrounds it, but I'm interested more in the demystification of that. The idea of presenting oneself as sophisticated is incredibly close to self-importance and snobbery. I think our culture has a jokey, ironic relationship to a lot of things. I like a serious relationship to everything, including art."

Tim is just one of the young people who are making the communities of the Big Bend their home. He tells us of a group of young people involved in the green scene in Terlingua. They live off the grid and are involved in green initiatives that involve the repurposing of buildings and objects for the good of the community and creating art out of refuse.

Members of a young musical group called Balmorhea lived and performed in Austin for years and then moved to Alpine. "They make really, really cool instrumental Americana music. These guys went to music academies, and now they play acoustic American music, between folk music and classical music," Tim says.

He believes that as economic conditions improve, many young people who would have left Marfa are now finding ways to stay and start businesses and raise families. The biggest employer in Marfa is the U.S. Border Patrol, so the families assigned to the Marfa Sector leave after their assignment is completed. The interns and participants in the Chinati and Lannan Foundations typically have three- to six-month residencies, then return to their permanent homes. "The time that they're here is long enough for them to become genuine participants in the community, and it also keeps the culture stimulated," Tim says. "Two thousand people can become socially claustrophobic, so when you have a constant arrival and departure of people who are here for three months or maybe six months, it makes it more dynamic in a genuine way. People do have a chance of getting to know each other. I think people move on because there are still not enough options here for people to make a life."

He is very happy with the size of Marfa. Economic improvement would increase the population, but the small-town atmosphere keeps him in there. He has friends who have come to visit Marfa and returned to make it their home. "I would love to spend my life here in Marfa," he says. "With this bookstore, or just anything, I will look for ways to stay in Marfa throughout my life and hopefully the bookstore will make it possible. I love this place."

The Swiss Alps to the Texas Alps

★

VERENA ZBINDEN

Across the street from the Marfa courthouse is a charming restaurant called Squeeze Marfa. The entrance is through a courtyard planted with trees. It is usually busy with breakfast and lunchtime customers. Coffee, croissants, sandwiches, and other items are featured on the menu. Chocaholics are usually gathered in front of a rack against the wall, well stocked with Swiss chocolates from the family business in Switzerland. The chocolates feature unusual designs and flavors, including a chocolate smartphone, which requires no monthly fee, as the staff and owner of the restaurant point out.

Verena Zbinden is the owner of Squeeze Marfa, which she opened with a business partner. She explains how the unusual name came to be. "We were brainstorming. We were going to do juicing, because in the beginning all we wanted to do was juices. Then we realized we needed to do more, because people said there was no sandwich shop, so we developed the idea," Verena says. "But the juicing part, that's where "squeeze" is coming from."

Verena was born in Winterthur, Switzerland, where her family has been for generations. She was twenty-six when she first arrived in the United States in 1969 with her husband,

Alexander. He had been to the United States before but had to leave—because he was nearly drafted into the U.S. Army. Since Switzerland is not part of NATO, the citizens of Switzerland can be drafted when living outside their own country. "All the other Europeans whose countries are part of NATO didn't get drafted," Verena explained. "My husband had already done his military service in Switzerland, which is compulsory there, and obviously you are not allowed to go and serve in a foreign army, so he was in between." If Alexander had served in Vietnam, he would have been imprisoned in Switzerland for treason.

Although he had a green card, he returned to Lysaach, Switzerland, and married Verena in August 1969. They stayed in Houston for three years, Alexander working in a salon, and Verena working as a pediatric nurse, but they returned to Switzerland in 1972, when Alexander took over his family's hairdressing salon.

Alexander and Verena lived in Switzerland, where their son Sven and daughter Kerstin were born, for the next eleven years. Then Alexander was offered a job in Houston to take over another beauty salon, so the family returned to the United States in 1983. Verena enrolled in the University of Houston and earned a B.A. and an M.B.A.

Alexander had trained in Switzerland, France, and England in hairdressing and was highly successful and much in demand, directing fashion shows in Paris, London, and the United States. With his mentor, Alexandre de Paris, he styled the hair of Sarah, the duchess of York, at Buckingham Palace.

In his spare time, Alexander, an accomplished pilot, also flew his own plane. In the midst of their busy lives, Verena wanted a change from their usual pace. "In 2000, I read in the newspaper about Marfa. I actually heard about Donald Judd for the first time in the seventies in Switzerland, when he moved to Marfa," she says. "There was a big article in a Swiss magazine about it. So when I read again about Marfa, I was curious, and so I took some trips out here without my husband since he was working."

After Verena returned a few more times to visit, the decision was made to buy a house in Marfa and retire. "I've always said I can't understand people who retire and go to some place they've never been. I couldn't understand that, and then here I go, and we're doing it ourselves. It's just really weird," she says. They were sure that when they put their house on the market in Houston, they would have at least a few months to make the transition between Marfa and Houston, but their house sold in four hours on the first of August.

Their realtor scheduled a luncheon open house for realtors at noon and then told Verena someone wanted to see the house at 2 p.m. It was sold by 4 p.m. Verena felt that was a sign. "I will never forget August 1st because it's a Swiss national holiday, so in August 2000 we moved out here. It was really weird; I have lived in many places, but immediately, I felt roots here," she says.

Verena and Alexander happily settled into retirement in Marfa, but in 2005, Alexander passed away from Alzheimer's disease. Verena decided to stay in Marfa but needed something to do, so she opened Squeeze Marfa.

Verena loved cooking and although she was not trained as a chef, she received training in cooking when she attended boarding school. Her parents believed it would be beneficial for Verena. "It was kind of a finishing school: 'So, otherwise if she can't cook, if she can't sew, if she can't do all this, we'll never find her a husband.' That was just the thinking in the sixties, and so I had a lot of cooking training there," she says. But Verena made nursing her career, specializing in pediatrics, both practicing and teaching, but she was still very interested in cooking. "In Switzerland, I took some classes in cooking. I just love to cook. My family doesn't just have chocolate, they have all kinds of baked goods and now have restaurants," Verena says.

Verena's son Sven, after graduating from Cooper Union, attended Rice University and became an architect. He has projects in Austin and Marfa. Her daughter Kerstin returned to Switzerland to work. "My daughter loved to dance, so she went to SMU [Southern Methodist University] for the dance program and graduated. She went to New York to dance, but her knees went out, then she lived in New York and worked, then her company

transferred her to LA. And now she works for my brother in Switzerland, doing PR and marketing," Verena says. Although her children are grown and on their own, Verena is part of a close-knit community, where she has found, as have the other residents of the Big Bend, that she can rely on her friends and neighbors. "You can drop into your neighbor's house and drink coffee. In the big city, you hardly know your neighbor. And if there is a problem or you need help, even the people who are not your friends stick together," she says.

Verena has found that her location in Marfa is actually more convenient for traveling than dealing with traffic in much larger cities. "If you think about it, it's two and a half hours to El Paso or to Midland. If I lived in a big city, the normal travel might be a good hour to go someplace, but then I am stuck in traffic for another hour, and so it's no big deal here," Verena explained. A woman who moved to Alpine from Houston told Verena that because she traveled a great deal, she decided to move to Alpine from Galveston. Verena was curious why she would make a move to a remote area if she needed to travel. The woman explained that to go to Houston International Airport from Galveston was a two-and-a-half hour drive, and two additional hours had to be added for traffic and getting through airport security, so it actually saved time to go from Alpine to Midland or El Paso than from Galveston to the Houston airport.

Verena has also found that many other activities are much less time-consuming in Marfa. "When people ask me, How do you like it here? I keep saying things that take an hour or whole day in the big city take ten minutes here—renewing your driver's license, paying your property tax. You are there ten minutes and it's done. So life is simple in its own way," she says. Since Internet access came to the Big Bend, most people find shopping online is very convenient.

As part of having a simpler life, Verena has recognized that advertising can affect what a person perceives as necessities. "I'm not the only one who thinks this, in the big city you see all this advertising, and it kind of brainwashes you. Here you see something, and it's like, I don't need that, I may want it, but I don't need it." In a smaller community there is less emphasis on acquiring whatever the latest fashion or trend may be. Since there is less attention paid to perceived need and want, it is indeed a simpler life. "I don't need that stuff, but it's also a simpler life because here I can walk around and go anywhere in jeans and tee shirt. When I'm in the city I like to dress up once in awhile and go out for a nice dinner and all that, but in the city you are under pressure to have the newest look," she says.

Verena is aware that the same distance that separates the Big Bend from major airports is also the same distance to major hospitals. When faced with a major emergency, the Alpine hospital arranges for flights out to the nearest big hospital. "I understand that there are lots of older people who move out because they need constant medical care. That is an issue, but I try to stay healthy," she says.

She does not miss the varied and extensive shopping in a larger city, although she does recognize that some cultural activities are not available in Marfa, such as ballet and more than one theater, but Marfa does offer many arts-related activities. "We have a lot going on here in Marfa, there's a lot of cultural events, like at the bookstore. You know the Lannan Foundation is a big asset to Marfa with their readings, and we have the Crowley Theater. There's a lot going on," Verena says.

She goes to Fort Davis as a change of scene from Marfa and does her shopping in Alpine. She loves Big Bend National Park and takes her guests there. She hikes in the Park, enjoying her favorite trail, the Lost Mine Trail. Another community Verena enjoys is Balmorhea, with its unique, spring-fed swimming pool. Once she vacationed in the country to escape urban life; now she vacations in larger cities instead of the country.

Verena thinks that Marfa and Switzerland are polar opposites in landscape. "I love Switzerland, but I don't really miss it because now I am so used to having the wide-open spaces," Verena explained. "When I go to Switzerland or, for that [matter], any big city, or even in the hill country—I love the hill country—but I get kind of claustrophobic with all the trees. I need to see. So yes, of course I miss the family and everybody in Switzerland, but I'm perfectly happy here."

Her life in the sparsely populated Big Bend in Marfa is very different from her life in Switzerland. "Switzerland is so small and densely populated, so I like to come back here," she says. "It's funny, every time I come back, especially when I come back from Midland, I come over the hill there and I see the wide open spaces, so I know, okay, I'm home."

VALENTINE

Along U.S. Route 90, 159 miles east of El Paso, is Valentine, Texas. Paralleling the highway, the main street, California Avenue, is lined with abandoned buildings, mostly former businesses with fading signage. On the opposite side of California Avenue are the post office, a war memorial, and a church. North of these structures and the railroad tracks is the hub of Valentine: houses, a community center, and the Valentine School, occupying a large and modern building.

There are two accounts of how Valentine was named. One is that on February 14, 1882, a crew from the Southern Pacific Railroad, laying tracks east from El Paso, stopped there and named it Valentine. The other, more likely story is that Valentine was named for John Valentine, a major stockholder in Southern Pacific and president of Wells Fargo. According to historian and columnist Lonn Taylor of Fort Davis, although railroad crews named crossings, the railroad executives themselves named the towns along their routes. Valentine was an important shipping point for the railroad because of its location between El Paso and Sanderson and was a stopover point for the railroad crews.

In 1914, Valentine was a thriving community of five hundred with ranches, a real estate office, grocery store, and a restaurant. In the 1950s, when cattle breeders began shipping their cattle by truck rather than rail, the Valentine depot closed, and local businesses soon followed. The population has steadily declined, but there remains a school district, church, post office, and an active high school athletic program.

Valentine has the high-desert climate of the Big Bend but does not have the tornadoes or hurricanes found in the rest of the state. However, on August 16, 1931, Valentine became the site of a 5.8 magnitude earthquake, the strongest ever recorded in Texas.

Fort Davis and Valentine are the only towns in Jeff Davis County. Although Fort Davis is

the county seat and has the county courthouse, Valentine is the only incorporated township in Jeff Davis County.

Predictably, on February 14, St. Valentine's Day, the post office receives a flurry of envelopes to be stamped with the unique Valentine, Texas, postmark. There are only four communities named Valentine in the United States, and the Texas Valentine community is one of only two towns that offer the special "Valentine" postmark.

Hollywood came to town when the 1998 movie *Dancer, Texas Pop. 81* was filmed in Valentine. A façade built for the film, called the Oasis Gas Station, remained on the filming site until 2005. Subsequently, Valentine has been the setting for other documentaries and films.

Valentine has received national attention for an outdoor art installation one mile west of town on Highway 90, called Prada Marfa. Artists Michael Elmgreen and Ingar Dragset completed

the project, commissioned by the Art Production Fund and Ballroom Marfa, in 2005. The architects were Ron Rael and Virginia San Fratello, and the project patrons were Suzanne Tick and Terry Mowers. Since the project is modeled on an actual Prada store, it is a startling sight, standing alone beside the highway in the middle of the desert. Behind the glass storefront, six Prada handbags and fourteen right shoes, selected by Miuccia Prada from their 2005 fall/winter collection, are displayed. The building was constructed with adobe bricks, so, as part of the vision of the artists, the building will decay over time and return to the original landscape. Occasional vandalism has plagued the art installation; three days after its opening all the handbags and shoes were stolen and were replaced by Prada. A sophisticated security system became a necessity. Prada Marfa, like other outdoor art installations in Texas, like the Cadillac Ranch outside Amarillo, remains one of the most talked about.

Rock-and-Roll Artist

★

BOYD ELDER

It is sunset in Valentine, and a documentary film crew is filming artist Boyd Elder; our interview is part of the documentary. Boyd proudly poses on the railroad track with a picture of his great-grandfather, W. E. Bell, his great-grandmother, and other family members, taken in 1896. This day, the filming is taking place outside the Prada Marfa art installation.

Boyd is the site representative for this installation and is well versed in its history. The vintage handbags and the single shoes are all handmade. "It's the line from the period when it was installed, so it's a time capsule. It's a funny story because friends of mine—Fairfax Dorn, Virginia Leberman, the founders of Ballroom Marfa, and the artists Elmgreen and Dragset—were driving around Marfa," Boyd explains. "I asked what they were doing, and they said they were looking for a place for a permanent art installation. I jokingly said, 'Well, hell, let's put it in Valentine.' Everybody laughed, then we wound up putting it here." Boyd and his daughters Flaunn and Shaula traded property with Smoky Carmen Hall to acquire land for the installation. Ballroom Marfa and the Art Production Fund created the site and arranged its maintenance.

Two days after the installation was complete, vandals broke into the installation. "Yvonne Force Villareal called and said the lights were out, and we came out and saw a car driving by, and they jerked the door off and they stole all the bags and all but six of the shoes, and then it got international press by the Associated Press and writer Michael Graczyk about an art site being vandalized," Boyd says. Prada immediately sent replacement bags and shoes, and Ballroom Marfa and the Art Production Fund asked Boyd if he could repair the damage. Boyd assembled a crew, and the site was restored. The process was filmed and titled *Stealing the Show*, and it was the subject of an article in *Artforum*, written by Adam E. Mendelsohn. Another documentary featured the business cards, shoes, and CDs that visitors left outside the exhibit. These days, Boyd monitors the exhibit from his home using security cameras that film any activity at the site.

The Prada installation is not the subject of the documentary being filmed today. The subject is Boyd himself and his highly successful career as an artist. Any fan of rock and roll in the 1970s is familiar with the famous rock band the Eagles. Boyd created the album art for three of their best-selling albums: *One of These Nights*, *Their Greatest*

Hits, and *The Very Best of the Eagles*. His photograph, showing him rolling a Bull Durham cigarette, is on the back of the *Desperado* album. The band made their first personal appearance at Boyd's art show "El Chingadero" in April 1972, featuring his work in polyester resin, seven and a half feet tall, cast, and laminated. "I've been really fortunate, I've met many extremely creative people, a lot of musicians and writers, a lot of actors, and my respect for them as talented artists and people is indescribable. This is an inspiration," he says.

Boyd is the subject of a two-part documentary by writer and filmmaker Jennifer Hamblett. The first part of the documentary is about Boyd and his work; the second part is about Boyd and Prada Marfa. The scheduled release date is 2012. Boyd also appears in the music video "The South Side of Heaven," featuring Ryan Bingham and the Dead Horses. Bingham is a close friend of Boyd, who considers him a brother. Boyd encouraged and supported Bingham in his career, suggesting he meet T Bone Burnett. As a result of that meeting, Burnett and Bingham co-wrote the song "The Weary Kind" from the 2009 movie *Crazy Heart*. Bingham performed the song in the movie, and it won a 2010 Academy Award, a Golden Globe Award, a Grammy, and a Critics' Choice Award. Currently, Boyd is facilitating a documentary with two professors from the University of Texas at Austin, Alex Bilcher and Teresa Hubbard Bilcher, on the remains of the movie set of the fictional Reata Ranch from the movie *Giant*—actually the Ryan Ranch, owned by Clay Evans.

Boyd has been involved with Ballroom Marfa since its beginning; his art was among the first works exhibited there. He participated in the April 2011 benefit held in New York City for the

Ballroom Drive-In, a nonprofit organization, by donating a work. He is also on the board of advisors for CineMarfa.

Boyd was born in El Paso to parents Hal and Billye, but he was raised in Valentine until the age of seven. Boyd, his brothers Howard and Mac, and their parents spent holidays, weekends, and summers in Valentine. Boyd and his brothers helped his grandfather Howard, a mechanic, and his uncle Howard Bell, Jr.—called "Buck Shot"—on the ranch; they also helped out at the garage, the Valentine Water Works, and the local telephone company.

Boyd was always intrigued by speed and drew pictures of fast cars and motorcycles; then he began painting decorative pin striping and flames for cars and motorcycles belonging to his friends. While very young, Boyd drew and did watercolor painting with his father, Hal, a railroad engineer and saddle maker. Boyd never forgot the experience of meeting his father's friend, the internationally known artist Tom Lea. He also inherited a love of music from his father. Boyd has had years of music lessons, which led to a friendship with the Fuller brothers, better known as the Bobby Fuller Four.

While Boyd attended Burgess High School in El Paso, he designed and painted backdrops and did makeup for school plays, designed the yearbook, and painted a mural in the school cafeteria. His teachers at Burgess, Jennie Weitz and Eugene Thurston, encouraged his talent. He won a gold medal from the National Scholastic Association. He studied art at the El Paso Museum, studying with Wiltz Harrison, Dorothy Guyer, and Jan Herring.

Bobby Fuller was an advocate and fan of Boyd's

work, but when he died in 1966, Boyd soon left for Los Angeles, where he was accepted at the Chouinard Art Institute. Walt Disney, among others, helped Melba Chouinard fund the school and offered scholarships for students in need of financial aid. Boyd submitted his portfolio, won the Disney Scholarship, and won it every year until he graduated. "Uncle Walt paid for my entire education. I never got to meet the man. I wish I had," says Boyd.

The Big Bend pulled Boyd back, though, even after years of living in Los Angeles, New York City, and other places. "I don't have to go to L.A. anymore, I don't have to go to New York, I want to and I do, but here I've got friends that are in the art world, in the film world, in the music world. But I still miss the throb of the big city," Boyd says.

With Boyd's long history in the area, he has seen great changes, particularly in Marfa: "Marfa's not the old Marfa anymore. Marfa's got an influx of people in and out, and Donald (Judd) was a close friend of mine, and I wonder what Donald would think of this," he says. "If he were alive, he'd be eighty. I think if Donald were alive he'd be living down at the ranch, down at his place where he's buried." Ranier and Flavin Judd, Donald Judd's son and daughter, have discussed this readjustment to Marfa after a visit to L.A. or New York with Boyd. "We wanted to create the New York to L.A. Marfa Deprivation Chamber so you [could] readjust yourself after all the sirens and phones and people," Boyd says. "When you get back here, all of a sudden you can hear your hair grow and your heart beat. I guess its just Mother Nature talking to you."

Boyd appreciates the quiet and solitude that

other residents in the Big Bend cite as a reason to make the area their home. The sparse population means that a social life is what you create for yourself. "I really stay to myself. I'm not really looking to go socialize in town. I have some friends I see every now and then, but I'm not looking for company," Boyd explains. "I appreciate having time to think and having time to concentrate. Every time I'm approaching home, whether it's from Van Horn or Marfa, Fort Davis or by plane, I always have this feeling of relief when I get back here."

Boyd has found he has less time for the creation of his art when he is at home in Valentine because of the ongoing responsibilities of day-to-day life: "It's not easy because you have to realize you can't call a plumber here unless you want to pay $400 or $500 just for him to come out and fix your drain or horse trough," he says. "You have to keep the place functional, the windmill, the troughs, the animals, the garden, the lawn, and the trees. I love being outside, and I do a lot of my work outside."

Boyd shows us the experimental pieces in his studio he is currently working on. "I don't believe in art factories," he says. Boyd shows us a negative that he will apply foil to the back of to achieve a reflection. He considers this new direction an experiment. His newest cover art is for an album by the band Yacht, *See Mystery Lights*.

He has also launched his own clothing line, with his striking designs as adornment on fine leather, which he brought to the Austin City Limits Music Festival in Austin. "I took three images and my logo, which is my signature, and had them digitized in the embroidery. All the hides come from Texas slaughterhouses,

everything's American made; nothing's made in Mexico, China, Japan, Korea, it's all 100 percent American, and to tell you the truth, the prices are probably about half of what they should be," he says. The products are available on his website.

Boyd was a young teenager when the movie *Giant* was filmed, one of the biggest events in Marfa. "I did hang out with that whole crew," he remembers. "I never paid any attention to James Dean, but I tell you what, when Elizabeth Taylor walked out of that trailer, at my age, hooo, baby!" Dennis Hopper befriended Boyd after the filming of the movie when Boyd arrived in Los Angeles, and he stayed in touch after Boyd left, but he was unable to return to the first Marfa Film Festival, which Boyd helped organize.

Although Boyd is a frequent visitor to other cities in Texas, particularly Austin and San Antonio, he doesn't have a favorite. "I'm particularly fond of all of them. Some action, music, art, film, good-lookin' women, as long as there's something to do and someone to talk to, someone you can relate to. With the economy the way it is right now, this is a real hard time for art and film," he says. Boyd travels to make money from his art since opportunities for that do not exist in Valentine. "I don't live in the city, I live outside the city limits, I come in, do my work, play my guitar, play my music, and now that I have the Internet I use that, and I come and go because I don't make any money in Valentine," Boyd says.

Boyd recognizes that he has a different reason for staying in the area than the newcomers, and he is more successful at making his life there because he knows the limitations of living in an area with a small population. "You have to realize that anything that you have, except your spirit and your body, if you're going to have it in this town you have to transport it in here or pay for it to have it shipped in—you can't buy gas, you can't buy a loaf of bread, butter, hot dog, cigarettes, or beer in Valentine," he explains. "People don't realize that. They have this really romantic vision about living out here, but they don't realize that you're so far away from everything. It's just ridiculous to me that a town like Valentine doesn't even have a pay phone, and a lot of time cell-phone towers don't work, and this is a very remote area."

In spite of those limitations, Boyd enjoys the fact that Valentine can be nearly invisible. He does not want Valentine to become what he calls "Texas shitty chic."

When asked what makes him come back to stay no matter how far away he travels, he quickly responds: "The one thing about Valentine that is so great are the people. I have to have peace of mind. It's a big peace of mind, a big slice of the sky pie. It's good for the soul."

The Land Stewards

★

CLAY AND JODY MILLER

Clay and Jody Miller live in the shadow of the Sierra Vieja Mountains southwest of Valentine, on the C. E. Miller ranch. Their front door is close to fifty miles from Marfa, the location of the nearest food store. A visitor must pass through several other ranches to reach their home, which is built in a cluster of giant pecan trees marking its location on an otherwise almost featureless prairie stretching north from the mountains to U.S. Highway 90. On the fence outside their house, there are signs showing their designation as recipients of the Lone Star Land Steward Award, honoring their conservationist practices. The Millers have been featured in *Texas Parks and Wildlife* magazine, not only for their land management, but also for their cattle and wildlife. The ranch is a destination for birders to view some of the estimated three hundred species of birds that have been identified on the property, and there has been a recent attempt to reestablish the Aplomado falcon, which has largely disappeared over its historic range, including the ranch.

It is obvious from the fence signs that Clay is not your average run-of-the-mill rancher. Graduating from the University of Texas with an undergraduate degree in biology, he continues his interest in science by contributing to natural history museum collections for the University of Texas and enabling scientific research on the property by university and avocational scientists. He regularly hosts field trips from the University of Texas and other schools and organizations. Recently, the Millers hosted the Texas Herpetological Society spring field trip, where members caught, identified, photographed, and documented numerous species of snakes and several additional "herps," including lizards, turtles, and salamanders. The most interesting animals Clay has found on the ranch were two desert shrews, which he captured and sent to the university. "They are known all over the southwest here, but they are quite infrequent in collections," he says. "As a student, I was involved in collecting small mammals in box traps, and so forth, but I had never taken in a desert shrew. I had been farming using irrigation techniques for several years. When the crops are harvested, the irrigation stops, the land dries, and cracks in the soil develop," he continues. "The next year when you put the water in, the cracks fill up. I happened to be there when one of those cracks was filling, and two shrews came out of the crack, and I managed to grab them."

The Millers' ranch is also a part of the history of nineteenth-century border conflicts. In

response to continuing threats by hostile Indians, Fort Bliss in El Paso County was established in 1849, and then Fort Davis in 1854. The line of forts was extended to include Fort Stockton in 1855 and then Fort Quitman in Hudspeth County in 1858. While there were no buildings at Vieja Pass during this time, the area became a prominent camping location because water and an easier route through the Sierra Vieja Mountains were available. With the Apache and Comanche menace receding, Forts Quitman, Davis, and Stockton were abandoned by 1891.

The second period of military activity on the ranch came in 1911, when the Mexican Revolution began to spill across the border into Texas. To provide protection for the cattlemen in the Trans-Pecos area, border posts were strengthened by the addition of federal troops. Camp Marfa (later Fort D. A. Russell) was built and became the command center for the Big Bend. A number of small camps were established, spaced ten to fifteen miles apart along the Rio Grande. A recommendation was made to secure land at Vieja Pass and construct a camp suitable for cavalry troops. The camp at Holland Ranch, later Camp Holland, was a pack-train base that supplied four camps west of the Sierra Vieja. It was quite active from 1912 to 1918, when permanent buildings were erected. When trouble was largely over, the camps along the river were abandoned. The buildings at Camp Holland were sold as surplus in 1921. Today, Camp Holland, once capable of housing some one hundred troops, is in ruins but remains a constant reminder on the ranch of the turbulent and dangerous years when ranching entailed more than a pleasant trot around the cattle by cowboys singing soothing cattle songs.

The ranch has survived the worst droughts Texas has suffered through the Millers' wise use of available water. They planted alfalfa and barley to be used for grazing during the winter and spring, but they have discontinued the use of irrigation beyond the confines of the yard at their home. "We've never had a registered herd. It's essentially been a cow-calf operation. We produce feeder cattle that go elsewhere," Clay says. "After they are weaned, we let them put on weight and then sell them."

For several years when he needed additional cattle, Clay went to the annual cattle auction in Globe, Arizona. "One of my father's cousins ran the wagon for the San Carlos Indian Reservation in Arizona. They have an odd situation. A lot of the individual tribal members have a brand on their cattle, and then they also have a big tribal herd," Clay says. Establishing ownership was a problem, so this cousin was hired as an outside manager. The reservation assembled several thousand cattle for the annual auctions. One time the auctioneer did not show up, and Clay's cousin became the annual auctioneer. Soon he retired as the wagon boss but continued to go back annually to auction the cattle. "I went out there with him and bought a bunch of those cattle," Clay remembered. "Lots of them were almost as wild as some Mexican cattle."

When an outbreak of hoof-and-mouth disease in Mexico resulted in their cattle being quarantined, U.S. ranchers were unable to get feeder cattle from across the border. Clay's herd was not affected with the disease, although Mexico is close to the Big Bend. "Fortunately, we haven't had a recent outbreak in this part of the world. I believe the last one was in California back in 1921," Clay explains. "When it showed up in Mexico, we were not directly impacted. We are so isolated from that country. This mountain range pretty well cuts us off. Although it's only about twelve miles to the river, we never had any actual contact with them. The whole U.S. cattle industry was concerned about the Mexican outbreak."

The ranch has been in Clay's family since 1925. His great-grandfather, Henry Clay Espy, the pioneer of the family, arrived in 1892. He first came to a place called Lobo, between Valentine and Van Horn. It was a depot and watering stop for the Southern Pacific Railroad. "He secured land from the state in that area, but on his way back home to San Saba County, he ran into a winter storm," Clay recalls. "He caught pneumonia and died. He left his widow, Amanda, and six children—two grown sons, three girls, and a younger son. She brought the whole family, and they built a tie house just across the highway from the Lobo station."

Clay explains that the tie houses were built of railroad ties, with the original ties made of redwood. "The railroad was being constructed from the west at that time. All the ties from the west were redwood. The ones on the eastern side were all cypress," Clay continues. "Both are highly resistant to decay, but the redwood [ties] are not very resistant to the pounding of the trains going over them, and they played out pretty rapidly and were replaced. So there were lots of those available. They just stood them up and put a roof on it and moved in."

Clay's grandfather Miller married the oldest Espy daughter. Clay's father was born in San Saba County and came to the Big Bend at the age of six months. When he was born, the youngest Espy son was only seven years older, so he spent time following his uncle around the Lobo Ranch. Clay's grandfather did not like ranching much, so he sold his interest in the ranch and became a successful businessman in Fort Davis, working for Whitaker Keesey, a banker who established the Union Trading Company. The complex had stables, a U.S. post office, a lumber yard, the first electric and telephone company, a general store, and a gentleman's club and bar, making Keesey the most successful and influential merchant in Fort Davis. There was also a branch of the company in Valentine, established when the railroad came through, where Clay's grandfather worked. "A year or two after that, Keesey decided to retire and sold both stores to a corporation formed by his employees, and my grandfather moved to Fort Davis. He was a stockholder and became manager of the store in Fort Davis," Clay says.

"The W. Keesey name is still on the building he built in Fort Davis. It's now the Fort Davis library. Many of the same stockholders, with some additions, organized Fort Davis State Bank in 1907," Clay continues. "Shortly after that, they built the Limpia Hotel and went through several managers for the hotel, and eventually it fell to my grandparents." The Limpia was across the street from the Union Trading Company, and Clay's grandfather managed both with the help of his wife.

His long family history in the area has created deep roots for Clay. "It's been home to me always," Clay says. "I wasn't actually born on the ranch. My mother was new to this country and didn't have much connection except through her husband. She went back to central Texas with her family, and I was born there, but my parents were living on the ranch before that time and brought me back when I was six weeks old."

Clay's mother, Lucy Foster, was an only child, and when her father died from tuberculosis, her mother ran a rooming house close to the University of Texas. Lucy graduated with a degree in library science and worked for the university. When Lucy bought a car, she decided to take a trip with her mother and two friends to Fort Davis. "The first visit was in 1922, and it was quite an experience at that time, four ladies driving from Austin to Fort Davis. My grandparents were operating the hotel." The ladies stayed at the Limpia, and that is where Lucy met Clay's father, who had a room at the hotel that he used as his base while he worked at several ranches. They married in 1925 and bought part of what is now the current ranch.

Clay lived in Fort Davis while he attended school and spent summers on the ranch outside Valentine. He was not particularly drawn to the life of a rancher. "At that time, there was hardly enough acreage to support more than one family, but in 1936 my father and uncle were able to purchase the adjoining ranch on the north side, and I spent lots of time over there. In 1946, they purchased some additional acreage on the north end, drilled a well, found irrigation water, and started farming down there," Clay says.

He joined the Army Air Corps at the age of seventeen during World War II. The war was beginning to wind down at that time. "They didn't send aviation cadets to active duty until they had been in the service for sixteen or eighteen months," Clay says. He was stationed at Keesler Field, Mississippi, and in Roswell, New Mexico. After his discharge in Amarillo, he traveled to Austin and enrolled in the University of Texas.

Clay had an initial goal of working for the state or federal government as a biologist. After graduation, he began work for three months for the Texas Game, Fish and Oyster Commission. The commission had established a new program of stocking pronghorn in areas around the state. "I didn't start with that program, but I participated that fall in trapping and moving pronghorns," he says. "We caught some east of Alpine and spent most of our time down around Big Lake and caught a good many animals and transported them to several locations over the state."

Clay also worked on the first mule-deer trapping the state of Texas had ever undertaken, on the Longfellow Ranch west of Sanderson, owned by the West Pile Cattle Company at the time. "It had several smaller pastures around Longfellow where they worked the cattle, and it had what they call the 'outside,' which was 250 sections in one pasture," says Clay. "I took the antelope truck to the Aransas Refuge and picked up a number of traps and brought them back and assembled them on the Longfellow Ranch. I set up the traps and managed to get the deer to begin to come into them. Then at the end of January I went back to school at UT to work on a master's degree."

Jody was born in Tulsa, Oklahoma, and was attending Texas State College for Women (now Texas Woman's University) when Clay's sister Betty brought her to visit the family ranch in 1946. She was a sophomore, and Clay had recently come home from his service in the Army. "She

and my sister had been schoolmates at Texas Woman's University in Denton. She brought Jody to the ranch with her during the summertime. I was here, and my sister always claimed she picked Jody out for me," Clay recalls. We ask if either thought it was love at first sight. "Not necessarily," Clay laughs. "Well, I don't know," says Jody. "He was out there driving the tractor all the time when we came to the ranch."

Jody graduated with a degree in physical education and health and taught for a year at Cottey College, a small liberal arts college in Missouri. Jody and Clay married in 1949. "By that time they had completed the irrigation well on the ranch and were beginning to try to get a farm going. There were better opportunities after we acquired some more land, and irrigation farming takes a lot of work, and there was a place for me here," Clay says. Since he had two sisters, one ten years younger and one who was married and living in Midland, it was assumed that Clay, as the only son, would take his place alongside his uncles on the family ranch.

Jody made the adjustment from life in much bigger cities to a more remote place. "I think I adjusted alright, after about a year. We were married on the seventh of June, and Albert was born on the ninth of June a year later. We started having babies, and we lived in a little isolated house at the other end of the ranch. We had a good life. I didn't have time to think about it. I had to learn a lot of things," Jody says. Mostly, she had to learn that town was a good distance away and that going to the grocery store was not an everyday occurrence. Clay and Jody had four sons, who are the current owners of the ranch. One son lives on the ranch, one lives in Valentine, one in Midland, and one in El Paso. "They are all partners in the ownership of the ranch, but only two of them are involved in daily operations. The others come along when they can and help. They are here lots of weekends," says Jody. "They look after us, that's why we had them all," she laughs.

Now that Clay has health problems that need more advanced medical care than the area can provide, he and Jody travel to El Paso to see their various physicians. This is very different from when the whole family would make one office visit. "We would all go to Dr. Stover in Marfa. All six of us at one time, and we'd come out with a $3 office charge. Tetanus, we kept up with. Everybody had a shot and that was it. We'd go in, and he'd see the whole outfit. But now I go every four weeks to have all these tests run," says Jody.

She showed us the many photographs and plaques that line the walls of their comfortable living room, full of books and art. She points to a photograph of Clay's mother in work clothes. "She was a genuine southern lady. She looks like this because she was a gardener, [but] by afternoon she would be all dressed. These are the hundred-year plaques from the Family Heritage Program because we have been here for a hundred years," Jody says, referring to the family.

It would be hard to envision Clay and Jody Miller living anywhere else since they are such a part of their beautiful land and all the plants and animals living there. As we were leaving, Clay rose from his chair and thanked us for the visit. "We have some of the most beautiful sunsets you'll ever see," he says. "In the summertime when the big cumulus clouds that build up over the Davis Mountains come this way, the sunsets get some of the most beautiful colors you'll ever see. If there happens to be green underneath them, it's that much better."

Mayor for Life

★

CHUY CALDERON

Jesus "Chuy" Calderon is the permanent mayor of tiny Valentine, Texas. "I've been the mayor here since 1974, and nobody has ever run against me," Chuy laughs. "Every once in a while somebody will tell me 'That's it, Calderon, I'm going to run against you this year,' and I say, 'You don't have to.' And they'll say 'Why?' and I'll say, 'I'll give it to you. I'll give it to you tomorrow if you want,' and they'll say 'Noooo . . . ,' and they'll back off."

Chuy was born in Valentine, delivered at home by a midwife. "I was born and raised in this little town, and the only time I was gone was when I went to Sul Ross for four years," he says. Alpine, the home of Sul Ross State University, is sixty-two miles from Valentine but seems much further away. A trip to another community in the Big Bend was a trip out of town, according to Chuy. "I remember when I was a kid, my mother would say, 'Let's load up, we're going to the grocery store,' and man, we had a lot of fun going to Marfa to the grocery store, and then we'd get out of there and go eat at a restaurant," he says.

In 1968, when he was a senior in high school, the superintendent of the school, Brit Webb, asked several of the boys if they would rather go to war in Vietnam or go to college. They chose

college. The superintendent took the boys to Sul Ross, guided them through the enrollment process and the financial aid forms, and was notified that the students were accepted for the fall term. Chuy finished in four years and, while searching for a job after graduation, was called again by Webb with a job offer to be a science teacher and coach for the Valentine Pirates, with a full athletic program and a six-man football team in the Valentine School. Except for an eight-year absence, when he ran a store located by the post office, he has been teaching since 1972.

He has also been working for FedEx since 1988. "So right now I get up in the morning and leave at 7:30 and don't get back home until 7:30. I go to the school and teach until lunch, and then I get out and get on with FedEx, and I go to Marfa and Presidio, get back and try to do the mayor's job somewhere in between," Chuy says.

He has known his wife Viola from childhood. They attended the same school in Valentine for twelve years and then attended Sul Ross together. "I was born in Marfa at the clinic there, but my parents lived here, so I've lived here all my life," Viola explains. Chuy and Viola had successful careers teaching at the Valentine School. Currently the student enrollment in pre-kindergarten to

grade 12 is fifty students. Although Chuy and Viola have retired from full-time teaching, Chuy continues to teach part-time, and Viola works with students individually.

The school has had several students who came from Mexico, and Viola, through intensive tutoring, makes them fully proficient in English, not just in reading and writing, but also in comprehension. Chuy also has had an impact on students who face a language barrier. He says of one of his students: "He had gone to school in Mexico and had learned quite a bit, so I have him in chemistry class, and he knows a lot of the stuff, he just doesn't know how to translate everything," Chuy says. "He knows elements, *elementos*, probably it's pretty similar [in Spanish]—atoms, *atomes*; *neutrones*, neutrons; protons, *protones*. It's very similar, the English and the Mexican languages; it's pretty easy to translate it, to learn it. Or learn both ways."

Since this year there are two seniors in the school, the numbers can work against them for state ranking. "What hurts us is the size. We have a class of two; if one doesn't pass that's 50 percent already," Viola says. The Calderons' son was ranked second in his class of fourteen, which turned out to be an obstacle when he tried to go to Texas A&M, Chuy says. "He was trying to get scholarships to go to A&M, and they said 'Well, you need to rank in the top ten percent,' and he said 'How can I rank in the top ten percent if there were only fourteen of us and I'm number two?' So they took that into consideration and they accepted him."

The student population of Valentine School remains stable because some graduates stay in Valentine and start families and some go away to college but choose to return to their family ranches to work. The new teachers and administrators who come to the school also add to the population. "Some of the teachers that come, bring kids. We have teachers right now, a couple, that have six kids. They came with five and just had another one," Chuy says. "The last superintendent that came here had five kids, and everybody said, 'They're going to hire him because he's got a lot of kids.' They hired him, but we are not just hiring people because of that," Chuy laughs.

Their decision to remain in Valentine was a sound one, Viola believes. "We were teachers here, and we started having a family. This was a good place to raise a family, and our lives in Valentine depend on the school, and everything that happens is school related, so we always knew where our kids were, what they were doing, who they were with. We taught our own kids, and they grew up to be good kids. We didn't have any problems," she says.

Chuy characterizes Valentine as a laid-back community. "Everybody here doesn't get in a hurry for anything; they don't worry about too many things. You can come to our house this weekend when we go to San Antonio, you'll probably find the doors unlocked. No crime, everybody just trusts each other," he says. It may be that the relaxed attitude in Valentine has a side benefit; it seems there is a large percentage of the 150 residents who are well into their nineties. "I heard somebody say, I think it was in Van Horn, that they had to kill somebody to start a cemetery," he says. "There's a man who moved here that said: 'I figured out why people live so long here in Valentine. There's no doctors in Valentine.' My granddad lived to be a hundred, my dad lived to ninety-two, and her mother lived to be ninety."

Chuy's grandfather died in his late nineties.

"Ninety-nine and three quarters, and he smoked all his life," Chuy says. However, it was not smoking that killed him. "Actually, he fell and broke his hip. I would peek in through the window at night when he went to bed, and he would say 'Let me get this bottle of Sotol.' Sotol is that moonshine whiskey, and he would pour himself one little jigger and that was it. Just one jigger, and put the bottle back down, made the sign of the cross and went to bed."

Possibly his long life was also a result of the laid-back attitude found among the long-time residents of Valentine. "He never got in a hurry, he was laid back, just didn't worry, 'Ah we'll do it someway,'" Chuy remembered. "He had a lot of faith. 'So don't worry about what we're gonna eat tomorrow, God will put it there for us. He'll find a way.'"

With the emphasis on family and community in Valentine, the divorce rate is very low. Chuy and Viola cannot remember the last divorce in Valentine. They remark that they have friends and relatives that live elsewhere who have been married two or three times. Although the community is a close one, Chuy says: "Nobody gets into anybody's business. We live out here so nobody can get into our business, and we don't get into anybody else's business."

Under his long stewardship as mayor of Valentine, he and his city council have accomplished what few city governments have accomplished. "The budget of Valentine has always been in the black. We're not in the red. We balance our budgets. The school and the city do, and there are just a few of us. We take care of our money, and we don't throw it away; we don't spend it, we try to be as conservative as possible," he says. A major project under way now is a sewer system funded through a Texas Water Development Board grant for two and a half million dollars through the stimulus funds provided by the Obama administration. Valentine also built a community center with a grant from the Department of Rural Affairs and has plans to add a kitchen, a dining room, central heating, and air conditioning.

There are two water towers in Valentine; the first was built in the mid-seventies with money borrowed from the Farmers Home Administration, in compliance with water commission standards for water pressure set by the Texas Natural Resource Conservation Commission, now the Texas Commission on Environmental Quality. When the regulations changed, the tower was found to not have enough water pressure to satisfy the new regulations. It was suggested that there may be a source for the funding needed to comply with the new regulations. "We had an option, I could have put a pump in there, a pressure pump, and we wouldn't have had to build the bigger tank," Chuy says. "I thought pretty seriously about it and I said, If we put a pump in there, it's going to cost money to run it; if we put a big tank over there that's going to be 100 percent grant, it's not going to cost us anything because it's going to work on gravity." Chuy brought an engineer in to draw up the plans.

"He said, You build it this high, put so much water in it, you're going to have enough pressure, even more than what [the Texas Commission on Environmental Quality] says that you're going to need. And we dug it, hallelujah."

On a more personal level, Chuy instituted the policy that anyone over sixty years of age who lives alone only pays $10.00 per month for trash disposal. Viola's mother lived in Valentine for ninety years. "Ninety, and she lived by herself for a long time, and she would take one little bag out there once a week, and I couldn't see myself charging her $30.00 for trash for one little bag a week," Chuy says. "So we did that, and we still have that rule. I don't want them to be overburdened by anything too expensive."

His FedEx run to Marfa and Presidio every afternoon has given Chuy a perspective on the different personalities of the communities of the Big Bend. The city government of Valentine, in addition to having Chuy as mayor, has two councilmen and a city secretary/water superintendent. "We just never argue; we always find a way to agree on something. Here in town we all get along, and if there's a law that says you can't do this, everybody abides by it. If there's something at the school, everybody's there," Chuy says.

He sees the differences between Marfa and Valentine from the viewpoint of a mayor. "You go to Marfa and the people there are very opinionated. They're all talking about each other, about the judge, about the mayor, about the alderman, about the superintendent," he explains. "You don't hear that here all the time. You go to their city council meetings, and there's a war, and you go to the county commissioners and read their paper, and it's like a soap opera every week. That's the difference between here and Marfa."

He finds Presidio a more relaxed community. "I think they're able to get along better in Presidio. They get a lot of things done, and the people are a little bit more positive over there, no big animosities," he says. On his daily FedEx delivery run, he hears very little gossip. He has found that his best source of information in Presidio is the newspaper. "I'll pick up the papers and read what's been going on over there and nobody told me this stuff! Somebody will die, and I never heard it," Chuy says. "They just want to know about you, what are you up to, how's Valentine, and how's your wife, and how's your daughter and your son?—instead of telling you all the bad things that happened in Presidio. That's the difference, I think."

On the main highway in Valentine, in front of the post office, there is a war memorial to honor the men of Valentine who served in the military during World War II, Korea, Vietnam, and Iraq. Chuy and Viola and their friends who live in or were from Valentine built it. Ramon Renteria, Chuy's childhood friend and columnist for the *El Paso Times*, returns often to visit family and take care of the memorial. "We plan meetings and get together, and we go out there as a group and clean up or repaint or whatever needs done," Viola says. Chuy also finds fun in this rewarding work. "We cook out and we party and talk and visit and get crazy."

They visit San Antonio frequently to see their daughter, a student at University of the Incarnate Word, and their son, who works in San Antonio. They have found that in two or three days they are ready to come home. Viola names the reasons: "All the traffic, just getting from place to place, and even going into the stores, the waiting in line. We can go from here to Marfa or Alpine and do our shopping and be back in two hours," she says. "At one store over there you can wait for almost two hours trying to get service." Chuy's perspective is the same. "I didn't know how small El Paso is until I went to San Antonio, and then I didn't know how small San Antonio was until I went to Houston. We went to Houston a couple of months ago. Man, that town is huge with the traffic and the people. You know the saying, 'You can take the kid out of the country, but you can't take the country out of the kid'? It's very true," he says.

They also find that the people in the Big Bend are more self-reliant than in the bigger cities of Texas and do more things for themselves. "I don't know anybody here that takes their vehicles to change the oil at a filling station. I change all the oil in my vehicles here. We do our own plumbing, our own electricity, I mow my own yard, we do everything ourselves," Chuy says.

Their ties and commitment to their community are strong and deep. Both Chuy and Viola are from large families but are the two who remain. Viola is one of ten children. "We all graduated from here. I'm the only one left. My mom just died this past year, and now it's just me here from our Segura family," she explained. "His dad just

passed away last year, two weeks after my mom did. So it's just his mother now. But all these large families on our side have passed away, and the kids left, and we're the only ones still here that were here originally."

When asked what they would want others to know about Valentine, Chuy responds: "I think that if there were jobs here, a lot of people would move here because it's the best-kept secret in Texas. Valentine's a good place to raise kids, and a good place to live. I think here in Valentine we stress God, country, and family." "And education," Viola adds.

Mayor Chuy Calderon sums up his mission for the city: "Every move that I make, everything that I do, I always have the citizens of this town in mind."

BALMORHEA

Balmorhea is located in Reeves County, forty miles from the town of Pecos, the county seat. The county is bordered by the Pecos River, Jeff Davis County, Culberson County, and Pecos County. Reeves County encompasses nearly three thousand square miles. The northern entrance to the Davis Mountains, the second-highest mountain range in Texas, is located at Balmorhea State Park. In addition to the Davis Mountain range, the Barilla Hills, with peaks of two hundred feet, also rise above the plains. Ancient Native American tribes lived in the foothills of the Barilla Hills in shelters of rock and caves.

The presence of water from San Solomon Springs, Toyah Creek, and Balmorhea Lake provided irrigation for the Jumano Indians, who raised corn and peaches. The Mescalero Indians also raised corn along Toyah Creek, as recorded in 1849 by Dr. John S. Ford.

The town of Balmorhea was named for the three men who established the township: Balcum, Moore, and Rhea. Balmorhea, Pecos, and Toyahvale are the only three incorporated towns in Reeves County.

Farmers and ranchers came from Mexico to settle the area and found a demand in the mid- to late 1800s for the beef, fruit, vegetables, and grain they produced in the nearby town of Fort Davis and the other developing settlements of the Big Bend. When the Texas & Pacific Railroad came to

Reeves County, Toyah, twenty-four miles from Balmorhea, became a trading post and shipping point for cattle, then a thriving community with businesses, restaurants, and a hotel. In 1881, a post office was built, and stagecoach service began from Toyah to Fort Davis and Fort Stockton. In the early 1900s, another railroad, the Pecos Valley Southern Railway, provided service from Pecos to Toyahvale, which provided additional transportation for cattle and crops.

Balmorhea remained the center of a large agricultural area but started developing as a town with a post office and a school in 1908. According to the 1910 Census, the population of the county had doubled, made up of people of Chinese, African American, Mexican, and Anglo descent. The drought of 1916 caused many to abandon their farms and move away. The Depression of the 1930s and the long-term effects of the drought continued to affect the population, although cotton remained a source of revenue. By the 1940s, the number of farms and ranches continued to decline, with the number of livestock and acres of farmland dwindling. Oil and gas production came to Reeves County, which increased revenue, and by 1950, crops made a comeback, but they declined once more by 1960. The discovery of three oilfields in Reeves County—the San Martine, Chapman Deep, and Athens Oilfields—produced millions of barrels of oil in the 1970s. Oil, livestock, and agriculture continued on the boom-and-bust cycle in subsequent decades. Today, although Reeves County has many ranches and farms, most of the farms operate at subsistence level.

While Balmorhea is still the center of an agricultural area, tourism brings the most revenue to the town. When the Civilian Conservation Corps built Balmorhea State Park, located four miles west of Balmorhea in 1933, the project provided employment for many people in Reeves County. They constructed a feature that is still very popular today, a spring-fed swimming pool with rock walls. The pool varies in depth, up to thirty feet deep, and San Solomon Springs feeds the pool from underground caverns. There are

fish, including the endangered Pecos gambusia and Comanche Springs pupfish, and aquatic plants in the 1.75-acre pool. The pool also provides an unlikely source of revenue: scuba-diving certification. Balmorhea has become such a popular dive site that up to ten groups of divers with up to fifteen students come nearly every weekend during what is considered the slow season in the park, from Labor Day to Memorial Day. The divers regularly come from Las Cruces, Roswell, and Albuquerque, New Mexico.

Tourists are also attracted to the San Solomon Cienega, a refuge for birds, fish, and amphibians on restored canals and desert wetlands. The disappearing horned toads can still be seen there. Birdwatchers have many species to observe: roadrunners, hawks, and migrants of all types are a few of the birds inhabiting the park and Lake Balmorhea.

The population of Reeves County has increased from 4,392 in 1910 to a population of 15,852 in 1990. Balmorhea's population, however, has steadily declined to a population of 497 in 2010. There are few businesses in Balmorhea, and Toyah no longer exists as an important railroad stop through Reeves County. Balmorhea residents continue farming the ancient land while serving as a tourist area, with a frijole cook-off and a cantaloupe festival.

The Grassroots Historian

★

ALBERTO ALVAREZ

Alberto Alvarez has a large collection of gray-green ledgers, the sort sold in the 1950s and 1960s. These ledgers contain the history of his family, stories, and recipes, told to him by his grandmother and written down every summer while he visited her and worked in the fields in Pecos and Balmorhea. Until he was seventeen, he worked harvesting the cantaloupe, cotton, and alfalfa crops. It was through these journals he developed a lifelong passion for history. He is what the southwest historian C. L. Sonnichsen called a "grassroots historian."

It was curiosity that fueled his habit as the chronicler of family history: "I really started doing this when I was about fifteen or fourteen because in the summer, I'd come to live with my maternal grandmother, Maria Renteria Talamentez, who lived to be 104, here in Pecos," Alberto says. "She was alone and we didn't have a TV or radio or anything, and we'd just sit down and talk, and I'd ask where she was born, who were her parents, and what were their names, who were her sisters, and who did they marry," Alberto remembers.

He also wanted to know what sort of music they enjoyed, what their everyday life was like and particularly about his maternal grandfather, Francisco Talamentez, who died in Toyah in a railroad accident while working at the Toyah Texas & Pacific roundhouse in 1928. "I always heard of him, and I think that is what started it all. I began writing things, whatever I could and as best as I could spell," Alberto says. "My grandmother said, 'I want to show you something.' She had a trunk and opened it and brought me a ledger, and it was handwritten in Spanish. She said, 'Your grandfather used to do the same thing you're doing.'"

His grandfather used his ledger as a journal, recording his everyday life, providing Alberto with an invaluable view into his grandfather's life. "He wrote about when his children were born, if it was cold or windy," Alberto says. "And he'd say something about the child, 'It's a beautiful child, like my mother.' He'd write, 'I think this one is going to be a good singer, she cries like the dickens, she's got a voice on her,' or he'd write, 'This one we're going to name Aurora, because of the sunshine she brings.' I thought, this is really poetic.'"

Alberto was born on Christmas Eve, 1945, in Brogado, previously called El Indio, one mile east of Balmorhea. His parents are Alberto Alvarez and Amalia Talamentez Alvarez. His mother was born in Toyah, Texas, which is about eighteen miles

west of Pecos, approximately thirty-six miles north of Balmorhea. It was a thriving community at the time. "My mother and seven of her nine brothers and sisters were born in Toyah. I spent many summers growing up in Pecos and Toyah," Alberto says. "My father was the second oldest of seven children, and he was born in the *cerro*, on that little hill I just showed you with the cross." His father has equally deep roots in the communities of Balmorhea. "My father is the son of Eduardo Fierro Alvarez, and his mother is Sylvestra Hernández Alvarez, she's the daughter of Mauro Hernández and is the granddaughter of Augustine Hernández, who was one of the first settlers of this area."

Alberto and his family moved to El Paso in 1952, where Alberto graduated from Bel Air High School. After graduation it was time to make plans for his life. "There was no aspiration or even an idea of going to college; it was a rich man's group. My dad was a mechanic, and I didn't have any skills other than farm labor because that's all I did in the summer," he says. His dream was to join the army, as his father and three of his uncles did in World War II. "My dad enlisted in the army in late 1939 and served as an infantryman with the 36th Infantry Division, 141st Regiment, the Texas Army, and they had a "T" patch, an arrowhead and a Texas "T," he was in G Company, and I memorized all that," Alberto says.

But the army wouldn't take Alberto because of a hernia. He could not get it repaired because he did not have health insurance. Undeterred, Alberto kept going back to the recruitment center. "There was a Sergeant Cortez from the Marine Corps, and they had just done away with the height requirement for the Marines, and he said, 'Come here, what's going on?'" Alberto told the sergeant that the army would not take him because of the hernia. Sergeant Cortez asked Alberto if he would enlist if he could arrange to have the hernia repaired.

The sergeant met with Alberto's father and arranged the surgery: "I joined the Marine Corps on August the second, 1964. I had never left El Paso other than to go to Pecos and Balmorhea," Alberto says. "I used to hear people talk about palm trees and my uncles talking about Okinawa when they were in the war and lots of war stories, and lo and behold, the day after I joined, August fourth was the Gulf of Tonkin incident."

After his grueling basic training, Alberto was sent to Hawaii, then on to Okinawa. "We went to Okinawa and got off the ships there and we went through Extensive Jungle Warfare School. When there was the opportunity to get out, I would wander off to the old battle sites. I was always amazed with the history of the war, and I'd go to these places I used to hear about," he says. Then they shipped out with no idea where they were going. After two days at sea, they found they were being deployed to Vietnam. "They gave us grenades and all kinds of ammunition, and then we hear that we were the last unit to go over the nets like in World War II into the landing barges," Alberto remembers. "We were going through the Perfume River that leads into Hue, and we got off on the beach real early in the morning. The

water was very choppy, and a lot of guys got hurt coming down the nets, so they were taken back on ship, and I guess they never went back out."

After his first tour of duty, Alberto returned to El Paso and renewed his acquaintance with a friend of his sister whom he had met in high school, when he was a sophomore and she was an eighth grader. They began corresponding. "She would write, and I would write, and I proposed by mail, and I said something stupid, she's still got the letter I think: 'If I get out of here okay and you're not doing anything, would you like to get married?' She said no initially, then later yes," Alberto says. They made plans to marry in December 1967, but Alberto became very ill within a few days of coming home on leave and spent three months in William Beaumont Hospital in El Paso with malaria and dysentery.

Alberto married Maria Ester Gallegos on January 21, 1968. Then he received new orders. "I was assigned to a very, very special unit that hardly anyone ever heard about; it was initially called Counter Insurgency but it became known as Combined Action Company, CAC," Alberto says. "Thirteen Marines and one corpsman were selected to live in a village out in the middle of nowhere and live with the people. We were helping train the local villagers and trying to find out who were the Viet Cong and where were they coming through. They told us the likelihood of getting help to us if something breaks loose is almost zilch."

One member of the company was from Canada and could communicate in French with the villagers. Alberto learned Vietnamese from the village children. "We were interviewed extensively to see about our attitudes about their culture and about the country and what kind of background we had," he says. "Most of us came from similar backgrounds working in the fields dealing with discrimination, even whites. It was like a brotherhood, and it was an experience of a lifetime; we saw a lot of action."

Alberto was then sent to Quantico, Virginia, to obtain a top-secret clearance for his new assignment to a base called "The Birdcage" within Fort Campbell, Kentucky, the home of the 101st Airborne. He was located in a top-secret area within the base. "There were fifty Marines guarding it, and we were armed to the teeth all the time. We really didn't know what we were guarding, but it was top security; we had to search people," he says. "We did patrols at night around this camp, like in Vietnam, armed. I began having dreams. I was sent to a psychiatrist, because I was waking up screaming."

The armed patrols were too similar to his experience of being point man on patrol night after night in Vietnam. Alberto had a close friend, Tom Greene, who noticed Alberto was biting his nails until his fingers bled, pulling the hair from his arms and throwing up at night. "Just being on the point every night, and I'm the first guy, and we had seen more action and more action and more action. One night Greene said, 'I'll tell you what buddy, I'll take it for you tonight, just get behind me.' He was a big guy. I felt so secure just because one guy was in front of me. About an hour later he was killed," Alberto says.

Once the psychiatrist helped him with survivor's guilt, Alberto decided he wanted to go back to Vietnam. His colonel wanted clearance from the psychiatrist, and it was given, although Alberto's wife asked if he was crazy, volunteering for a second tour. Before Alberto left Quantico, he was decorated with the Navy Commendation Medal with a Combat V, for valor. "I was sent back, and the war was worse. Somebody found out I had been in a CAP [Combined Action Platoon] unit after I got back to Vietnam, and I got called up and was told, 'We need an experienced CAP marine, would you be willing to go back, we're sending you out further than any other CAP,'" Alberto says.

He survived this tour of duty but found civilian life grim when he returned to El Paso. He was lacking civilian job skills, and couldn't even get a job in manufacturing. Desperate for work, Alberto made up his mind to reenlist. "I was already a sergeant when I got out, and I said, I'm going to go back into the Marine Corps, they'll give me a bonus and another stripe, but chances are they're going to send me back, and it's not getting any better," he says. "On my way [to reenlist], I'm driving on Delta Street, and I saw the juvenile center, and I was familiar with it because I had friends who were there." Alberto stopped to ask if they had any job openings for any kind of work. After he filled out the application and was getting into his car, he was called back into the center. "I got hired that day cleaning offices and stripping wax, and I was glad I had a job."

He stayed and was offered a higher-paying position. A Korean War veteran at the center asked why Alberto was not attending school through the GI Bill. "I never was told about the GI Bill," he says. "We didn't get any information that we qualified for unemployment, or that we qualified for school, or that we qualified for a house, zero, good luck, thank you." Alberto then enrolled in El Paso Community College but had a hard time because of a lack of study skills.

After accumulating enough credits, he enrolled in the University of Texas at El Paso but stopped during his first semester because he was failing the three classes he was taking. Then the government wanted its money back. "I kept getting letters, and I start throwing them away, and I say, Come on, a million guys like me out there, and they're going to come after me. Well, they did. It just worried the heck out of me, how am I going to pay these people back, and I didn't throw the money away," he says.

The men called to the hearing, who were in the same situation as Alberto, found advocates in the community from a counselor at the community college and two UTEP professors: Ellwyn Stoddard, from the Department of Sociology, and Joseph Graves, from the Department of Criminal Justice. "One of the professors said I sat in front, always on time, but I had no business [being] in college yet," he recalls. "Another of the professors said, 'You people are something else; these guys come back and you put a carrot in front of them, and you think they're going to say no to that? Free money? They're not thinking about I need to pass and get a degree or whatever; they need something. You guys don't give them any counseling, nothing.'" Because of their intervention, the veterans got to stay at UTEP, but received remediation to bring them up to university-level classes.

It took Alberto eleven years to complete his education while working full-time to support his family: "I loved college and I did well, better in history and sociology than anything else, but I got my degree in criminal justice," he says. Alberto became a juvenile probation officer and was promoted to director of training and program development in El Paso. When the position of chief juvenile probation officer became available for Reeves County in Pecos, Alberto immediately

applied. "Reeves County was looking for a trained, experienced, bilingual state-certified juvenile probation officer because they were mandated to have a juvenile probation department and remove kids from jails. I came here to start a department from scratch," he says.

He returned to his childhood home, bringing his wife and two young children, which was an adjustment from living in the big city of El Paso. "My wife is a city girl, she had a hard time adjusting. The first thing she said when we came here was 'There's no Walmart, there's no McDonald's

189

here.' I think she cried for two or three years, and now you can't get her out of here," Alberto laughs.

He returned to a changed area. Reeves County had always been agricultural, and African American families from the South had come to the area and had stayed for generations, as did families from Mexico. Segregation of African Americans, Mexicans, and Anglos had been commonplace. But when Alberto and his family returned to Reeves County, it no longer existed.

During segregation, "We had a number of theaters downtown, and of course they were all segregated, and whites sat downstairs, and the Mexicans sat upstairs, which we thought was great, we get to sit upstairs, nobody's ever been upstairs before," Alberto says. "That part on the top of the theater was segregated because it was a law, blacks sat here, and the Mexicans sat here, and the whites sat there." He remembers the walkway that would allow two people at a time from upstairs to visit the snack bar, but they were not allowed into the snack bar. They were served through a sliding window.

One constant in Balmorhea and Reeves County is the steady migration of young people in the community away from home. Alberto's son and daughter moved away to attend college and stayed away, finding more opportunity elsewhere. "My son and daughter had some schooling in El Paso, but then we moved here, and they were in shock,

I guess. My son was probably the only kid in Pecos who subscribed to *Rolling Stone* magazine, but they were very active in school and they graduated," he says. His daughter is a social worker in Los Angeles, helping the homeless and drug addicted on skid row. She also hosts the *Feminist Magazine* public radio program.

Alberto's son started out as a cinematographer in Los Angeles but changed careers to art installation. "He got a job in an art storage facility where they store very, very expensive art. He got internationally certified, and sometimes he goes to Spain and escorts paintings here and sets it up for celebrities or museums," Alberto says.

Long before Alberto retired from Reeves County, he was asked to create the permanent Hispanic Heritage Room in the West of the Pecos Museum. His lifelong curiosity about the lives of not only his family but the people of the Big Bend was an invaluable asset in the creation of the exhibit.

Now retired, Alberto is a sought-after speaker on the history of the area, talking to civic and museum groups in Pecos and Fort Davis, such as the Texas Heritage Trails Association. He now happily spends his days interviewing the older residents of the Balmorhea and Pecos area; most of them have connections to his own family. He is firmly rooted in the area: "Here in Balmorhea, this is home. I always loved it here."

The Memory Keeper

★

EDUARDO ALVAREZ

Across the road from the small home of eighty-eight-year-old Eduardo Alvarez is the house where he was born. "I was born about five hundred feet from here. Everybody else goes to another state, and I only traveled five hundred feet in eighty-eight years, except when I was in the army for eighteen months," Eduardo says. His military tour was at the end of World War II, and his assignment was supply clerk for his division. His nephew, Alberto, urges Eduardo to show a photograph of himself in his army uniform. He was a handsome young man in uniform and is pleased to display his picture. He had no desire to go to faraway places, even on leave. "In the army, they wanted to give me a thirty-day pass in Germany and come back. Nope. I didn't dislike the army, but I felt like I didn't belong there," he says.

When Eduardo returned home, he worked for the State of Texas for thirty-two years, maintaining the highway signs in south Reeves County. He married a hometown girl. "She used to live right next door," he remembers. "Actually, I lived on the other side of that grocery, that's where I lived when I was young, but when I got married I moved to this house in 1949; I lived here all the time."

Eduardo built the home he lives in now. "When I got married I had a little house, a two-room house. Then I started building, and I finally got what I wanted, I built it myself. I'm surprised it hasn't come down yet," he laughs.

Eduardo and his wife had three children. One lives in Wink, one in Pecos, and one son died last year at fifty. Eduardo shares his home with his nineteen- and seventeen-year-old grandchildren. One granddaughter, married to a navy corpsman stationed in Japan, has a six-month-old baby who is part of the household.

Eduardo and his brothers all attended school in Balmorhea in a segregated school. "They called it Balmorhea Mexican School, it was only to the fourth grade, then we had to go to the other school then, the one where the white people went," Eduardo says. They were honor students. Although Eduardo only completed the sixth grade, he was a substitute teacher for the fourth grade.

Eduardo is a self-taught guitar player who began playing in a band. "One time a band came over, they didn't have the guitar player with them, and the leader came over to my garage where I was working, I had a filling station. He came over and said, 'Can you help us tonight? I hear you play the guitar.' I told him I couldn't play that well because I hadn't even practiced with him. I didn't think I could play with him. It was a wedding dance," Eduardo recalls. "He got his saxophone out and started playing and said: 'Let me be the judge.' So I played, and [he] said, 'Well, you play with us tonight.'" Eduardo continued to play with various musicians at different venues around the Big Bend when a band was needed; the group did not have a name.

Now that Eduardo is retired, he spends time with his nephew Alberto and shares his memories of the history of Balmorhea and the small communities of Calera and Brogado. Tiny Brogado once had another name. "Before Brogado? El Indio, that's what we called it, there was never a post office or anything," Eduardo says. Alberto points out the reason for that name was because of the artifacts left behind by the Jumano and Apache tribes, arrowheads, hollowed grinding stones, and broken arrows. Augustine Hernandez, the grandfather of Eduardo's wife Sylvestra Hernandez, was one of the first settlers and owned most of the surrounding land, Eduardo remembers. "He came up from Mexico, and he bought land over here, and he had a big ranch up there in the mountain. They had a big ranch in Mexico, too, then on account of the revolution they moved over here."

There is a cross on the hill overlooking Balmorhea that served as a lookout point for the Indian tribes. "There were some Indians over here on the top of that hill where the cross is, all the time they were watching, watching, and if they saw something, they ran to the chief there in Calera, and he would prepare to fight or run," he says.

The cross that stands on the top of the hill, called El Cerro, has a story, Alberto says. "This cross is called 'The Devil's Swing.' The story is that a devil appeared at a dancehall here that was getting out of hand, so the devil made a swing on the cross and would swing and laugh loudly at the people around here, he says: 'I'm going to take over.'" Eduardo adds: "Well, at that time the devil was pretty popular."

Alberto researched the naming of the town and the story of the cross and found that the first priest to come to the area was named Father Brocardo Eekan. "His native country was the Netherlands, his baptismal name was Nikolaus Eekan. He took as his religious name Brocard, which in Latin, German, and Dutch is Brocardus. El Padre Brocardo, as he was called by the Mexican community, served as pastor of eleven missions in the Big Bend, including southern Reeves County from 1895 to 1935," Alberto explains. "When the Anglo community moved in, they set up the post office, and when they were asked what's the name of this community, they didn't know how to pronounce Brocardo so it became Brogado. The reason the cross was placed there was because he blessed this valley for good crops."

In addition to recording Eduardo's recollections and family stories, Alberto also began drawing the sites important to his family. He shows one of those drawings. "Before my Parkinson's was diagnosed, I used to go around sketching the old parishes from this area, and this is from where that old Carrasco's Mercantile stands. That was where I was baptized, my uncle was baptized, my dad, and my grandfather. My grandparents were married there, and that was the church Father Brocardo started, and it doesn't exist anymore," he says. Alberto traveled Reeves County sketching new and historic Catholic churches before he had to stop. "I began experiencing trembling spasms which prevented me from holding my pencil steady," he says.

Many of the people Eduardo has known all

his life in Balmorhea are moving away to larger towns to have easier access to medical services. Their children and grandchildren usually do not move back home. Still, his favorite community in the Big Bend is, and always will be, Balmorhea.

Although he does travel to Pecos and occasion- ally to Odessa, he is content in the house he built as a young man home from the war, in close proximity to the house where he was born. Eduardo does not think Balmorhea has changed. "I don't think things have changed at all. I don't think so, except for me. I think I've changed a lot."

Turkish Dreams

★

DENISE DOBYNS

When Denise Dobyns opens her front door in Balmorhea, she is dressed in hijab, traditional Islamic dress, a manner of dress we haven't seen in the Big Bend before. The term "hijab" has two meanings: the traditional head covering worn by Muslim women, and the style of dress, emphasizing complete modesty. Usually, only the face and hands are allowed to be visible in public.

Denise asks us to remove our shoes on entering her home. In the living room, she has graciously prepared an elaborate tea for our visit, served with a wide assortment of pastry and candy. This is a Turkish tradition, Denise explains. Although she was not born to Turkish parents, she has embraced that country and culture as her own.

Denise was born in Houston but raised in Rosenberg, thirty-six miles away, considered part of the Houston-Baytown-Sugarland metro area. She never felt that she fit in while she attended high school in Rosenberg, so she moved back to Houston as soon as she could. She trained as a nurse and worked in neonatal pediatric nursing in Houston, including a job at Sharpstown General Hospital. She met her future husband, Thomas Dobyns, while she was in training. He was her preceptor, which is the assigned role of an experienced nurse as a mentor and role model to nurses in training.

"Tom's Cherokee Indian, which means, and you can research this one, that he is actually Turkish, because the Cherokee Indians are part Turkish. They're Melungeon," Denise believes. (The term "Melungeon" characterizes some American groups that are tri-racial, and there is an ongoing DNA testing project for these groups.) "That's an interesting bit of history that most people don't know about. His mother used to get royalties from oil from tribal land. But, when the storm hit, all of his people went, so he doesn't get any royalties," she says. "He lost all of his heritage, paperwork, and that's hard to get to be part of the tribe, but he says he doesn't want to be part of the tribe."

The storm Denise refers to is Hurricane Ike. Denise and Tom lost their home in the Galveston area to the devastating hurricane. "You just can't get insurance down there. With every storm, they increase the things you have to have on your house. So we were going to have to raise our house another ten feet," she explains. "Now you have to have your house thirty feet in the air. To take a $34,000 house and raise it that much, we're not going to pay for that." Her home was located on Gilchrist, a community situated on a peninsula across from Galveston Island. The city of Galveston is on the island and a ferry ride away from Gilchrist. "It was ground zero. They sensationalized Galveston like it had a lot of damage. Yeah, the university was torn up, but it didn't have the damage that Gilchrist did. It was completely wiped off the map," Denise says.

She was exhausted with living on the coast with its constant worry about hurricanes. So in 2008 she moved to Balmorhea to accept a job with the Texas Department of Corrections as a nurse in a nearby prison. Tom remained in Houston. "He stayed in Houston for awhile and kept my house up, and he was working a baby ventilation job. Then I came here and I thought, well, I'll just work this prison job, and you know it'll be okay. It was awful!" she says.

When Tom moved to Balmorhea, he also began work with the Texas Department of Corrections in the same prison. "He's been with TDC longer than I have, and I couldn't stay there because we were going to get engaged, and it was going to cause problems with the other nurses on the unit because he's in charge, and I can't be in charge of him, and he can't be in charge of me," Denise says. Tom is content with his job and likes living in Balmorhea, but Denise feels the pull of another culture and wishes to live in Turkey.

When she befriended a young man in Houston who was from Turkey, she became a second mother to him since he was so far away from home. Denise calls him her son. She fell in love with his culture and traveled to Turkey to meet his family, who made her welcome. "I love Turkey, you know. To me that's my paradise," Denise declares. She is looking for a job to finance a trip to Turkey, but the opportunities are limited in Balmorhea. "There's a place in Odessa that's a group home, and they take in preemies or kids that have shaken baby syndrome. They're on

vents and that's what I do. I'll stay there when I work, then I'll come home after three days. You can't work a fourteen-hour shift and drive one hundred and forty miles home," she says. Denise told us that Odessa Regional Medical Center has plans to build a one-hundred-bed nursery, a neonatal intensive-care-unit women's center and nursery. This is her area of specialization, so she looks forward to an opportunity to work in a hospital again.

Denise feels more at home with her Turkish son and the people she met in Turkey than with her own family. She is estranged from her one sister and her mother, who still lives in Rosenberg. Her mother, at seventy-seven, is not in good health, but, as Denise says, "My sister has kids; I have a niece and a nephew and a great-niece and a nephew. But I don't really know those people," she adds. "I can trust the Turkish people more to take care of me. I can trust my adopted Turkish son more to take care of my money, because he's in finance. And those people would not do anything to hurt me."

When Denise lived in Houston, her neighborhood was home to drug dealers. In moving to Balmorhea, she did not expect to find a drug situation in such a small community. But there was. Fifty percent of the prison population where Tom works is there because of drug-related crime. In considering the effect of drugs and drug laws on the communities that she has lived in, Denise reflects, "I don't care if it is illegal. Frankly, I would like to see it all legal, but that's only my opinion. It hurts me to see the kids and know that they are suffering and that they are suffering in school, too, [and I know] because people talk."

Denise is not alone in thinking that if drugs were legalized, they could also be taxed and controlled. Denise concludes, "If you do that, it's going to turn an ounce of marijuana that's two hundred dollars to ten dollars. But the way it's going now, it's not working. It never has worked," she says.

For the moment, Denise continues living in Balmorhea, and she knows she may be living there for years to come. She enjoys the swimming pool, where she swims regularly in traditional modern hijab swimming attire. In addition to the traditional head covering, which can be a hood for swimming, hijab swimming attire includes a loose-fitting tunic and pants. If she moves to Turkey, she will miss the Balmorhea pool. "I'll have to give up the swimming pool, but they have a lake in Turkey, and they have clear rivers, and you can swim in them. You know, they do get warm enough [for swimming] in the area where I'll be living."

With teatime over, Denise is eager to show us something dear to her, her large number of cats. We go outside and walk to the back of the house where there is a large enclosed patio area with high chain-link fence on the sides and the top.

A doorway from a bedroom leads directly into the area Denise calls the "cattery." "I'm going to show you my pride and joy," she tells us. "That's one of them, Charito, he came from Pecos, and there's my show cat. We call that one Hissy. I just bought a bunk bed for that area, and I put a real thick comforter on it and a heating blanket. We have a heater in there. I wish my Turkish cat would come out."

Since our interview with Denise, Tom has retired, but at sixty-six, he does not see Turkey as his next home; perhaps, he considers, it could be a second home. Denise, at forty-six, has made a life for herself in Balmorhea, but she does not see herself living permanently in the Big Bend, which she realizes is not a good fit for her.

Denise is part of a small segment of the Big Bend population who have found themselves living there because of circumstances not entirely of their choosing. Many find that what is charming to others—the isolation, desert landscape, and lack of urban amenities—is for them daunting. The Big Bend is not their permanent home.

LIMPIA CROSSING

Limpia Crossing is a rural development eight miles west of Fort Davis on Texas Highway 118 toward McDonald Observatory. The lots in Limpia Crossing are five acres or more and have spectacular views from every direction. It is situated along Limpia Creek at the foot of Arabella Mountain, with vistas going up the Limpia Valley toward Blue Mountain and to the north, the McDonald Observatory.

The altitude is above 5,000 feet, and the unobstructed view of the night sky has attracted many amateur astronomers to the development. The vast majority of the residents are very active retirees, coming to Limpia Crossing from careers and homes across the United States.

The Great Escape

★

RESIDENTS OF
LIMPIA CROSSING

During a wine and cheese gathering of friends living in Limpia Crossing, the conversation centers around why so many people from such disparate walks of life have come to the area to retire. In the beginning, there were only a few homes in the community, but since then, the small development has gotten bigger, and what once was a majority of part-time residents owning second homes is now a majority of full-time, permanent residents. As more people have made Limpia Crossing their home, they have become acquainted and set up an e-mail network to keep each another informed of social events, such as monthly garden parties.

A former local resident, Tom Hobby, recalls, "I think we have a retired orthopedic surgeon, biologists, helicopter pilots, U.S. marshals, schoolteachers, construction engineers from Saudi Arabia, lawyers that can practice before the Supreme Court, you name it," he says. "We've got the wildest assortment of people out here that you've ever met in your life. They all get along with each other, and they leave their titles at home. You wouldn't know who any of them were when you're enjoying a garden party."

The eight guests at this gathering are all living in Limpia Crossing full-time but have come from a variety of jobs and backgrounds. Madge Lindsey recently retired as the director of the Audubon Society of Mississippi. Jimi Lowry and his wife Connie are former Florida residents. Jimi was a longshoreman and amateur astronomer who searched the United States for the darkest skies and chose the Davis Mountains. Dave Hedges retired from AT&T in Lee's Summit, Missouri, and married Linda, the daughter of friends of his parents. Linda is now an interpretive specialist for the Texas Parks and Wildlife Department. They traveled the United States by motor home for three years before making Limpia Crossing their home.

Nancy and Van Robinson came from Dallas, where Nancy taught school and Van was a petroleum engineer by day, working for DeGolyer & MacNaughton, and an astronomer at night. Ann and Howard Adkins came from Austin, where they owned a graphic design and marketing company. Ann is another astronomer.

Jimi starts the conversation. "There's something in common we all have, the people who live here. People that don't like it, don't stay. They leave. A lot of people think they want to live out here and then they come out and stay two or three months, and either he doesn't like it, or she doesn't like it,

and soon, they're gone. So there's something that all of us have in common that really love this type of setting. It creates a bond that we have between us. I think that's why the friendships are so much easier to have out here." Anne agrees, "You find that some people come to visit you, and they get it immediately, and others don't. It's not that they don't like you, they would just rather meet you somewhere else. Dave observed that many come for a sense of adventure and the urge to test themselves."

Van Robinson remembers why they moved to Limpia Crossing. "I had been coming to Fort Davis for the Texas Star Party for several years. When I was ready to retire, I wanted to move to a place with dark skies, low humidity, and at a high elevation to indulge in amateur astronomy. The presence of the world-class, cutting-edge McDonald Observatory was the icing on the cake. There are now twenty private observatories located in Limpia Crossing," he says. "We built our home

and our observatory, and then we developed even more interests, including birding, gardening with native plants, and horses. Fort Davis is friendly; it's filled with people who love the land and want to keep it safe."

There was another reason that Van and Nancy left Dallas for the Big Bend. Nancy was active in a gardening club in Dallas and enjoyed her activities with that organization, but her arthritis became severe. She had always been interested in horses and longed to take riding lessons, but her condition prohibited that. Van and Nancy had tired of urban life with traffic noise and crowds, so in addition to their interest in astronomy, they were looking for a small town. The future for Nancy was uncertain; her condition could deteriorate rapidly, making a wheelchair a necessity. When she settled into her new community, she heard of a nationally ranked dressage rider nearby who ran a stable and gave lessons. Nancy did not imagine she would be able to actually ride but went to see

201

the stables, anyway. Much to her surprise, she has been able to ride, starting slowly, and she has become an accomplished rider. Most important, her arthritis has improved greatly, which she credits to a stress-free environment and being able to fulfill her dream.

"While we were building our house," Anne says, "We met a fellow from Mano Prieto (another community near Fort Davis), Rick Herman, who had built a home out there. He said one of the reasons they came out was to see the Marfa plains. The people who come out here all share one thing, and that's a love of the land. It's a strong connection and bond. It's a pace of life. You get up in the morning and have this long list of stuff to do, and suddenly it's late afternoon and the day is gone."

"It's like the clock runs differently," Anne laughs. "People ask what in the world do you do out there, and your day is just gone like that!" Jimi says it is more than that. "There's something else that's in all of us that stay here. The longer I am here, the more I see it, and I've been here five years this month! It takes a certain kind of person

that doesn't mind going three hours to Home Depot or Lowe's or something like that," he says. "We don't want them any closer," Ann observes. "Actually, there is probably a whole kaleidoscope of reasons that bind everyone out here together," Dave Hedges remarks.

Love of astronomy, bird-watching, escape from the frenetic pace of the city, horsemanship, an interest in geology and mountains, and the love of photography drew them to the Big Bend. There are many individual reasons that led to their decisions to make their homes in Limpia Crossing, beyond the fact that the majority of the group are retired baby boomers. They are reinventing retirement. They live in their small, close-knit community instead of choosing to live close to grown children, grandchildren, and family. This is active retirement, taking advantage of a chance to choose where to live, not to stay where their careers took them. They are able to enjoy pursuing the interests that urban environments did not offer. The isolation of the desert has provided the oasis for the next stage of their lives.

The Survivor

★

RUTH ABEL

It is early evening in Limpia Crossing when long, blue shadows fall over Arabella Mountain and quiet descends in the desert. Every day, a voice can be heard calling "Putzele, Putzele" (sweet little gnome, sweet little nothing). In answer to that call, the deer slowly appear, silent, ghost-like in the slanting light, walking up from the brushy arroyos and from behind the trees and crossing the open land toward the double-wide mobile home. The bucks, always wary, usually follow the does. The voice belongs to seventy-eight-year-old Ruth Abel. "I feed the deer and walk right in the middle of them. They grew up here, and the bucks are now six pointers. This morning, I had two inside my fenced yard, and I walked out, and I said, 'Get out of here,' and they waited until I opened the back gate. What you do not do with wild animals is surprise them. First of all, talk to them, sing, talk to yourself, and let them hear your voice. Don't look at them in the eye; that's a threat."

When asked if the deer have become bilingual, Ruth replies: "I'm pretty sure they understand German. Even the javelinas understand German because I cuss at them in German. The things you never forget in your first language are that you cuss, you pray, and you count in your mother language. That comes automatically, you never forget."

It was a long and perilous journey in 1950, when seventeen-year-old Ruth undertook to leave her native East Germany to cross the border to West Germany. She was born in Plauen, in what is now the Free State of Saxony, fifty miles from the Czechoslovakian border in 1933. Her father was a guard for the king of Saxony and became a soldier in World War I.

When the war ended, her father joined the border police: "When Hitler came to might and power, he got fired because he did not join the party. That pressure started way before 1933." Her family moved into the schoolhouse, where her father found employment supervising the cleaning crew and making repairs. "I grew up there. It was beautiful. I had a little castle in that school."

The school was near the city's main train station. As the Nazi regime arrested people and sent them to camps in Eastern Europe, arriving trains at night brought detainees from France. "The Nazis kept them in the school building. They had the benches and desks removed and brought in straw for them to sleep on." British prisoners

of war were transported to the school to remove the desks and prepare the classrooms for the prisoners. Ruth had just begun to learn English in school, so she spent time talking to them. "My sister was seven years older, and she fell in love with a pilot named Bruce, and he had one of those thin mustaches. He was one of the prisoners. Weeks later, he escaped and showed up in the middle of the night at our house. Naturally, my mom kept him. Before long, he disappeared. They didn't tell us kids. My mom and my dad always said don't ask."

"One night," Ruth recalls, "I heard a commotion, and my mom went out to see what was happening, and the guards weren't there, but they had the people locked up, and they couldn't go to the bathroom or anything. So somehow, I don't know how she did it, she got a key and got to talk with one of the trusties, and she told them she would open up, room by room, and let them go to the bathroom if they promised to not escape. They actually did cooperate with her, and then the next day they left."

A few times, a baby or a toddler was left behind by a desperate mother hoping to save her child from near-certain death. "I came in the kitchen and my mom had a toddler that they left behind," Ruth says. "Sister Gertrude of Lutheran Welfare was called. Sister Gertrude and my mother gave the kid a bath and food and everything. In retrospect, now I know they were Jewish. But, I knew of five [of those] children that grew up as good Lutherans. My mom always said, 'If somebody asks, you never talk to anyone about what goes on. No one! But if somebody says something to you kids, you say it's a cousin of yours. His mother is in the hospital and we have to take care of him.'"

When Ruth was eleven, she came home to tell her mother what she heard on the radio: "There's a special bulletin, and we are going to win the war, they killed forty thousand Russian soldiers. My mother looked up at me and said, 'There are forty thousand mothers who are crying.' That just stuck with me; that was my mother. Yes, forty thousand mothers who are crying."

Ruth's father was drafted in 1943, although he was in his fifties. Ruth's mother took in refugees. "She had a big heart," Ruth recalls. "She took in refugees in 1945 when they came from Silesia and from what is now Poland. She took them in, and I had to sleep on the couch because all the beds were occupied. She never asked if somebody needed help. My mother was there. We were twenty-two women and children in a one-bedroom apartment. As a mother, she took women, children, old folks, old couples she found sitting on the side of the road—refugees—she brought them home."

Plauen was heavily bombed, the destruction was massive. In April 1945 the Americans occupied the city. On May 8, 1945, the Germans surrendered. Ruth was twelve years old. "Then the Russians came. Oh God, what a difference! The Americans came in the jeeps, but the Russians came with wagons with wooden wheels drawn by horses. My mother said, 'Get away from the window. Get away. Get away.' At the neighbor's house, there was an old German lady. She was a Nazi. Everybody knew it. She was fat, and when the Russians came in, she mooned them out of the window, and one of the Russians took a pistol out and shot her in the back. She squealed like a pig.

"After the Russians came," Ruth continues, "there was no more food. At four o'clock in the morning you went and stood in line at the grocery store, but there was nothing. For about two years we had no meat, you know in the stores. No eggs. No meat. No protein whatsoever." Ruth, then fifteen, worked as a saleslady in a three-year apprenticeship program that included learning bookkeeping and other office skills. The Russians still occupied East Germany, and the privations continued. One evening when Ruth, nearly seventeen, came home from work, her mother had prepared a meat stew: "I said where in the world did you get it? She said, 'Well, your father was able to get some sheep meat.' Well I ate stew and that was good. The liver sandwich was delicious at noon. She said, 'You really like it? How was your sandwich?' Where did dad get the meat? After I was through eating, she said, 'Was it really good?' I said, 'What's wrong with it?' She said, 'There was nothing wrong. It was German Shepherd.'"

Ruth and some of her friends began buying in the black market, which was dangerous because she faced being picked up by the authorities and placed in a state school. "Someone turned me in, and my dad, who played cards once a week, came home and woke me up and said, 'They're going to come to pick you up. You've got to make up your mind if you stay or go to West Germany,' So I went."

Plauen was thirty miles from the West German border. Since the border was officially closed, Ruth had no choice but to swim the Saale River, which formed the border between Plauen in Saxony and Hof in Bavaria. Ruth was one of many young people who were forced to flee, either by going through Poland or by swimming across the river. On September 9, 1950, Ruth escaped. It was a cold night. She dressed in her good suit and shoes, and she walked to the border: "There was another family there waiting for another party to cross with them, and they couldn't keep their traps shut and were screaming and hollering. The East Germans started shooting, and they panicked and ran back, and it was my good luck because I went through while the border patrol was busy with them."

With her tight suit skirt hiked up and her shoes tied around her neck, Ruth swam the river. When she reached the other side, exhausted and wringing wet, family members of the group detained at the border in East Germany beat her badly, assuming she was to blame for the detention of their relatives. She escaped into the woods and spent her first night of freedom in a barn. She had some money from the black marketeering but had to hitchhike to Munich. "I slept on pool tables and park benches. I was hoping to get a job in Munich because it was the start of the Oktoberfest. In West Germany it was the law that if you don't have a job, you cannot find a place to stay, and if you have a place to stay, you have to prove you have a job."

There were people in Munich that Ruth's mother had taken in as refugees. Ruth's mother had told her they would take her in now. "They took me in for two days, and then I heard a big argument between the husband and the wife that he was not too happy to have me there. I hitchhiked back to Neuhof [a district in Hof]." A woman and her husband, who had known Ruth and her mother since Ruth was small, took her in. Ruth then went to work for the Winterling Porcelain Factory, located in the two small towns of Kirchenlamitz and Marktleuthen.

Since Ruth was not yet eighteen, and a minor, she did not have work papers. The authorities wanted to send her back to East Germany or to

a refugee camp. "Then I met my first husband, he was a good man; he was working in [the] porcelain factory, and so I married when I was eighteen." Over the next eleven years, she worked her way up from making porcelain, the lowest and dirtiest job in the factory, to painting porcelain. Then Ruth's husband died of kidney disease, and she was a widow at twenty-nine.

Back in Plauen, her father worked at the only job he could get, as a "powder monkey," the man who set up the explosives in the uranium mine. "He died of colon and liver cancer because they didn't have any protective clothes. My mom got Alzheimer's, but she lived to be ninety-three." The rest of Ruth's family made the same decision her parents made, to stay in Germany. Ruth returned for her father's funeral in 1956.

Ruth moved to the city of Hof and found work as a waitress and then found a job on the American air force base as a waitress in the non-commissioned officers' club. There she met her next husband, the father of her daughter. When he was transferred back to the states, he urged her to join him and move to the United States. Ruth was reluctant: "I'd seen too many German girls coming back with three, four kids. I said, 'I'm not going to come until you get out of the military.' He had his years in and retired, and then I came." She moved to San Antonio and became an American citizen, but her husband became abusive and the marriage failed.

After the divorce, Ruth worked as a waitress in San Antonio and then worked at Shultz Nursery in Marion, Texas, located between Randolph Air Force Base and New Braunfels: "That's a big, big nursery. After a while, I thought, People always come and say 'We're going on vacation, will you take care of my plants?' So I start running around with a watering can to restaurants and office buildings and watering plants and replanting them. It became a business I called "Babysitting Your Plants." I had an herb farm and a nursery; I gave lectures about cooking with herbs and cutting down on salt."

It was while Ruth was tending the plants for a restaurant client that she met Don Abel, who would become her next husband. He came to the restaurant with a group of friends and always managed to be there when Ruth was on duty. Going through her divorce, Ruth soon began to rely on Don's help with bookkeeping, a chore she did not enjoy. The relationship blossomed, and Ruth and Don married. "Don ran the plant care in San Marcos, New Braunfels, and Seguin, and I had all San Antonio. We made good money."

It was Ruth's severe allergy to insect stings that changed their lives: "I got stung a few times, every time by bees or yellow jackets, and every time it got worse. One morning, I went out to water, and three yellow jackets went in my blouse and got me. I just remember trying to give myself a shot, and then I was out. I was in the ambulance, and the guy says, 'Mrs. Abel, Ruth, Ruth.' I say: 'Where am I?' A few days later, I woke up with a preacher praying over me. I'll never forget that. I heard a mumble, mumble, mumble, and I turned my head and I saw that white collar, and I looked up and said, 'Not yet.' And those faces started to laugh and I was gone again. I woke up in the [intensive-care unit]."

The doctor informed Don that a heart specialist, pulmonary specialist, and allergist had worked on Ruth and had determined that one more sting would prove fatal. He was advised to move with Ruth to a higher and drier climate. "I don't know how often he told everybody that Guadalupe Peak was already taken, so the next best thing was Fort Davis."

Ruth and Don sold their land and the greenhouse and bought land in Limpia Crossing. There were two houses available in Fort Davis, but with her menagerie of animals, Ruth did not want to live in town. All that was available in Limpia Crossing was a manufactured house. "The house was here, but there was nothing else. The house and the pump house, and two trees, and they were little. First we put in the fence because, when we moved, I had four dogs and nine cats in my car. All I needed was the band, because I was the clown and the rest was a circus."

Ruth has not been stung since the move: "Don't forget, San Antonio has higher moisture, and down there we had yellow jackets that are so much more aggressive than what we have here. They also had killer bees and fire ants. I got stung by fire ants and couldn't breathe anymore. Out here we have yellow jackets, and I'm careful about them."

Their original plan was to build a house after a few years, but by that time, Ruth no longer saw the point in building a house, she was content to live without a mortgage and build onto the existing house. "This place is very well built," she says. "It's solid here. Manufactured houses are warmer in the winter and cooler in the summer, plus Don put a lot of improvements in here. I said, No, why should I get into a mortgage and all the headaches with the people coming to build it, right?" Ruth has lived in Limpia Crossing for thirteen years and has watched the steady influx of people moving to the area. "Now when somebody says to me, 'Oh you live in Limpia Crossing with the millionaires,' I say, 'Yup, I live in a doublewide mansion!'"

With Don gone, Ruth is even more appreciative of the friends she has made in Limpia Crossing: "They are helpful if you need them, but they are not on your back. I respect other people's privacy. I don't go and visit, even though they were [like] Why don't you come over? That's Texas, isn't it? You respect others' privacy. But I try to be a good neighbor, and you cannot explain it to anybody else, that out here you don't have to constantly be on each other's porches to get help or give help. And I just love it."

When Ruth is asked what she misses from a larger city, she says: "Well, I'm too old now to miss too much. Mass transportation maybe, transportation to be able to come and go." She also finds it more difficult to access more than routine medical care, which requires a trip to Odessa. "I love it out here. I really do. That would be the only thing I really miss."

She is adamant that she has never missed a Walmart, and a visiting neighbor agrees: "What do you need a Walmart for? Tell me. Some people need it." Ruth explains why she has not regretted the limited shopping in the area: "I've never been a shopper. Never! First of all, there was never anything to shop for, and I always worked and took care of myself. When I came to my dad and said I need some money and said I wanted shoes, if there were shoes you could actually put on your feet, not made out of plastic, he said, 'Do you want them or do you need them?' Because what I made, I had to bring the money home. If I said, 'I really want it,' he said, 'Save up, work overtime. You have to go with the economy, buy some food, some food we can split.'"

Ruth's daughter lives in Maui, Hawaii. Ruth has no plans to move closer to her daughter now that she is widowed, although her daughter wants

Ruth is an accomplished weaver; she learned to weave at the Southwest School of Arts and Crafts in San Antonio, studying under Robert Hills. It is a skill that she has shared by teaching weaving classes in Alpine, but she has not done much weaving in the last two years. Don developed severe health problems that required Ruth's care; he died in 2009. Ruth is just now returning to her weaving: "We are planning now to get some women together after this week; they can crochet or knit or get on my weaving looms. We call it 'Stitch and Bitch.'"

her to. "Oh, she wants me to move, but there's too much water. If you go to Maui, first of all, it's overpopulated, too many tourists on top of the natives. And then you drive to the north. and you end up on water. You drive south, you end up on water. I mean, no matter where you drive, there's water. And I hate water, that big water. No, I love it out here."

Ruth lives in Limpia Crossing surrounded by her adopted animals. She now has one dog, Bonnie, that she adopted from the humane society, and four inside cats. There are nine outside cats she feeds from the boxes Don constructed to feed the animals. She has also dealt with the occasional mountain lion: "It was about three or four years ago. I came down to feed the cats, I had more cats then, and came around that barn and there was a lion eating on a deer and that time I always had a pistol on me because we had herds of javelinas, twenty or thirty down here.

I shot at it, and I almost got in hot water because you're not supposed to discharge weapons in Limpia Crossing."

At the time of this interview, Ruth could not imagine leaving her animals and her friends in Limpia Crossing, but now, a year later, she has had to consider moving. As time passes and the need for medical care becomes more important, it becomes more difficult to live in a sparsely populated area. She is considering moving back to San Antonio, but her life philosophy serves her well: "There are no hard times, there are interesting times; it depends what you make out of your life. My husband died, and I have my ups and downs since he died, but I have to go forward. I'm not going out and dance, but my life goes on, and the whole picture shifts. You know, you have to look at it from another way, you have to use another sidewalk to get towards the end, and that's the way it is. I'm easy."

The Reluctant Goodbye

★

THOMAS HOBBY

Thomas and Carol Hobby came to visit the Big Bend for the first time in 1991 with a fifth-wheel trailer. On their second trip in 1997, they came in a motor home and stopped overnight in Fort Davis at the state park. "We didn't know Fort Davis existed. That night we learned of the McDonald Observatory, and I am an amateur astronomer," Tom says. "We learned that Fort Davis is on a major bird migration route, and Carol is a birder. There are deer and javelina running in the park; wildlife was everywhere. Thirty days later, we owned five acres in Limpia Crossing and never made it to Big Bend National Park." After looking for a place to retire in several states for nearly four years, they found their home. Tom and Carol built in Limpia Crossing in 2000 and moved into their new home in 2001.

Tom grew up in a rural area outside of Tulsa, Oklahoma. Born in 1930, he is a product of his times. "A friend of mine who was a professor of psychology at Colorado University said that we're like computers, we are 'value programmed' in the first seventeen to twenty years of our life," Tom says. "The first part of my life was during the Depression Era and World War II. So I'm programmed with a lot of insecurity and conservative values from the Depression Era and the patriotic values of World War II. Even as school children, we bought the little 'savings' stamps and pasted them in a booklet until we had enough to buy a $25.00 savings bond to help the war effort."

During the Depression, Tom's father was fortunate to have a job, and since they lived on rural acreage with animals, they were able to raise everything they ate. When Tom's father died in 1939, times became hard for the family he left behind. It was then Tom realized the advantage of a small, rural, close-knit community. "My Mom and brother and I ran out of resources, and the community gave us what they call a 'pounding.' A pounding is when friends go throughout the community and say the Hobbys are out of food and everybody donates a pound of something," Tom says.

On that day, Tom and his brother and mother were invited out separately for the day. When they were taken back home, they were greeted with a welcome sight. "We go back to our house, and there was food all over the place, you never saw so much food in your life. We had participated in these so many, many times during the Depression, but we until now, we were always on the giving end," Tom says. "There were about fifteen people in the kitchen cooking supper, and it was just a banquet. That's the kind of community we were raised in, part of those values. It is similar to the ones that attracted us to the small rural town of Fort Davis."

Another lesson in values that programmed his life happened while he was a teenager. When Tom began his senior year in high school, his mother passed away. He lived in the YMCA in Tulsa until he could graduate. Customarily at graduation, the girls would wear white dresses under their gowns, and the boys would wear suits. Tom did not own a suit or even a pair of jeans; he wore overalls. "Just before graduation, Mr. Godown, vice president

of the Public Service Company of Oklahoma, who had been a Mason with my Dad many years before, came to the high school, picked me up, and took me to Harrington's, the nicest men's store in Tulsa. He bought me everything from the skin out: underwear, socks, shoes, suit, and tie, even a hat. None of these things I'd ever owned before," Tom says. "We were in the car, and he's taking me back to the YMCA with all of this and I'm embarrassed at his generosity. I said 'Mr. Godown, I'll never be able to repay you.' He said: 'Of course not, but some day you'll be able to help someone else, and when you do, you will have passed the gift on.'" Tom later became a Mason, and he has been committed to passing that gift along throughout his life.

Tom began his military career when he was drafted at the beginning of the Korean War. He rose rapidly in the enlisted ranks and was then given a commission. He was a first lieutenant when the war ended. With nothing to go home to, he chose to make the military a career. He served two tours in the Pentagon, was a battalion commander during the Vietnam war, and retired as a full colonel in 1979.

While stationed at Fort Meade, Maryland, he met his wife Carol. She was hired as a temporary replacement for his stenographer, who had been transferred. It wasn't until the following spring, during Secretary's Week, that Tom really noticed Carol. "That was when they were wearing loose sweaters and long skirts. The general and all the other colonels were going to attend, so jokingly I told her to buy a sexy dress so the general would notice her and the rest of us could enjoy lunch," Tom says. "Today, I would probably be accused of sexual harassment for saying that. She showed up in a knockout dress; we all noticed her." On

their first date, both made it clear they would never remarry. One year into the relationship, Carol changed her mind, and two years later they married. They will celebrate their thirty-fifth anniversary in 2012.

After Tom retired from the army, he worked as a management consultant in Atlanta, Georgia. When he and Carol sold their home, three cars, and most of their possessions, they bought a thirty-eight-foot yawl sailing vessel, making the

ocean their home for the next two years. It was during this experience that Tom found a new calling. "We visited many small churches along the East Coast and in the islands that could not afford a minister. I told Carol that as a retired army officer, I could afford to pastor small churches. It was something I had considered previously but rejected. We sold the yawl, and I went to seminary," Tom says.

Tom was ordained in the Christian Church

(Disciples of Christ), established by two Scottish Presbyterian missionaries to the United States in 1730. It split during the Civil War, with the Southern division becoming the Church of Christ, and Tom was ordained in this division. "I pastored small churches in Oklahoma and Colorado full-time for fifteen years. I made the mistake of taking a big church in Canon City, Colorado. It wore me out, and I retired. After retirement, I did 'interims' for several years for churches that were in between ministers."

When Tom and Carol moved to Limpia Crossing, Tom did not tell anyone he was an ordained minister. He knew from his experience in Colorado that people will treat a minister differently. Since Tom and Carol were retired, they did not want to be known by titles anymore. However, when he gave part of his seminary library to three local ministers, one of them, after promising secrecy, leaked the information that Tom was a minister. Eventually, Tom began doing "pulpit supply," preaching at four Methodist and two Presbyterian churches in nearby towns. "Full-time ministry is 24/7, pulpit supply is just on Sunday. It's the cream of ministry, and I enjoyed it," Tom says.

Tom and Carol are an integral part of Limpia Crossing, and Tom is a one-man welcoming committee to new residents. He greets new

homeowners with a bottle of wine and a map of nearby homes labeled with the neighbors' names.

Although Tom and Carol love living in the Big Bend, they have confronted the lack of medical and other facilities in this sparsely populated area, particularly as they have become older. They made the difficult decision to leave Limpia Crossing, their dear friends, and the area they love to move to Las Cruces, New Mexico. Tom is eighty-two and fourteen years older than Carol; he does not want to leave her alone in an isolated area if he predeceases her.

Tom and Carol have bought a home in the Las Cruces area, only thirty miles from El Paso. Las Cruces is a small city surrounded by mountains, home to New Mexico State University and the necessary medical facilities. Their home, a few miles outside Las Cruces, is in the foothills of the Organ Mountains. Their home in Limpia Crossing is now for sale, and until it sells, they plan to visit their friends whenever they can. Tom says, "We are moving to Las Cruces with mixed emotions because this is home, and we would really like to stay. All our core values are here. Personally, I'd like to die here—not that I want to die, but this is the place I'd like to stay forever."

On October 21, 2012, Tom Hobby passed away peacefully at his new home in Las Cruces, New Mexico.

FORT DAVIS

Most people have scant knowledge about the illustrious—and long—history of the area surrounding the far-west Texas community of Fort Davis or of the community itself. It seems very likely that early Paleo Indians lived in or traversed the Big Bend area soon after humans first came to the New World.

The area remained largely unsettled except for a few ranches and settlements along the Rio Grande until 1848, when Lieutenants William Whiting and William Smith traveled west from San Antonio and established the Whiting-Smith Route to El Paso, passing through the Davis Mountains. Limpia Creek and Wild Rose Pass were both named by Whiting; the creek was named for the word *limpia*, which is Spanish for "clear," and the pass was named for the Demaree rose, found only in the Davis Mountains.

The federally funded westward expansion of the mid-1800s was in response to the demand for transportation routes across Texas and was usually accomplished by military explorers, including Major Jefferson Van Horne and Lieutenant Francis T. Bryan. With the discovery of gold in California, there was a need for a route through the area. In 1849 Lieutenant Colonel Joseph E. Johnston founded a route through the Davis Mountains, which became the main route to California for the forty-niners. With the establishment of trails, settlers followed. In 1854, the U.S. War Department established the military post of Fort Davis—named for Jefferson Davis, then the U.S. secretary of war and later, and most famously, the president of the Confederacy—to protect the area and travelers. The location of Fort Davis was an important one because it was situated at the junction of two major trails, the San Antonio–El Paso Trail and the Chihuahua Trail, and a small settlement outside of the fort became a town with gambling halls, saloons, and businesses. Soon, the town of Fort Davis grew around the fort.

Cattle drives made of longhorns, some herds of nearly a thousand, came down the Butterfield Overland Trail, crossing the Pecos River at the famous Horsehead Crossing and through Wild Rose Pass and Limpia Canyon. Cattle ranchers came to the area during the 1880s, making the town a supply center for ranchers who were attracted to the sparsely populated area, with many escaping a fever epidemic ravaging the rest of the state.

When the fort closed in 1891, cattle ranching and tourism became the mainstays of the town

of Fort Davis. In the early 1900s, affluent Texas families, particularly those from the Gulf Coast, were drawn to the cooler temperatures and altitude of Fort Davis to escape the oppressive heat of summer in the rest of the state.

Fort Davis is the largest town in Jeff Davis County, one of only two; the other is Valentine, the only incorporated town in the county. In the 1880s, the Southern Pacific Railroad laid tracks east of El Paso and into the Big Bend, and towns grew around the railroad depots. The only two other towns in Jeff Davis County no longer exist: Chispa, established when the railroad came through, is now only a railroad siding, and Madera Springs, which was a resort destination in the 1920s. Over time, the springs dried up, and the town became known as the smallest town in Texas in 1970, with a population of two.

Fort Davis has the distinction of being the county seat of two counties. In 1871, Presidio County included part of what is now Jeff Davis and Brewster Counties, and Fort Davis was the county seat of Presidio County. When the railroad, which bypassed Fort Davis, came to nearby Marfa, many felt the county seat belonged in Marfa. A courthouse fire in Fort Davis had destroyed the original voting records from the county seat selection process, leading to disputes over the previous decision. Marfa prevailed and became the county seat in 1885. Those defeated in the second election joined forces to create a new county with Fort Davis—a thriving town with over two thousand residents, several churches, cotton gins, and a weekly newspaper—as the county seat. The Texas Legislature passed the act in March 1887, creating the new Jeff Davis County, and Fort Davis was once again a county seat.

Tourism to the area was boosted in 1932 when the McDonald Observatory of the University of Texas was built at the summit of Mount Locke. Scientists from Harvard took up residence in the Limpia Hotel for an extended time during the construction and initial operation.

The Davis Mountains State Park followed in

1934. Congress designated the Fort Davis National Historic Site in 1961, and its four hundred and sixty acres became part of the national park system in 1963. Twenty original structures of adobe and stone from the early days of Fort Davis were restored. Today, the site features extensive hiking trails, nearby campgrounds, and a visitor's center, with tours of the grounds and media presentations. Employees in historical dress conduct tours and give historic military demonstrations in the summer. Alpine's Chihuahuan Desert Research Institute operates an arboretum on three hundred acres close to Fort Davis, which also draws tourists. A well-known institution in Jeff Davis County is the Bloys Camp Meeting, established in 1890 by William Benjamin Bloys. This popular event is held annually in Skillman Grove, a few miles from Fort Davis.

Fort Davis is located 209 miles southeast of El Paso and 80 miles northeast of Presidio on Limpia Creek. Jeff Davis County is best known as the location of the Davis Mountains, called the "Texas Alps"; they are the second-highest mountain range in Texas and the highest entire range within the state. Mount Livermore has an elevation of over 8,000 feet, the fifth highest in Texas. Other Davis Mountain peaks are over 7,000 feet in elevation.

Although the population of Fort Davis has fluctuated, it has held steady at approximately twelve hundred residents over the past few decades. The town attracts families as well as retirees. The athletic events of Fort Davis High School, home of the Fort Davis Indians, are well attended by the townspeople. It is an active and involved community, and this was never more evident than when catastrophic fire raged through Fort Davis and much of the surrounding area in April 2011. Neighbors helped neighbors through the crisis, knowing they could rely on one another—not a common occurrence in a sprawling urban environment. There is a sense of pride, rightfully so, shared by the people of Fort Davis that their town is a wonderful place to live.

Fleeing the Fire of April 9, 2011

★

LUCINDA TWEEDY

On April 9, 2011, Lucinda Tweedy, the manager of the historic Limpia Hotel in Fort Davis, arose to a great day. The wind was blowing briskly from the south, but the temperature was mild and a welcome relief from the extreme winter, where the outside wind chill temperature plummeted as low as minus thirty-five degrees. The extended sub-freezing weather resulted in broken pipes throughout the Limpia Hotel complex, and the staff spent many hours trying to stop the leaks in the historic plumbing.

It was the annual Hammerfest bicycle race weekend in Fort Davis, so the hotel was fully booked with bicyclists from all over the state. Lucinda was working the front desk with her staff all day, and everything was efficiently planned and running smoothly. The staff posted the results of the previous day's races, and the riders were already well along the scenic seventy-five mile loop. No broken pipes to worry about today.

Lucinda has lived in Fort Davis for about six years. Her parents loved the Big Bend and spent their honeymoon here. In 1951, they answered a newspaper ad and rented the old fort grounds in Fort Davis. As Lucinda recalls, "That's when the fort was private property. And so they rented the fort and started renovations and founded the Fort

Davis Historical Society and got things running." After the two oldest children were born in Marfa, the family relocated to western Pennsylvania. Lucinda was born in Geneva, Pennsylvania, about sixty miles east of Pittsburgh. Her parents came back to Fort Davis in retirement and bought the Stone Village Motel in 1978. "We had been coming back and forth to Fort Davis all of our lives," Lucinda says. "Mother was in Mexico with Aunt Flora, a very good family friend from Fort Davis, and she came back through Fort Davis to drop Aunt Flora off and called Daddy and said, 'Honey, I just bought a motel.' Daddy said, 'Okay!' So they moved down here that summer."

As an adult, Lucinda has moved around, enjoying new places and meeting new people. For a time, Lucinda lived in San Diego but left to attend Humboldt State University in northern California, then lived in San Francisco for eighteen years. "I always said, 'Why go where there's family? I might as well go where I can meet all sorts of new people.'"

After her mother's death in 1984, her father became ill, so she returned to take care of him until his death. "Daddy's health was starting to fail, and I was at a crossroads where it was a really good time for me to make a change," Lucinda says.

"I just decided I'd move down here and spend the rest of Daddy's life with him; which I did. The day that daddy had his stroke, my sister from Chicago and her family were already coming down here for vacation. They arrived and were able to see Daddy alive for the last couple of days. It was good to be back."

Around midafternoon of April 9, Lucinda began to see smoke or haze toward Marfa, only twenty-five miles to the south. Curious, she began streaming the Marfa public radio station on the Internet and learned that a fire had started at an old abandoned rock house about two or three miles west of town on U.S. Hwy 90.

By now the winds had increased to gale force, gusting to seventy miles per hour. Guests were stopping by the front desk to inquire about conditions. "I'd say that I thought everything was really okay. They were not saying anything about evacuations on the radio," Lucinda recalls. Then, about 4:30 p.m., she heard that they were evacuating Mano Prieto, an outlying development eight miles south of Fort Davis. The fire was headed straight toward town.

Lucinda had planned to have drinks that evening at Sutler's Club with a writer friend who was in town, but the smoke was so thick that guests began coming to the desk to turn in their keys

219

and leave. "At that point," Lucinda remembered, "Marfa Public Radio was knocked out of service, and so I had no other way to know where the fire was or what was going on. I got hold of Joe Duncan, my brother-in-law and the owner of the Limpia Hotel, who was up at his mountain house, and I said, 'Joe, I think something really serious is starting to happen here. We seriously need to get into some sort of evacuation plan.'"

Joe quickly drove back to Fort Davis and arrived in about twenty minutes. Joe's wife Lanna, Lucinda's sister, drove out to Mano Prieto to check on the fire. "She called and said, 'Lucinda, I think everything is fine. It's just getting to Mano Prieto but I think everything is okay.'" Although the report set her mind at ease, Lucinda advised the guests coming into the lobby: "Everyone sort of has to take care of themselves and listen to what's going on. If you feel you will be safer leaving, then please, by all means do so."

Once Marfa Public Radio went off the air, there was no information available. "We didn't know where the fire was," Lucinda explains. Diane, the Limpia gift shop manager, came in and said, "I've heard that Fort Davis is being evacuated." There was a line of people lined up at the desk to check out, but since the smoke was increasing outside, the guests were told just to evacuate and the refunds would be sorted out the next week. "You couldn't even breathe it was so full of smoke inside by then," Lucinda says. "People were in and out of the doors constantly, bringing in the smoke from outside. There was an orange-pinkish glow out there. Very weird."

It never dawned on Lucinda that the fire would get to the hotel. She began to worry about Molly, her cat. "Everybody was just so in the dark about what was really going on. I realized the smoke was so thick outside and the color so fiery that there was definitely a big problem. I just ran out of the lobby door." Before she reached her car, she saw her friend Kay Crum running hysterically down the street. Five or six houses were on fire on Front Street, and one of them was hers. Since she was not listening to radio or television, she did not know about the fire until she smelled smoke and saw the flames. Kay was able to take two computers and her two dogs before she drove through the fire on her driveway. "I gave her a quick hug and ran to my car," Lucinda recalls. "I am so close to my house I could get there in a heartbeat. I didn't look to the side of me or look up. I just focused on the road and getting there."

Lucinda had driven only a short distance when she saw a car weaving around in front of her. She soon realized it was a police officer blocking her way. "I pulled to the side and he said, 'Ma'am, you can't go that way.' I said, 'Officer, I'm sorry but I have to. My home is right there'—you could see my house from where we were—'I have to get to my house and get my cat.' He said, 'I can't let you.' I said, 'I have to, I'm going.' He said, 'Okay. Go get your cat and then get the hell out of there.'"

At that point Lucinda had no idea the fire was that close. She ran in the house to save Molly, but the cat was frightened and hid under the bed. "I can't get her out from underneath the bed, but I know I've got to get out of here, and I finally got a broomstick, and I just swatted her out from under the bed and grabbed her, grabbed her kitty litter and her food, and we jumped in the car. I wasn't even in the house a minute and a half, I bet."

In that short time, the smoke was so thick Lucinda could not see the front of her car. She began driving back to the hotel. By the time she reached her neighbor's driveway, a wall of flames confronted her nearly four feet high. Visibility was zero. "I'm not a movie watcher, but I've heard that they do this kind of thing in the movies where you can drive through flames if you go through it fast," Lucinda says. "So Molly was sitting on top of the passenger seat, and I just said, 'Okay Molly, I've heard that they do it in the movies.' I just floored it." After Lucinda cleared the flames, she began inching her way down the road, not sure if emergency vehicles were in her path. "My knees were like jelly. I've never in my life had adrenaline going like that," she says.

When Lucinda reached the Limpia, Joe Duncan and she began checking that everyone had evacuated the hotel. They were unable to check the rental houses up the street from the hotel, but they were sure everyone had left. Lucinda had just checked on the people who rented the carriage house two hours before the fire. When radio contact was lost, they came to the hotel and checked out. That turned out to be a wise decision because the carriage house burned to the ground that night.

When the Limpia was evacuated, a sign was posted on the unlocked front door welcoming emergency workers to stay there to rest. "After we made sure everyone was gone from the properties," Lucinda recalls, "Lanna and I got into our cars. She had two dogs and a cat, and her rig was dubbed Noah's Ark for days because she wouldn't even go shopping without taking her animals with her because she was so afraid." At this point, the emergency workers were diverting all vehicles toward Balmorhea. Lucinda waited for Lanna to find Joe so they could leave town together. The smoke was thick, the wind was howling, and embers were flying through the air.

"There was a lot of sound from the wind," Lucinda remembers, "but what is funny is that I never heard a siren, even with so many police cars around. I must have just blocked it out. Others later said that they were blaring everywhere. We headed out of town toward Balmorhea to spend the night in Van Horn at the El Capitan Hotel. After we passed through Balmorhea, they stopped the evacuation going through that way because the fire was approaching."

When Lucinda and Molly finally arrived in Van Horn that night, dozens of people were there with their dogs and cats. Joe and Lanna, the owners of El Capitan, opened up the rooms to all the evacuees. After things calmed down a bit, Lucinda, Lanna, Joe, and the other evacuees gathered in the lobby for cocktails.

Joe was talking to some friends from Fort Davis when he looked over along the wall and noticed ten or twelve bulky pillowcases lined up. "He didn't think much of it," Lucinda says, "but suddenly, he caught a glimpse out of the corner of his eye of one of the pillowcases hopping around. He wondered, 'What in the world is that?' Each pillowcase contained a live chicken saved from the fire. Oh my God, it was classic! So in the dining room we had chickens. We had dogs, we had cats. My goodness, if the Health Department would have come in, they would have had a cow," Lucinda remembers.

The next day, Lucinda and Molly headed back to see what remained of the town. Twenty-four houses had burned. The fire continued burning until it consumed some 317,000 acres, making it the largest prairie fire in the history of Texas. "It was creepy," Lucinda says. "We were coming up through the Bloys Camp and past Davis Mountain Resort coming into town; I came up over this rise, and everything was just black and smoky. And

I didn't want to look too much, because I knew there would be animals out there. It was really hard. It was scary, because we really didn't know what we were coming back to."

Someone had sent Lanna pictures of the carriage house burning, "So we knew the carriage house was gone. We had heard that my house was still standing, but because of it being a hundred-year-old or more adobe house, I didn't know if that meant it was just a shell standing or whether it was still intact."

As Lucinda neared Fort Davis, it was black and smoky. Although nothing was actively burning, hot spots could be seen where smoke was rising from the ground. The town looked nearly normal, but was very quiet. "We drove to Lanna and Joe's house and dropped off the animals, and then we all got in her car. We wanted to just slowly drive around, and we wanted to be together, because we didn't know what . . . we just wanted to be together." When they arrived at Lucinda's house, they found it was completely intact and not even very smoky. Lucinda heard that morning that the shed behind her house was destroyed in the fire. Their family history was in the shed, all the photographs of their parents from their child-hoods and their wedding. "That was where all my history was stored. Photographs, papers, the only thing that survived were some christening cups and my Dad's Purple Heart."

Lucinda also lost a small box of her personal things that contained her kindergarten scrapbook and a newspaper clipping of when she was saved from drowning: "I had fallen into the stream when I was two years old during the spring floods," she explains, "and they found me about half a mile downstream with my foot caught on a root, and I was unconscious because I had been in the water. I was saved, and I had that newspaper from that. There were big, black, bold headlines of the newspaper reading, 'Rector Woman Saves Child from Death.'" Lucinda also lost love letters from the love of her life.

The destruction was random and seemed capricious. The ever-changing wind moved the flames in random patterns. Her barn, over one hundred years old and very unstable, survived. "Everything was black up until the other side of my driveway. The whole field was completely black. Why didn't that thing burn? That's unbelievable! My Volkswagen bus would have gone up, and then the house. The wind was so erratic that day and shifting. And I really think that's the only reason my house was saved. It had to have shifted just the time when the flames were coming."

Lucinda is moving from Fort Davis. Although things have returned to normal in many ways, there is still a lot of recovery to be done. The costs of the fire were devastating, not only financially but also, and perhaps mostly, in emotional terms. The ranchers who represent the backbone of the area lost cattle that burned to death, and much of the value of the remaining stock had to be sold at a loss because the grass also burned. Miles of fencing costing close to $15,000 per mile had to be replaced. Tourists, believing nothing remains but burned countryside, have not returned. Lucinda lost her job as manager of the hotel since it was sold, and the new owners have taken over the operation.

Lucinda is not distressed, acknowledging that it is time for her to move on again. The wanderlust is back. "I have always done this," she says. "I have always picked up and moved somewhere else. You know, I just get itchy feet, and I just go." She is drawn to New England, where she will have a definite four seasons in the year. She would also like to be closer to a larger town. Most important, it is time for new adventures. "When I was eleven years old," she recalls, "we had this beautiful house in the mountains in western Pennsylvania with this white picket fence the whole way round it, but I was this wannabe hippie. My eldest sister in the sixties would jump in the love bus with her sweethearts, and I would want to go in that bus! During all weekend long of Woodstock I paced that white picket fence. I wanted to know why couldn't I go there, it was only one state away."

The Entrepreneurs

★

JOE AND
LANNA DUNCAN

The one certainty in teenager Joe Duncan's life was that he was never going to live in Fort Davis after high school graduation: "I left. I could hardly wait to get away from here," he says. During high school and summers while he attended the University of North Texas, Joe could be found helping out in the Hotel Limpia dining room. His parents owned the hotel. "I would come home for the holidays, for spring break and Christmas, and I would wash dishes and wait tables, and all my friends would go skiing and have a good time," Joe remembers. "When you're that age you want to stay up all night and sleep all morning; that didn't work. We used to serve breakfast, and I was the fry cook most of the time. So I decided [that] whenever I graduate, I'm never, ever coming back to Fort Davis."

Both of Joe's great-grandfathers Duncan and McCutcheon came to the area in the 1880s from the Texas Hill Country. When the railroad came to the Big Bend, cattle shipping began and attracted ranchers to the area. They established their very large ranches and raised families. Joe's father J. C. and his mother Isabelle married and continued the family ranching tradition until the devastating seven-year drought of the 1950s.

J. C. and Isabelle moved to town, and J. C.

decided he did not want to ranch anymore. "My father bought the Hotel Limpia in 1955, I wasn't even born then, and he felt like tourism was the future here, not ranching. Everybody thought he was crazy, that that might be something viable for the future."

J. C. bought the hotel shortly after a fire in August 1953 nearly destroyed the top floor—and the tourist trade that he anticipated didn't happen. So he remodeled the ground floor and turned the second floor into apartments. He leased the hotel to Harvard University. "They were looking for headquarters for their West Texas radio astronomy headquarters, so he leased

the hotel to Harvard for twenty-five years. The ground floor was used as office space, and he reconfigured the second floor as apartments for their astronomers, and that was really the best use of the building in the fifties and 1960s." When the lease was up, J. C. remodeled the building again, restoring it to a working hotel since tourism was beginning to have an impact on the economy of Fort Davis. A historic hotel in downtown Fort Davis drew visitors.

Joe's wife Lanna is Lucinda Tweedy's sister, and they are part of a West Texas ranching family as well. The Tweedy Ranch is located in Tom Green County, where San Angelo is the county seat. Joe and Lanna's parents became friends in the 1950s when her parents came to Fort Davis on their honeymoon: "They liked it so much they stayed and leased the fort, before the fort was a National Historic Site. They lived out on the fort grounds and tried to get a tourism thing going out there. But they were young, they were in their twenties, and he quickly found they couldn't make a living out here, but our parents became good friends," Joe says. Lanna's parents moved to Pennsylvania but continued to visit Fort Davis, and the families remained close. Joe and Lanna married after Joe graduated with a business degree from the University of North Texas, and they moved to Dallas.

Until 1990, Joe worked in commercial real estate, and Lanna was a counselor in the Highland Park schools in Dallas. Joe's father passed away in 1982, and the family soon sold the Limpia. "But three years later, [we] got the property back in foreclosure. We arranged a buyer again in the summer of '90, and we were going to get rid of it once and for all, and I'm helping my mother get rid of it, and my brother was involved, and basically we were giving it away again," he says. Joe and Lanna came out that summer to visit Joe's mother and Lanna's parents, who had retired to Fort Davis, and to attend the annual Bloys Camp Meeting. The friends who came with them from Dallas could not understand why they would not want to buy back the hotel and move to Fort Davis to run it again.

On the return trip to Dallas, the friends persuaded them to consider not selling the hotel to an outsider. "We got back, and we called my brother, who was in charge of the family business, he lived in Dallas, too. We said we want to buy it, don't sell it; we want to buy it from the family," Joe says. "He said 'No, you all are set up in Dallas,

you have good jobs, we'll sell to anybody but you all. Are you crazy?' We said 'Well, maybe we are, but we really have thought about this, and we want to buy it.'"

After six weeks, Joe's brother relented, and Joe and Lanna bought the hotel on New Year's Eve 1990. "We drove out in our car on New Year's Eve and got here about midnight and came in the front door of the hotel and looked at it and asked each other, What have we done? Our house sold immediately in Dallas, so we were homeless at Christmas," Joe says. "We had three employees: a front desk clerk that held things together and two housekeepers."

Lanna was still under contract to the Highland Park schools, so they came to Fort Davis every two weeks during the spring of 1991. When they made the permanent move in June, Joe's adolescent dread of washing dishes, cooking, and waiting on tables was a fact of life for him again. These chores were in addition to the extensive refurbishing and remodeling the old hotel required. "We were painting in the daytime, cooking at night, remodeling in between meals. She would call over, I would drop the paint brush over there, and she'd say there's an order up over here, so I'd come over and cook and put the order out, go back, and we would paint," Joe says.

They persevered and were able to get the hotel fully functional and successful enough in the first year to buy back the annex building behind the hotel, originally owned by Joe's father and converted to apartments in the 1980s and early 1990s. This gave the Limpia a building of suites behind the main hotel that offered larger rooms with kitchens.

In the midst of remodeling and running the hotel, Lanna discovered she was pregnant. This prompted their move out of the hotel into Joe's grandmother's house, which they purchased from the estate. Although the pregnancy ended in miscarriage, they decided to have a child. The birth of their son prompted a reevaluation of their life: "We've already moved out of the hotel, but we needed to do that to get away from the business, we needed to get a real life, and so that helped us become a little more grounded," Joe says. "I think we would have burned out and gone back to Dallas in three or four years at the most if we hadn't done that." Their son began attending a film-and-arts boarding school in California, established by the University of Southern California Film Department, during his junior year in high school after attending Fort Davis High School through his sophomore year. Students from this school have competed at the Sundance Film Festival. He is considering coming back to Austin to attend the University of Texas Film School, ranked third in the nation.

Joe and Lanna acquired the historic Hotel Paisano in Marfa in 2000 under very unusual circumstances. The hotel, well known as the residence of the cast of the movie *Giant*, had steadily deteriorated over the years. It was a time-share property by the 1980s, so nearly eight hundred people had time-share ownership in the derelict property. Much of the hotel was boarded up, and the hotel was in foreclosure. All the time-share investors had to be contacted because the hotel was abandoned, a process that took six years.

The hotel sale was to take place on the courthouse steps in Marfa. This event had attracted attention, even in the *Wall Street Journal*. Joe suggested that they should go to the sale to congratulate the new owners and welcome them to the area. The odds were on Charles Tate from Dallas, one of the owners of the Texas Rangers, to become the new owner of the Paisano. On the way to the sale, Lanna suggested that they should bid on the property. Joe said that this certainly was not something to do casually on a Tuesday morning. The atmosphere was party-like at the courthouse, with coffee and pastries and a crowd of nearly two hundred people. Tate was there with his architect and his wife, but a few minutes before the auction began, he crossed his name off the bidding list. When Lanna became aware of this—and that there was only one other person on the list, an agent from Florida bidding on behalf of a client—she urged Joe to bid. "The opening bid was $158,500. That was the amount of the taxes owing on the building, and I said, 'Okay, but we're not bidding, we've not seen the building, please Lanna, do not make a fool of us in front of everybody.'"

The auctioneer started with the $158,500 bid; no one bid, and no one raised. After one more raise, Joe and Lanna placed their bid and bought the property for $185,000. "We got our financing together, and on the day after the required six-month waiting period, it was ours," Joe says.

They renovated seventeen rooms and opened for business on Thanksgiving weekend. All the rooms were booked. The renovations were done a section at a time. The Paisano is now a very popular destination hotel in Marfa.

Joe and Lanna expanded their Fort Davis business by purchasing several old historic homes in town and renting them out as cottages as part of the Limpia Hotel. They bought an old tourist court in Fort Davis, named it Stone Village, and remodeled it. Lanna opened a whole foods market with a delicatessen and bakery, offering another choice besides the Thriftway grocery store.

Renowned Southwest architect Henry Trost of El Paso, who built the Paisano, also built four other hotels in west Texas and eastern New Mexico, in addition to over five hundred buildings in the Southwest. Joe and Lanna purchased El Capitan Hotel, one of Trost's hotels, in Van Horn, Texas. "When the interstate came through in the sixties, it became derelict, and it was off the beaten path, and so the bank bought it, the Van Horn State Bank, so it's been the home of Van Horn State Bank since '73. We bought it from the bank and turned it back into a hotel," Joe says. "When the bank bought it, they turned it into an office building, they took all of the bathrooms out of it, so we've built fifty-four bathrooms, with the same style tile and fixtures as the 1930 original work, redone all the electrical, redone all the plumbing, and put in an elevator."

They found that Van Horn has thousands of cars and trucks passing through town daily, and three hundred of those stop for the night. They hope that by advertising they can capture 10 percent of that market. The restaurant and bar at El Capitan are scheduled to open in a few weeks.

Their businesses continue to flourish, and they have created a niche for themselves in the Big Bend. "We're different from the rest of West Texas in that we have a good little economy. We've created a market and a job base for ourselves here, and it's been good. We're in our twentieth year this year; we said we'd do it for three years. We're getting a little worn down, but we'll see."

Since the interview, Joe and Lanna have sold the Hotel Limpia but still own El Capitan and the Paisano. They continue to maintain roots in the community and come to Fort Davis often.

The Rambling Boy

★

LONN AND
DEDIE TAYLOR

When Lonn Taylor's father brought him out to the Big Bend on a highway inspection job, it was summer, and Lonn was out of school. "I just fell in love with this volcanic landscape; I had never seen anything like it in my life. I have remembered it since then."

Decades later, Lonn and his wife Dedie were contemplating retirement. Lonn went to Sul Ross State in Alpine on business and drove through Fort Davis on his way to Midland. "I stopped at the drugstore for breakfast, and it was a beautiful spring morning very much like today, and I went to the pay phone in the drugstore and called Dedie and said, 'Dedie, just sell the apartment, quit your job, and get down here, this is the place,'" he remembers.

Lonn is a historian and a prolific writer. He found himself in print at the age of fifteen. "I was a footnote in the second edition of C. L. Sonnichsen's *I'll Die before I'll Run* because, in the first edition, one of the chapters in that book is about my grandmother's cousins, about the Border-Wall feud; my grandmother was a Border," Lonn says. "He got some fact messed up about the Border family, and so, you know, being fifteen, fourteen I guess at the time, I sat down and wrote him a note and said you have this wrong, and when that second edition came out, there was a footnote in there that says 'Lonn Taylor of Manila, P.I., set me straight about the Border family,' and he wrote me a very nice letter, and he must have been able to tell from my handwriting that I was a little kid."

Lonn, much in demand as a speaker on a variety of historical subjects, has published many books. Most recently, *Texas Furniture: The Cabinetmakers and Their Work, 1840–1880* (University of Texas Press, 1975), co-written with David B. Warren, will be re-released in a second edition, and *Texas, My Texas: Musings of the Rambling Boy*, a collection of his very popular column "The Rambling Boy," appearing weekly in the *Big Bend Sentinel*, was published by Texas Christian University Press in the spring of 2012.

Although Lonn was born in Spartanburg, South Carolina, his family always considered themselves Texans. "Jimmy Byrnes, who was the head of Franklin Roosevelt's Office of Economic Stabilization and was from Spartanburg, moved all the federal offices in the South to Spartanburg, South Carolina to rescue his hometown from the Depression, so that's how my parents happened to be living in Spartanburg when I was born," he explains. His father was born in Fort Worth, and his grandmothers from both sides of the family

lived there, so Lonn's family considered Fort Worth their hometown, and the family spent their vacations there.

Lonn and Dedie met while working in Washington, D.C. Lonn worked at the Smithsonian and lived in Washington for eighteen years. Dedie retired from the *Chronicle of Higher Education* as senior editor, her career for thirty-two years. They both knew they did not want to continue to live in Washington when they retired. "When we started talking about retirement, we first thought about retiring to Dedie's hometown, which was Astoria, Oregon, which is also an incredibly beautiful place right at the mouth of the Columbia River," he says. "But Dedie remembered that it once rained sixty-three days and sixty-three nights without stopping when she was in high school, and we decided that might not be too attractive."

They began spending extended periods of time in the Big Bend, first staying at the Gage Hotel in Marathon, then the Chisos Lodge in the national park. They went by rowboat across the river to Mexico, escorted by Enrique Madrid. The next year they came for a two-week stay at the Limpia Hotel in Fort Davis and decided they would retire there. Lonn identified their reasons for picking Fort Davis. "What impressed me about the town was really three things: at the time the public library was in the jail, and they had a very, very good library, which included two of my books, so it was bound to be good, right?" he laughs. "They had an English literature cell, an American history cell, and an American literature cell, and each cell had a big easy chair and a lamp in it, and I could just see myself spending the afternoon sitting in one of those jail cells reading. So I thought that was a good sign."

"Then a friend, Larry Francell, took us over to meet the newspaper publisher Bob Dillard, who has a little two-room office on the town square. We went over there three times, and all three times there was nobody there, the door was unlocked," he says. Since they were coming from Washington, D.C., they regarded the unlocked door with amazement. "We lived at the time in downtown Washington, D.C. We were on the garden committee of our apartment building, and if you set a trowel down on the edge of the little strip of lawn and turned your back, it would be gone. So we were very impressed with the fact you could just leave all that equipment in an unlocked building," Lonn says.

Besides those two reasons, the most important one became evident when Lonn and Dedie visited Clay Miller's ranch. "He and his wife are very well-educated people, and they were so hospitable to us and so friendly and took us all over their ranch. We thought we really would like to live around people like this," Lonn remembers. "We discovered how nice everybody was, not that the people in Washington aren't nice, but they're all short tempered, they're all workaholics. Washington is a huge city, and it's gotten more and more congested. So that's how we decided to move to Fort Davis." In addition to those reasons, the temperate climate and sparse population were factors in the decision to make Fort Davis their home.

Dedie, born in Oregon, recognized after years of living in Washington what was missing. "What I missed was not water but the ability to see forever, and out here in the Big Bend you can stand on the ground and see forever. You don't have to look around over anything or around

231

anything, you could always see the sun and the sky, and that's the big draw to me," she says.

Lonn and Dedie agree that the people of the Big Bend are a more independent and self-reliant population. Familiar with the theory of Texas exceptionalism, they feel that the Big Bend may very well be one of the last outposts that attract a particular sort of person, attracted to the sparsely populated, small communities.

Lonn offers a historical perspective: "Historically, the first Anglo settlers that came out here, people in the 1870s and '80s, probably came because they didn't get along very well at home, they were individualists, and they still value individualism and then they attract people who are individualists, which is why I think the artists and the ranchers down in Marfa get along together so well," he observes.

They have also noticed the differences between the communities of Fort Davis, Alpine and Marfa. Lonn notes that all three rely on tourism: "I think Fort Davis is still, in many ways, a ranching community. There are still two or three big working ranches near Fort Davis, and every morning if you get up early enough you can see cowboys going to work with their saddles, horses, and trailers behind them."

Lonn continues: "Marfa has currently become an international art center, and it has attracted the kind of wealthy people, urbanites, who like to be around artists. There's two or three good restaurants and a good bookstore, and it's really a very cosmopolitan community." Alpine, the largest community of the three, is more difficult to characterize: "Alpine is a college town in some ways, although it's kind of a cow college, but it's got an academic population and a good library, and there's a certain amount of boosterism in

Alpine that you don't find in Fort Davis or Marfa, maybe just because it's bigger. It has a very active Chamber of Commerce, and it's a railroad town to a greater extent than Marfa; the train stops in Alpine, it doesn't stop in Marfa, that's part of it."

There is one common element among the three communities, Lonn notes. "One thing that is characteristic of all three towns is they're very sharply divided between the Anglo population and the Hispanic population."

Lonn refers to the history of the region, when soldiers and the contractors necessary for construction and the provision of food and building materials at Fort Davis, a military installation before it was a town, intermarried with the families relocated from Presidio del Norte (now Ojinaga, Chihuahua). "Discharged soldiers tended to marry Hispanic women. So the three oldest Hispanic families here in town are named Dutchover, Hartnett, and Webster. If you look at the census record for 1870 and 1880, you'll see that there was a lot of intermarriage between Anglo men—or to be more precise, I guess, Anglo and European men—because a number of the soldiers were Irish or German, and they took their discharges and married Hispanic women and had very large families," he says. "So there was historically a certain amount of intermarriage, but the children of those families tended to remain Roman Catholic and married other Roman Catholics, so the families became more and more Hispanicized in each generation."

Lonn explained the geographical divisions within the towns. "The bottom line is that all three towns had divisions. Here, the Mexican community was called Chihuahua, and it's over on the east side of town; and in Alpine it's south of the railroad tracks; and in Marfa it's called

'Sal si Puedes,' which means 'get out if you can,' and it's on the east side," he says. Although there were residential divisions, the realities of small-town life bring everyone together, whether through church, civic, or school functions or in helping neighbors through a difficult time.

"If you go to a Friday night football game in Fort Davis, everybody in town is there, and it doesn't matter what church they go to, it doesn't matter what race they are, it doesn't matter at

all, everybody is there," Lonn says. "It's six-man football and it's just stunning. At half-time the football players are in the band and the cheerleaders are in the band because there aren't enough kids to go around."

Dedie is also impressed with the children of Fort Davis, raised in a simpler environment than on the East Coast. "The children here, three-year-olds, speak in complete sentences and think it's their social duty to carry on a conversation with you if there's no adult around," she says. "And they all stand ramrod straight and look you right in the eye and say 'Yes ma'am, No ma'am,' and they never say 'like' or 'uh,' and there's never any of this running around and hiding behind their mothers." Dedie contrasts the behavior of the children of Fort Davis to children on the East Coast. "That happens all the time in the East. I also see the kids doing unsupervised play; I grew up with unsupervised play, and around here they do, too, and I think that's just a gift."

She has noticed that residents of Fort Davis tend to socialize with others in Fort Davis. "The focus of a lot of the socializing in town is through the churches in town and the school," she says.

Shortly after Lonn and Dedie moved to Fort Davis, they were able to participate in and see for themselves how the people of their new home came together as a community to help a family in distress. An elderly mother and her daughter, who suffered a brain injury, sold their home, planning to move away. They were not well loved in Fort Davis. "They were not popular in the community because they kept to themselves; they had been extremely rude to people who had gone to their house to solicit help for various good causes," Lonn explains. When it was discovered that the movers were coming in forty-eight hours and that nothing had been packed, a community call to action was issued. "In every church in town an announcement was made that these people needed help packing up. We don't go to church in town, we go to church in Marfa, but somebody put it on the e-mail that they needed help," Lonn says. "About twenty people got together the next morning, and Dedie was one of them, went to their house and packed everything, and it was

a huge house with a lot of stuff in it, packed up everything, got it all ready for the moving van."

Dedie recalls her early experience as a volunteer in her new town: "Sally Espy, the wife of a big rancher here, took it upon herself to be the coordinator for this effort, and through the course of the week we found several thousand dollars in cash in with the towels and in with handkerchiefs and in with underwear; nobody took any of that, it was all consolidated and given back. It was just amazing, and people worked their tails off, I was there for five days, everyday, and I wasn't the only one," she says. The people of Fort Davis stepped forward to help people who had not made themselves a part of the community, but they were there to help anyway, which is part of the experience of living in the Big Bend.

Typically, in a small town, everyone knows everyone else, and it is assumed that small towns are hotbeds of gossip. Lonn found a very different experience: "We go to church in Marfa, and most of the members of that church come from old ranching families, and you will never hear anyone say anything negative about anybody else. It's just an ethic. There's absolutely no gossip, no backbiting," he says. "I always think about Gene West, who was an old rancher and managed the Comb ranch, which is one of the bigger ranches near Marathon, for years and then had his own, his wife's families' ranch, and Gene was my first source on the history of the area. I would ask Gene about somebody I knew, somebody dead who I knew had a very bad reputation, and Gene would always say: 'Well he was kind of an interesting old boy, and maybe some people didn't like him, but I always got along with him.'"

Lonn has a favorite story of going on his daily

morning walk with Dedie; a car pulled up beside them. The driver asked if he was Lonn Taylor. Lonn says he was, and the man asked if Lonn would sign two books for him. Lonn, puzzled as to how the man recognized him, was told that the driver was directed to where Lonn and Dedie were walking down the street by several helpful townspeople. Lonn thinks that story sums up one of the delightful experiences of living in a small town.

Lonn and Dedie have lived in Fort Davis for nine years now and have never regretted making Fort Davis their home. Dedie observes that people who need to shop in a store and not by Internet will not be happy at the lack of those opportunities. They have embraced their community and are an integral part of Fort Davis.

Dedie gives the reasons she loves Fort Davis: "Being anywhere else for very long gives me claustrophobia. I love being in a city for a little while, but after a while, the traffic gets to me really fast depending on the city," she observes. "The number of people and not being able to see the sky makes me crazy. There's a point at which you've lived here long enough that you can't go stay anywhere else very long."

The Snake Man

★

BUZZ ROSS

The Rattlers and Reptile Museum in Fort Davis is on State Street off Highway 17, the main road through town. There is a large painting of a snake on the side of the building, no doubt giving first-time visitors arriving from transcontinental I-10 an uncomfortable feeling about the town they are about to enter. Next door to the museum is the stone house where owner Buzz Ross lives with his family. Across the street in front, the historic Fort Davis National Historic Site draws thousands of visitors each year.

The museum has a front room with a counter, and you will most likely see Buzz himself lounging in an easy chair. The large room in the back has all sorts of snakes, venomous and otherwise, along with Gila monsters and Mexican beaded lizards and other desert creatures in lighted glass boxes. The room itself is dimly lit; if you are afraid of snakes, particularly in enclosed areas, this could be your worst nightmare realized.

Buzz Ross was born in Essex, England, in 1944 during a buzz-bomb raid: "My mother was standing outside the air-raid shelter, and she ran down the stairs of the shelter, tripped, fell, and went into labor." No one but his wife Brendy calls him by his given name Jeffrey. "She decided that she liked Jeffrey better," he says. "She believes it has more class. I don't want class; I'm not the classy guy. I didn't know my name was Jeffery until I was in the third grade." At the age of seven months, Buzz and his family came to the United States.

His adult life is centered around reptiles and the creatures of the desert. Buzz has spent most of his adult life hunting snakes along the highways and back roads of Texas. He was the head of the Reptile Department at the Fort Worth Zoo. He began coming to the Big Bend in the 1960s to hunt snakes in his spare time. When Buzz began going to Terlingua in 1972, he was offered the opportunity to run river trips: "Ken Barnes was there, and he asks what am I doing tomorrow, and I said I don't know, why? And he said: 'Do you want to run a river trip?' and I said 'Yes, but what do I do?' He says, 'I'll put you in the river, and when you see me stand on the bank, get out.' I ran the Colorado Canyon, and I stayed there. I had a house in Fort Worth that didn't cost much, and all winter I'd work and pay up all my bills and come down to Terlingua and spend all summer running the river trips from 1972 to 1975."

Buzz had a compelling reason to move to Fort Davis: "The snakes got me here. That was the reason I came to Fort Davis, I had that feeling when I got here, it was like I never forgot Fort Davis, and at least once or twice a year I was here hunting snakes; I liked it here."

In 1979, Buzz was offered the opportunity to partner in a taxidermy business in Fort Davis. "When I moved out here July the second, I was sleeping in the motel room under a blanket with no mosquitoes and I thought I had died and gone to heaven because since May I'd had the air conditioner running 24/7 in Fort Worth. If I went back to Fort Worth in the summer, I would remember exactly why I left. When I'd come out

here snaking, as soon as I'd get back toward San Angelo, I could feel the humidity, and it just got worse and worse. I didn't notice it coming out, but going back when you went into the humidity it got really bad. I always wanted to live here and got the chance." Buzz bought out his partner in January 1981, and for the next three years he raised lizards to sell to pet shops and operated the taxidermy side of the business.

When there was less demand for taxidermy, Buzz converted the business to a snake museum: "Everybody said they would like to have a reptile building in Fort Davis. I always wanted to do this, and it was a transition; I was still doing taxidermy work, still had the freezers in here and stuff on the walls. I was building the cages all in the same building. It just evolved and the other evolved away, and I started in April of 1999, and I got it open by July." The busiest times at the museum are the summer months and during spring breaks, during the tourist season. It can be a struggle to hold on during the winter months.

Herpetologists have been a welcome source of income in smaller far West Texas communities during the summer months. The grey-banded king snake draws reptile searchers from across the globe. In 2007, the Texas State Legislature banned the hunting of snakes, as well as other high-desert reptiles. The ban was in effect and enforced by game wardens for four years. Then the ban was lifted during the 2011 legislative session. Snake hunters are now required to have a stamp from the Texas Parks and Wildlife Department and must wear reflective clothing. Searching can take place only on the side of the road, and no artificial light can be used. The lifting of the ban means Buzz can continue to legally search for snakes.

Fort Davis was a smaller place when Buzz moved to town. "They didn't speak to me for three years. I came in here with a beard, and after three years they decided I was going to stay. The town used to be run by ranchers and their families and the people at the state park and people at the Fort. Then somebody like me moved in, I was looked at like, what's this guy all about? In thirty-one years, people change. There's a lot of people here we don't even know anymore, the newcomers. Now, they wouldn't notice me."

Buzz made Fort Davis his permanent home when he was in his mid-thirties, and over time he has developed a reputation as a citizen who does not hesitate to say what he thinks about the future of his town. "There's the story of the tomato farm," Buzz recalls. "Everybody raised hell about that, and we had a big town meeting, and one of the owners was there explaining how much water they were going to take out of the ground, and it's all recycled water except for what actually evaporates out of the buildings. But all these people said they didn't want change here. I'd been here seventeen years at the time, and I stood up and said: 'All you people that are complaining didn't ask me if you could move here, and all of you have been here less than five years, and you want to change it for me.' And I sat down. I just used to stand up for everyone's rights and wouldn't let anyone get stepped on."

It was his outspoken reputation that nearly cost him the introduction to his future wife, Brendy, in the fall of 2005. They met at a local bar called Sherlock's. She was with a group of people, including some members of the Chamber of Commerce. "The lady in the Chamber said, 'You don't want to talk to him, he's a bad guy' because

I had raked the Chamber over the coals." Brendy had been through a difficult divorce and took her time getting to know Buzz. By December, the month of the Cowboy Christmas Ball, things changed. "She walked up to me, and she said, 'You're taking me to the Cowboy Christmas Ball tomorrow night.' I said yeah, okay, and she said, 'Can you dance?' and I said 'Oh, yeah!' So a two-step came on, and we two-stepped and had a great time. That was the beginning." Brendy is an accomplished singer and has performed the national anthem at the Fourth of July celebration in town. According to Buzz, "She sings Patsy Cline better than Patsy Cline." They married in 2006. Brendy's son lives with them and attends Fort Davis High School.

Buzz does not see dramatic changes coming to Fort Davis in the next ten years. Although the population has increased from eight hundred in the 1980s to over a thousand now, a 20 percent increase, two hundred additional citizens over that period of time is not a population boom. He sees the newcomers as equally divided between retirees and young families. "They'd be leaving town as soon as they got out of high school, but by the time they're thirty, they're trying to figure how to move back because they've gone out in the cities and found out what it's like. Then they want to raise their kids here," he says. Although the lack of specialized medical facilities keeps some retirees away, the reported life expectancy of Fort Davis residents is eight years more than the state average.

Buzz observes there are a lot of ninety-year-olds in Fort Davis and sees the lack of stress in everyday life as a reason for this. "Any job you have in the city is going to be stressful; there's the

stress driving to work, there's the stress coming home in the traffic, there's the stress of whatever happens at work, and most people have fairly boring regimented lives. You get up, shower, eat breakfast, go to work, drive, get to work, have a lunch break and a break, and it's the same thing every day. Nothing ever changes in their lives, and they do that for years. You can't do that your whole life and not put stress on your body."

Once a reporter from the *Houston Chronicle* interviewed Buzz for a story about the museum, and a photographer came from the newspaper to shoot pictures. While the photographer was there,

Buzz had a visitor. "A lady walks in and she was blind, she was from Fort Worth, and I told her I couldn't charge her, and she says, 'Yes you can, I can feel.' So I got a tarantula out, and he got the picture that was printed in the paper with the tarantula on her hand. Then I got a rattlesnake out and put it in a tube and let her feel it. He got to witness all that. They did a real good article, it got five pages in the *Houston Chronicle Texas Magazine*, front page, and five pages inside." That article has drawn tourists to the museum.

Although Buzz struggles during the winter months to survive, he has no intention of ever leaving. The snakes and reptiles, the temperate climate, the lack of mosquitos, and the people of Fort Davis have kept him in the Big Bend. "I'll probably never be a true resident of Fort Davis, I don't know. Once I walked up to one of the county commissioners, and I told him, 'You're getting old,' and the judge's secretary asked me, 'You looked in the mirror lately?' I said that was the point. You come into a place when you're thirty-five years old and then all of a sudden you're sixty-five, and you don't know what happened."

After thirty-one years in the same town, even among the independent and self-reliant residents of Fort Davis, he is indeed at home because he shares the love of the Big Bend with the people of the town. "If I could make it here my whole life and die of a heart attack that I could have been saved from if I was sitting in San Angelo, I wouldn't trade that. I'd rather be here."

One Step from Heaven

★

GREG AND MYRA MEADS

Gregory and Myra Meads have lived in Fort Davis, where he is the minister at the Fort Davis Church of Christ, for six years. He began his life-changing second career at the age of forty-eight. Greg was born in a very small rural area between Labadieville and Napoleonville, Louisiana. He served in the U.S. Air Force, stationed at Carswell Air Force Base outside Fort Worth. When he was discharged, he stayed in Fort Worth, where he met Myra, from Mount Pleasant.

"I was bettering myself at Tarrant County College," Myra remembers. "He sat in front of me, and he was just bragging, 'I'm just here to get my money.' He was fresh out of the air force. 'I have a house. I have a car, but I don't have much time because I have to be at work.' I thought, black man, house, car, job, I'll take this one! It took a little doing, but I did get him."

Myra attended church with her family on a regular basis. Her uncles were builders in Mount Pleasant and built the Methodist Church, the Church of Christ, and the Baptist Church. Myra says that Greg was a "CME Christian" at that time. Greg explains, "Yeah, Christmas, Mother's Day, and Easter. Those were the days when I usually went to church and she went sometimes, but I didn't." It was the birth of his granddaughter Jazmine that changed his attitude about his role in life.

"When I was in Louisiana, they raised me [telling me] 'You are Gregory Victor Meads,' that's why I use my whole name. I grew up with this idea that I was above everything; there was nothing or nobody greater than me. In fact I grew up and ended up with the attitude that the only person that I would admit that was (this was before I was a Christian) as good as me, possibly, maybe was Jesus Christ," Greg says. "I grew up with that attitude. That was the way I lived, and the most important thing in my life at the time was my job. My job came first and family second, because you've got to have a job to take care of your family."

Greg's career was in management at the post office, and he was not a well-liked manager. He did not understand why his employees would ask for sick leave since he never took any himself. "I was real focused on the job. The only thing I cared about was the job and that everybody knew the job; that was the most important thing. I told a person one time that was sick, 'I don't believe in sick leave, and if you're sick you're no use to me,

you're no use to your family, you might as well go home and die,'" he remembers.

The day Jazmine was born Greg left work and went to the hospital to see his brand-new granddaughter: "I was the first one to pick her up. I held her for hours and hours. That's the first time I understood there was something more important than me. So with my granddaughter I understood what pure love was, then I wanted to live another life," he says.

Greg usually would wait until Myra left with Jazmine for church before coming home from work on Sunday. One morning, he mistimed his arrival, and Jazmine, a toddler then, was fussing and crying, and when she was asked what was wrong, she said, "I want my papa to come to church with us." So Greg began attending church with his wife and granddaughter.

After attending church regularly for six months, Greg professed his faith and became a Christian. Church members started encouraging him to be a preacher. His mother-in-law Irene had another opinion, though, that she could not stand a "shade tree preacher" and that he should go to school to become a minister, which Greg did. He attended the Center for Christian Education, although he still resisted the idea of becoming a preacher. "In Louisiana, when I was little, people were telling me, 'You're going to be a preacher.' Being black, this was me saying, 'Every black person is a preacher or a teacher, and I'm not going to be either one. I'm going to make it in this world without being a teacher or a preacher.' That was my attitude, so I resisted. I made a deal with the Lord, and I said, 'Lord, I'm going to go to school part-time, I'm not going to go full-time, I'll preach on the side for you because my job is real important, and you really need me on that job, because you know we got some real sinners on that job.'"

For three years, Greg attended school part-time. Then he was at a point in the curriculum where he either had to attend full-time or repeat courses. And things were not going well on the job at the post office. Since he had become a Christian, the cynical, driven Greg was gone; his attitudes and manner were different, and employees who used to be his friends were not adjusting well to the change.

On his way to work, he would have conversations with God. During one conversation, he recalls he said, "'Lord, I thought you said if I served you, you would never leave me and never forsake me. Where are you Lord? Where are you?' The second time I said, 'Where are you?' an empty truck came out of the sky and landed on my car. I was on the freeway in the Dallas/Fort Worth area on I-20 going about sixty miles per hour early in the morning, and this empty truck went bam! right on the hood of my car! The only place you could have lived in that car was where I was sitting. I opened the door and my body was all twisted."

A truck had flipped over the overpass and landed on his truck. He prayed that when he pulled himself to the side of the road that he would see a familiar face. When he got to the side of the road, he saw a woman he knew from the post office, Rita Murray. Greg had lost his glasses in the accident and could not see well. Rita calmed Greg down and kept him from going into shock. When others arrived to help, Greg asked that Myra be called, but she wasn't at home. "Then Rita Murray told me, 'If you need me, call me. Here's my number,' and she stuck the number in my pocket. I looked at the paramedics

and looked back at Rita and said, 'You aren't Rita Murray are you?' I looked at the paramedics, and I looked back at her, and she was gone." Myra believes it was an angel sent to save Greg.

It was miraculous that Greg survived. The empty truck fell onto Greg's vehicle when a truck driver parked his truck on the top of Cedar Hill: "He was driving through from North Carolina and he parked his truck on the top of that hill. He was tired, and when he got out of his truck, it rolled on the side of the road in the embankment, rolled all the way to the bottom of the hill, and I was coming up the hill, and when it hit the ramp it went airborne and landed right on my car. When they were wheeling me into the ambulance, I said: 'Lord, I will do whatever you say. Whatever you want me to do, I will do.'"

Myra felt that was a strong message that Greg should return to school full-time. She had the ladies class at church praying that Greg would see the light. After six months of continuing to work at the post office, Greg came to Myra with his plan, which included giving up their house. "I was ready to give up the house, but I had to go home and tell Myra. I said, 'Myra, I'm going to quit the post office, and I'm going to go to school full-time.'" He fully expected Myra to object since he thought they would have to sell their home to finance this venture. He was surprised by her reaction: "She said, 'Praise the Lord!'"

They did not have to sell the house after all and were able to stay there until Greg graduated. Instead of quitting, he went on leave from the post office. It was a precarious existence, but Greg found that the friends he made in his new life as a Christian, and even those he had not treated well before, admired his transformation and were there to help. "They saw the difference in my

life, and it was those people who took care of us and enabled us to stay in our house. Nobody ever said, 'We are going to give you enough money to stay in school and pay your house bill and all that until you graduate.' Nobody ever said that, but every month those people that I mistreated and other people . . . I would go to the mailbox and there would be a check. If we needed a thousand dollars, there would be a thousand dollars."

Churches would pay ministerial students a hundred dollars per Sunday to come to their churches and assist in the services. One Sunday, Greg's check was forgotten; he did not mention this oversight. Soon, on a subsequent Sunday,

Greg was handed an envelope with a check. It was not for the missing hundred dollars but for a thousand. That small congregation would continue to make that donation at various times during the rest of Greg's schooling. His former employees from the post office would also send money. Greg remembers, "That's how I stayed in school full-time. The other people at the post office got me through and kept us going for three years. When I graduated from school, I retired from the post office."

Strangely, Greg was promoted at the post office while he was on leave. However, he would not have much retirement income because of his age and years of service. He was told that if he paid twelve thousand dollars into his retirement account, he would receive his full salary, but since they did not have the money to pay into the account, he would receive a much smaller retirement benefit; five hundred dollars per month would be all they would receive. Six months later, Greg received two letters in the mail the same day. One offered him the same opportunity to pay the shortage of twelve thousand dollars, which Greg and Myra still didn't have, but the second letter contained good news. While reviewing his retirement papers, the post office discovered that because of the many jobs he had held at the postal service, some of his pay increases had not been carried forward. Greg had been shorted $12,800. That same day, Greg and Myra paid the twelve-thousand-dollar shortfall into his retirement. "We ran down and paid those people," Myra remembers. "And then we went to the Big Bend!"

Greg and Myra had been visiting the Big Bend since 1983. A television commercial had aired in Dallas about Alpine, calling it "the heart of the Big Bend." Greg was intrigued and decided to take a vacation there. A coworker advised Greg that if he was going to the Big Bend, reservations were needed. "We made the reservations, but we didn't know where we were going. I was telling Myra, 'Okay, we are going to this resort place and don't you be dancing all night.' I didn't have a clue where we were going, and we got there in the middle of the night." They were both under the impression that they were going to a destination resort, with all the amenities. "We were going to this famous place, and there was going to be tons of people there. I am thinking I am going to Yellowstone or something. We got there in the middle of the night, and it was so dark! We ended

up in the Big Bend National Park. We stayed in the basin, and nobody was there to greet us or anything." There were no dancing halls there. They were wearing shorts and sandals, what they thought was appropriate attire. The first day they were there, they were told that a movie was being shown. It was how to survive in the Big Bend.

Myra thought she brought what they would need in a remote area: "I worked at Safeway. These guys would always come in and they'd be going hunting and they would always buy all this food and chips and soda and beer and candy. I was thinking: 'What kind of hunting are they going to do, it seemed like they were just going to eat a lot.' So when Greg said we were going to the Big Bend, I bought lots of soda and candy and chips and everything." Myra didn't bring water.

The scenery worked its magic on Greg and Myra; they both responded to the vast spaces. "I saw the splendor of the emptiness and the grandeur of the place. We started going once a year and then we would go twice a year," Greg says. "Then we would go every time we had extra money. He had to buy a Jeep, and we had to buy binoculars, and we had to buy hiking boots," Myra says. They enjoyed hiking and began going to other areas of the Big Bend, bringing Myra's mother and, years later, their grandchildren.

They stayed at Lajitas, Presidio, and Cavern Post. Finally, after six years of trips, they went to Alpine, the only place where Greg's brother-in-law could get his flat tire fixed. They decided that the next trip would be to Fort Davis. Before they made that trip, Greg became a Christian. "I stopped being one person overnight to being somebody different. I thought God was going to let all that junk I did in the past stay hidden." But Myra heard of his past indiscretions, and the week after Greg was baptized, she left. "I come home, and the house is empty. Myra was gone," Greg says. They reconciled, but it was a difficult six months. Greg drew on his faith to see him through by promising God that, even if he never saw Myra or his grandchildren or children again, he was committed to serving Him.

After Greg and Myra reconciled, they returned to visit in the Big Bend and stayed in Fort Davis. One of Greg's fellow classmates became a preacher in Fort Davis, and they became close to his family. "He was the preacher here, and they lived in this house, and in fact they built the house for them. So then we used to come here all the time to see them. That's how we ended up coming to Fort Davis all the time, and I would preach while I was here."

After graduation, Greg interviewed for jobs as a minister. He was only the second black person to graduate from his school. He was called to interview with a church in Meredosia, Illinois. "This old guy called me and said, 'Greg we're looking for a preacher, how about coming in and checking us out?' I could tell he was an Anglo, and I said, 'You do know I'm black, right?'" Since Greg is from Louisiana, he did not want to return to an area where he could encounter prejudice. "Even though I come from Louisiana, I hated Louisiana. I couldn't stand the bugs. I didn't like the sugarcane. In fact, when I was eighteen, I graduated on a Friday and I was in Texas that Monday, because I always wanted to come to Texas. For some reason or another that was just in my heart." Greg tried not to go, but every reason he thought up not to go, God removed that obstacle.

"Myra said they were thinking because we would be the first black people in this community,

maybe we would want to live outside the town. And Myra said, 'No, if we are going to be the preacher here, we are going to live in the community,'" Greg recalls.

It was an uphill battle to overcome the prejudice they encountered from some of the townspeople, but they persevered. Through their volunteer work with Meals on Wheels and their sickbed visits, even to those who opposed their arrival, they won over most of the opposition. The ice was broken when Greg and Myra had an open house for the small town in the house they rented. That house was infamous because the heirs of a reclusive resident, newly wealthy, built the house, but no one was allowed on the property. The whole town showed up because of their overwhelming curiosity about the interior. Greg and Myra stayed almost two years: "It's one of those things where God worked it out. It was time for me to leave Meredosia, because I was having a hard time at the church. I had this one old guy, the very old guy that had me come to Meredosia, ended up giving me the hardest time. I was trying to decide what to do, and I prayed and I prayed and I prayed about it. The whole town was upset and so mad at that guy."

Once the decision was made to leave, Greg took Myra to Fort Davis, and while he was back in Meredosia to pack, he heard from the minister in Alpine that Fort Davis did not have a Church of Christ minister, so Greg interviewed for the job and told them the truck was packed and he needed to tell the driver the destination. "So God worked it all out. I ended up right here."

Greg and Myra have an active life through the church and volunteer work. Jazmine, who is now at the University of Texas at Arlington, comes to stay with Greg and Myra every summer and during the holidays. She volunteers at the fort along with her grandparents.

Greg feels that the time in Meredosia was well spent: "We interacted with the community, we loved them, [and] they loved us. God arranged it, but while I was in Meredosia, God used that time to prepare me for being here. We are the only black couple in Jeff Davis County."

The Meadses have been welcomed into their community in Fort Davis. The sparse population means that people connect with one another out of necessity. "You have to speak. You have to speak to everybody. You wave at everybody, because you don't know when you are going to need that person. You could have a flat or they could have a flat. So everybody waves. You see everybody, they wave out here because everybody needs everybody. Nobody is better than anybody," Myra says.

That was the first lesson Greg had to learn in order to become a Christian and change his life: "When I came in 1983, I felt something, and I knew I would be back. I can't tell you why exactly. . . . The only way I can explain it is that I felt there was something here that was greater than me. I guess that's when, if I was able to hear God, I was able to hear him saying, 'You're not much. Look at what I made and compare yourself with all of this.' I didn't become a Christian until thirteen years later, but being here is when I got on the road. First I had to realize that there was something greater than Gregory Victor Meads."

Greg and Myra are very popular in Fort Davis and with the congregation. Their community service and volunteerism extends throughout the Big Bend, not just Fort Davis. They have found their home. Greg knows why he stays: "Whenever I leave here, I always know I am going to come back because the next stop after the Big Bend is Heaven. There is no greater place than here. This is the best place that you could live, a certain calm, a certain peace comes over you until you just feel like this is home."

Acknowledgments

There are many people to thank for their assistance in developing the *Authentic Texas* project, none more important than the interview participants themselves. They graciously welcomed us into their homes and their lives and were pleased that we wanted to hear about their experiences and their opinions of their corner of Texas. Because of their kindness and friendship, *Authentic Texas* quickly became more than a book project; it became a labor of love for the people of the Big Bend. In addition, there were others who suggested names of persons we should contact. We greatly appreciate the tips and suggestions and located many participants whom otherwise we would have missed.

We thank our friend Bobbi Gonzales, who skillfully and sensitively transcribed many of the interviews. Amanda Jones played an important role in assisting with organization, transcription, and research. Their work is greatly appreciated.

We are grateful for the continuous support and enthusiasm from our spouses, Alice Wright and Howard Daudistel. They held down our respective home fronts in Abilene and El Paso while we traveled around the Big Bend talking to people and taking photographs. We are also grateful for their patience as we edited photographs and text and fumed over missed opportunities or unfocused images.

Finally, we must express our appreciation for the encouraging and positive response we received from Joanna Hitchcock and Dave Hamrick, past and present directors of the University of Texas Press and our wonderful editor, Allison Faust, who kept us on schedule with gentle suggestions and accurate advice.

MARCIA HATFIELD DAUDISTEL
BILL WRIGHT

About the Authors

MARCIA HATFIELD DAUDISTEL
El Paso, Texas

Daudistel is the editor, most recently, of *Grace and Gumption: The Women of El Paso* and the award-winning *Literary El Paso*. She is the West Texas/Trans Pecos Regional Editor of *Texas Books in Review*. As the former Associate Director of Texas Western Press of the University of Texas at El Paso, she established the bilingual imprint, Frontera Books. She was inducted into the El Paso Commission for Women Hall of Fame in 2013.

BILL WRIGHT
Abilene, Texas

Nationally known author and photographer Wright has published six previous books, including *Portraits from the Desert: Bill Wright's Big Bend*, *People's Lives: A Celebration of the Human Spirit*, *The Tiguas: Pueblo Indians of Texas*, and *The Texas Kickapoo: Keepers of Tradition*. He has exhibited his award-winning photographs internationally and in the United States in hundreds of solo and group exhibitions. He is a member and former president of the Philosophical Society of Texas.

Photo Captions